# DRAMACONTEMPORARY

SPAIN

# THE DRAMACONTEMPORARY SERIES

DramaContemporary is a series specializing in the publication of new foreign plays in translation, organized by country or region. The series developed in response to the increasing internationalism of our age that now links world societies more closely, not only economically, but culturally as well. The last twenty years, in particular, is characterized by cross-cultural references in writing and performance, East and West and throughout the Americas. The new drama series is designed to partake of this movement in world patterns of culture, specifically in the area of our specialty, theatre.

Each volume of DramaContemporary features a selection of recent plays that reflects current social, cultural, and artistic values in individual countries. Plays are chosen for their significance in the larger perspective of a culture, as a measure of the concerns of its artists and public. At times, these plays may find their way into the American theatrical repertoire; in other instances, this may not be possible. Nevertheless, at all times the American public can have the opportunity to learn about other cultures—the speech, gestures, rhythms and attitudes that shape a society —in the dramatic life of their plays.

The Publishers

IN PREPARATION:

DramaContemporary: France
DramaContemporary: India
DramaContemporary: Latin America

# DRAMACONTEMPORARY

# SPAIN

plays by

## Antonio Buero-Vallejo
## José Martín Recuerda
## Jaime Salom
## Francisco Nieva

## Edited, with an Introduction, by
## Marion Peter Holt

**Performing Arts Journal Publications**
New York

Library of Congress Cataloging in Publication Data
DramaContemporary: Spain
CONTENTS: *The Foundation, The Inmates of the Convent of Saint Mary Egyptian, The Cock's Short Flight, Coronada and the Bull.*
Library of Congress Catalog Card No.: 85-60188
ISBN: 0-933826-85-0 (cloth)
ISBN: 0-933826-86-9 (paper)

Graphic Design: Gautam Dasgupta
Printed in the United States of America

Publication of this book has been made possible in part by grants received from the National Endowment for the Arts, Washington, D.C., a federal agency, and the New York State Council on the Arts.

General Editors of the DramaContemporary Series:
Bonnie Marranca and Gautam Dasgupta

# Contents

# Spain's Theatre of Transition

## Marion Peter Holt

Serious Spanish theatre of the Franco era attracted little international attention. Although the brisk, popular comedies of the 1950s enjoyed successes with bourgeois audiences in Latin-American countries, from Mexico City to Rio de Janeiro, committed drama and experimental works of the period seemed too narrowly focused on situations peculiarly Spanish for export. Plays overtly political in theme, or those dealing with certain taboo subjects were, of course, simply suppressed in Spain, and such major dramas as Buero-Vallejo's *La doble historia del doctor Valmy* [*The Double Case-History of Doctor Valmy*] and Sastre's *La sangre y las cenizas* [*The Blood and the Ashes*] were not to be seen until after the passing of the dictatorship. Even when a dramatist did circumvent censorship—and this occurred more often than is supposed—the play was seldom given consideration by foreign directors and producers, who assumed, sight unseen, that it had been hopelessly neutralized. A group of marginal "underground" playwrights began to emerge in the 1960s, and a number of their plays were published in Spain and circulated abroad. However, these generally short allegorical or absurdist works had limited production potential at best and suffered from a lack of opportunity for experimental development. The situation was hardly ameliorated by the cafe-theatres that sprang up in Madrid in the late 1960s, providing limited forums for political satire much as cabaret theatres in some Eastern European countries offer in the 1980s. The *café-teatro* movement was short-lived, and within a few years all but one or two of the small performance spaces had closed for lack of an audience.

Only after the discovery of Buero-Vallejo's *El sueño de la razón* [*The Sleep of Reason*] by Andrzej Wajda, Liviu Ciulei, and other prominent directors of Eastern Europe and Scandinavia did a post-Civil War Spanish playwright succeed in breaking through the cultural and intellectual ostracism of the Franco years. In the decade following its Madrid premiere in 1970, Buero's powerful multimedia drama on the effects of repression and violence on the creative mind was translated into a dozen languages and performed in as many countries of Europe; in 1984 it became the first important contemporary Spanish play to reach a professional stage in the United States.* *The Sleep of Reason* was not, to be sure, an isolated instance of a Spanish dramatist's protest against current absolutism through historical or fictional parallels and not-so-subtle allusion. Enrique Llovet's updated version of Moliere's *Tartuffe*, which opened in 1969 despite censorial objections, was so brazen a satire of the technocrats of the Franco regime that audiences cheered it for months. In 1972, *Tiempo de espadas [Time of Swords]*, by the Catalán dramatist Jaime Salom, depicted the participants of the Last Supper as a group of revolutionaries of conflicting ideologies whose revolt against foreign occupation is doomed to failure. Although Salom maintained that his principal aim had been to demythicize the apostles and to strip away the cultural encrustations of centuries, the political stances voiced by the updated characters resembled those espoused by various still-clandestine political associations in Spain. But other committed playwrights, particularly those of the group known as the *"generación realista"* or realistic generation, who favored a more direct confrontation with Spanish social ills, had less success in obtaining authorization for performance of their works. Lauro Olmo, José Rodríguez Méndez, Carlos Muñiz, and José Martín Recuerda remained on the sidelines, writing plays that had little chance of reaching the stage.

The decade of the 1970s was to be a period of uncertain transition for the Spanish theatre. After the death of Franco in 1975, the change from dictatorship to constitutional democracy was more rapid and orderly than anyone would have predicted; however, cultural institutions were not suddenly transformed, nor were ingrained attitudes and habits so easily altered to accommodate the new freedoms. As censorship faded, the most conspicuous effect on the theatre was in superficial aspects of production. Isolated instances of semi-nudity (first tolerated in the production of *Equus* in 1975, shortly before Franco's death) gave way to a rash of nude scenes, more often than not gratuitously grafted onto a conventional play. Transvestism soon became fashionable, resulting most notably in a production of Lorca's *The House of Bernarda Alba* with a popular male actor in the title role and, in 1980, an intriguing though historically dubious play—Francisco Ors's *Contradanza [Contredance]*—that depicted Elizabeth I of England as a transvestite.

Plays long prohibited because of their political or sexual themes could now be viewed by the public and judged on their merits. Buero-Vallejo's *The Double Case-History of Doctor Valmy*, dealing with the torture of political prisoners, opened for a long run in 1976; but it was the production of Martín Recuerda's *Las arrecogías del beaterio de Santa Maria Egipciaca [The Inmates of the Convent of Saint Mary Egyptian]* in 1977 that became a symbol of the departure of censorship and the beginning of the new era of post-Franco theatre. Directed by Adolfo Marsillach (who had staged the unconventional *Tartuffe* some years before), Recuerda's accusatory drama on the imprisonment and execution of the nineteenth-century

---

*Produced by Baltimore's Center Stage, under the direction of Travis Preston. This followed a nonprofessional tryout at Theatre Converse (S.C.) under the direction of Hayward Ellis in April, 1983. Three years earlier, Recuerda's *The Inmates of the Convent of Saint Mary Egyptian* had been staged by the resident company of the Pennsylvania State University, using both professional and student actors, under the direction of Manuel Duque.

liberal Mariana Pineda surrounded audiences in the venerable Teatro de la Comedia with the dramatic action, challenging them to re-examine the question of imprisonment for political belief.

The penchant of Spanish playwrights to explore their country's troubled past to find parallels with the present and the use of allegory to comment on contemporary events did not abate. Buero-Vallejo's first play completed after Franco's death was in a sense a companion piece to *The Sleep of Reason*, investigating the effect of political hypocrisy, censorship, and social pressure on the decision of the nineteenth-century social critic Mariano José de Larra to take his own life. *La detonación [The Detonation]* (1977) was a stunning experiment in total theatre, featuring human and animal masks, startling sound effects, and the slowing down or acceleration of the action to suggest the altered perceptions of a man recalling some ten years of his past in the moment preceding the firing of the bullet that will kill him. Manuel Martínez Mediero, one of the "underground" writers who appeared in the 1960s, enjoyed a major success in the 1975-76 season with *Las hermanas de Buffalo Bill [The Sisters of Buffalo Bill]*, a grotesquely amusing allegory on sexual repression and the effects of the passing of a dictatorial big brother on two reclusive sisters. Ann Diosdado's *Y de Cachemira, chales [And from Kashmir, Shawls]* (1976) and Antonio Gala's *Petra Regalada* (1980) were also pointedly allegorical plays—one set in a metaphorical department store following a nuclear holocaust, and the other in a musty brothel. While these plays were quite obviously dramatic studies of Spanish social and political institutions, they succeeded in transcending the immediate national concerns through their striking theatricality and provocative treatments.

Playwrights who had lived in exile from political necessity or personal choice returned. Madrid audiences had their first opportunity to see Rafael Alberti's *El adefesio [The Ridiculous Person]* in 1976 and Fernando Arrabal's *El arquitecto y el emperador de Asiria [The Architect and the Emperor of Assyria]* the following year. It was, however, the multitalented Francisco Nieva—a near contemporary of Arrabal and a resident of Paris in his formative years—who exerted the most conspicuous influence on the early theatre of transition. Through his own brilliant stagings of his flamboyantly irreverent "Furious Theatre," he brought a new look to productions that complemented his critical view of traditionalist Spain.

Independent experimental groups and collectives have become increasingly influential in Spain's recent theatrical life, extending even into some venerable institutions. The most promising of the new generation of Spanish playwrights, Fermín Cabal, began his career as a participant in collective theatre and in 1984 ventured successfully into the commercial theatre with a prize-winning neo-naturalistic drama. The "Centro Dramático Nacional" at the Teatro María Guerrero is now headed by the young director Lluis Pascual from Barcelona's Teatro Lliure—long recognized for its individualistic stagings of classics and avant-garde contemporary works. Another Barcelona-based troupe, El Joglars, performs throughout Spain and abroad, while independent groups have come into existence in virtually every Spanish city. Although frequently criticized for their artistic choices, the subsidized theatres have served an indispensable function in developing new audiences. The María Guerrero has sponsored such worthwhile productions as those of Cabal's *Vade Retro [Get Thee Behind Me]* (1982) and Angel García Pintado's *El taxidermista [The Taxidermist]* (1982), as well as new stagings of a variety of classical and modern European plays. Restored in 1980, following a devastating fire, Madrid's municipal Teatro Español has offered two unorthodox productions of Calderón, an eccentric adaptation of *The Tempest* for Nuria Espert, and a spectrum of experimental groups from Europe and America.

For all the flurry of production—much of it hotly debated—Spanish theatre faces a variety of internal and external problems. Audiences have become fragmented or alienated; with the rapid shift of population to new suburban areas and the rise in street crime, theatre attendance has become increasingly erratic and unpredictable. While a theatre can be filled to capacity by an enthusiastic young public for a few performances of an avant-garde work, few serious plays have demonstrated drawing power for a prolonged run. Commercial producers now show a fondness for imported plays requiring only two or three actors, and talented new Spanish writers find themselves compelled to mold their scripts to compete with *Agnus Dei [Agnes of God]* and *Buenas noches, madre ['night, Mother]*. Only the subsidized theatres can attempt such elaborate stagings as the María Guerrero's recent revival of Jardiel Poncela's *Eloisa está debajo de un almendro [Eloise is Underneath an Almond Tree]* or the Español's admired production of Odon von Horvath's demanding *Cuentos de los bosques de Viena [Tales from the Vienna Woods]*. With government subvention so essential, competition has become intense, creating dissension and causing playwrights to withdraw into opposing camps.

Spanish critics have been neither helpful nor consistent when evaluating the multifaceted post-Franco theatre, particularly in their appraisal of works by dramatists who have sought to deal with the actualities of modern Spain without the familiar obliqueness. When Buero-Vallejo explored the inner world of a corrupt bureaucrat of the Franco regime who rises to prominence in the new democratic government in *Jueces en la noche [Judges in the Night]* (1979), the critical reception was overwhelmingly negative and there were unfair allegations that the playwright had chosen his theme merely for exploitation. It was hardly surprising, even in 1980, that Jaime Salom received threats of physical reprisals from *franquistas* of the extreme right when it became known that his *El corto vuelo del gallo [The Cock's Short Flight]* dealt explicitly with the private lives of members of the Franco family. However, it seems odd that hostile charges of opportunism, unfairness, and "bad taste" were leveled at him by theatre critics as well. These reactions suggest that some of the taboos of a departed censorship have remained engraved on the psyches of many Spaniards—including some of the guardians of critical values—preventing them from reacting objectively to a play that deals with the present or recent past with a political or sexual directness that was forbidden less than a decade ago.

The four plays in the present collection, covering the period 1974-1982, are representative works by committed playwrights of distinctly different aesthetic and thematic approaches. They are but a part of the remarkable variety of drama to originate in Spain in the years of political and social transition. Included are: a major work by Buero-Vallejo, utilizing the immersion techniques so characteristic of his theatre; Recuerda's challenging historical re-creation of the imprisonment and execution of Mariana Pineda that became an outcry for amnesty at the end of censorship; and Salom's expressionistic treatment of the liberal-conservative schism that precipitated the Civil War, illustrated by a paradigmatic family named Franco. The final selection, the most Iberian of the group, is a prime example of Nieva's "Furious Theatre," a scenic and verbal *tour de force* ridiculing, with unabashed irreverence, blind adherence to tradition.

## THE FOUNDATION

Buero-Vallejo's *The Foundation* reached the stage in 1974 after a two-year prohibition by the censors. Unlike the plays in which Buero shows the effects of political oppression or rigid social custom on a single, near-mythic historical character to draw parallels with contemporary events, *The Foundation* is pointedly set in an unnamed country, and the characters are given names that suggest neither Spain nor any other specific nation. However, Buero's melding of a theatre of images and sound with dramatic discourse is closely akin to the scenic techniques employed in his more expansive historical dramas.

While writing *The Foundation*, Buero drew from the experiences of his six years of imprisonment at the end of the Spanish Civil War—years in which he was shunted from prison to prison after the commutation of his death sentence. He has acknowledged two other specific sources of inspiration for the play: the first, H.G. Wells's novel *Mr. Blettsworthy on Rampole Island* (1928), whose protagonist-narrator, having suffered a mental collapse from being adrift in mid-ocean, believes New York City to be the island of Rampole until he is cured of his delusion; the second, Cervantes's Don Quixote, the crazed knight errant who moves from a delusion in which windmills are giants to a final stage of lucidity. In both cases, the parallels with the delusion of the young political prisoner (Thomas) who envisions his cell as a comfortable studio in a modern philanthropic institute are obvious.

*The Foundation* presents an inversion of Buero's usual *efectos de inmersión*, or immersion-effects, which recur in his plays as a device to achieve a participatory theatre in which the audience is drawn into the mind of a character or toward intensified personal identification with a physical or psychical defect. In *The Sleep of Reason*, when the deaf painter Goya is on stage, the audience hears only his reaction to the silently-mouthed dialogue or sign language signals. In three of Buero's plays dealing with blindness, the theatre is plunged into absolute darkness for varying lengths of time, or the scene is suddenly transformed to represent the distorted imagined reality of the blind character. However, Buero had always initiated the immersion-effect from a base of normalcy; in *The Foundation* the process is reversed, and the actions begin with a view of Thomas's abnormal world. In the course of the four scenes the set is stripped of its illusory features until it is totally revealed as a stark prison cell.

One of Buero's dramatic signatures has been the musical motif, used not merely for mood or identification but in varying functions that are ancillary to his immersion-effects. On some occasions they also provide a signal to the audience for a metafictional association. In *Las Meninas*, a play on Velázquez, a musical theme is used synesthetically to suggest a work of art unseen by the audience; the "pastorale" from Rossini's overture to *William Tell* is repeated as the motif of

Thomas's imagined landscape in *The Foundation*, and at the end of the play it is heard tauntingly as the possible re-initiation of the delusion for the new occupants of the cell. It is significant that the music never progresses beyond the quiet pastorale interlude to the faster section of the overture (a section all too familiar to American ears) with its suggestions of the more dynamic events of the opera and the Schiller play on which it is based. Nonmusical sounds also achieve a striking dramatic impact in *The Foundation*. The chants of the sentries at the end of the third scene, varying in volume until they are lost, and the pounding on the cell doors in the final scene need no accompanying dialogue to convey their meaning.

As the unmasking of delusion progresses, the dialogue becomes increasingly direct in its references to concerns beyond the confines of the prison cell. One character in particular (Asel) becomes the bearer of the play's most urgent plea for an end to all forms of violence practiced by humankind against its own. While Buero's characters are obviously spokesmen for his own views on occasion, seldom has he provided a speech within the context of a dramatic situation so unequivocally accusatory as Asel's impassioned indictment of fratricide and genocide. Goya's long speeches in *The Sleep of Reason* on the effect of fear on art, or the lines of social criticism lifted directly from Larra's essays in *The Detonation* are, of course, equally pointed in terms of their own time frame and transcend that frame when the audience draws the obvious parallels with contemporary ills. Asel's words, however, speak directly to the contemporary predicament, and his observation that escape from the punishment cell in the prison basement may only lead into another larger prison is a universal warning that sudden liberation at a point in time does not signify the end of a struggle.

## THE INMATES OF THE CONVENT OF SAINT MARY EGYPTIAN

More than a decade before he wrote *The Inmates of the Convent of Saint Mary Egyptian*, José Martín Recuerda had won the prestigious Lope de Vega Drama Prize for *El teatrito de don Ramón [Don Ramon's Small Theatre]*, a moving study of the failed lives of a group of vivid characters aspiring to artistic expression in a small Spanish city. After the almost totally negative critical reception for this masterly drama when it was staged, Recuerda resolved that his future work would feature characters who took a stand against whoever their oppressors might be. *Las salvajes en Puente San Gil [The Savages in Puente San Gil]*, his play on the revolt of a touring theatrical company against small-town reactionaries who attempt to suppress their performance, was successfully produced in 1963 and later made into a film. But *The Inmates* focused so strongly on political oppression that its prohibition by the censors was inevitable. When the play finally reached the stage in 1977, in Adolfo Marsillach's stirring production, it became not only a symbol of the liberation of creativity from censorial restraints but served as well as a cry to the new Spanish government for political amnesty.

Martín Recuerda sees his plays as "fiestas" or theatrical celebrations that transform the playing space into something resembling a street spectacle in which actors, singers, and dancers challenge the spectators directly. The premiere production of *The Inmates* came close to realizing this dramatic vision even though it was performed in one of Madrid's older proscenium theatres. Marsillach used the faded auditorium to good effect, unfurling banners from the tiers and placing the actors in the aisles in deliberately provocative confrontation with the audience.

The events dramatized in *The Inmates* take place during the reactionary reign of Fernando VII—the period that Buero had depicted in *The Sleep of Reason*. One of Garcia Lorca's less familiar plays, *Mariana Pineda* (1927), also deals with the same story as Recuerda's but from an entirely different aesthetic perspective. Lorca's version is a poetical treatment which takes considerable liberty with historical fact and focuses almost entirely on Mariana's personal emotional drama; only the final act is set outside Mariana's house in the Convent of Saint Mary Egyptian. The historical Mariana Pineda was an active participant in the liberal opposition in Granada, and for Martín Recuerda her martyrdom continues to have relevant political significance. Unlike Lorca, he is quite specific about the nature of the "beaterio" where the young woman was imprisoned. The convent was actually established as a place of detention for prostitutes and other undesirables, and the word *arrecogías* in the play's Spanish title is a local euphemism for "prostitute." It has been documented, however, that some of the so-called "*arrecogías*" were in fact political prisoners whose jailers were nuns. While Recuerda retains Mariana's intimate personal drama, the dramatic action becomes collective as the "inmates" unite in protest against injustice, lending an epic quality not even hinted at in Lorca's more closeted treatment.

The theme of torture for dissident political acts is introduced in two powerful scenes. The first, involving a fifteen-year-old girl whose hands have been broken for alleged complicity with Mariana in embroidering the liberal flag, emphasizes the collective nature of the play as the "inmates" join Mariana in tearing strips from their dresses to bandage the girl's mutilated hands. It is a scene that leads to the impassioned choral response that concludes the first act. The second instance presents Mariana's lover, Casimiro Brodette, whose tongue has been so severely burned by his captors that he cannot speak. Although the mute Casimiro attempts to silence her, Mariana confesses to him her active role in the liberal cause, knowing that her confession is being overheard and that it may result in her execution.

Director Marsillach added a note to the play by allowing the actress who played the leading role to return to the stage after Mariana's final exit and step out of character to announce that Mariana's life would have been spared had Fernando VII's amnesty decree come a few months earlier. Obviously, this skillful politicizing of the production, even beyond the play's fundamental political statement, contributed to its exceptional success at a critical moment in Spain's post-Franco transition. But even without the excitement generated by these special circumstances, it is probable that *The Inmates of the Convent of Saint Mary Egyptian* would have been successful. It is an epic drama of compelling theatricality—Spanish in essence but not narrowly so, and accessible to audiences unfamiliar with its special historical background.

## THE COCK'S SHORT FLIGHT

Jaime Salom's early plays reveal a continual experimentation with form, from the most conventional two or three act linear structure to the episodic and, eventually, the skillful non-linear interweaving of past and present, of real and imagined events. Time fluidity, with a complementary shift from scenic realism, has now become the most constant feature of his theatre. Both *Los delfines [The Heirs Apparent]* (1969) and *Tiempo de espadas [Time of Swords]* (1972) were performed on a series of platforms, with only the most basic furnishings and properties. Salom has also used the device of character doubling to good effect in several of his plays. In *The Cock's Short Flight*, doubling and the assigning of multiple roles to a single performer permit eighteen characters to be played by only eight actors. With a similar selectivity of means, Salom's terse scenes and incisive dialogue move the action of his plays quickly—though seldom through sacrifice of mood or, when required, metaphorical allusion. A close observer of British and American theatre, Salom has no doubt been influenced as much by foreign currents as by Spanish tendencies in developing his own quite distinctive dramatic techniques. To an American audience, *The Cock's Short Flight*, with its non-linear structure and manner of treating a personal drama against an historical background, might seem closer to David Hare's *Plenty* than to the work of any Spanish dramatist that comes to mind.

Salom uses the Franco family in *The Cock's Short Flight* as a paradigm for the two Spains that entered into fratricidal battle in the Civil War of 1936-39. With the exception of Ramón Franco, who achieved fame as a pioneer aviator, the family of the late dictator is unknown outside Spain, and the father himself was little more than a non-person from the time his son assumed power in 1939 until his death in 1942. Although Francisco Franco is a constant influence on the events of the play, he is never actually seen on stage; however, through repeated allusions in the dialogue, he becomes a spectral presence as a child, an ambitious young man, and ultimately, the absolute ruler of Spain. In the single scene in which he does figure directly, the audience sees only an empty chair.

The play unfolds on two levels, with two interweaving time spans. The realistic events cover only the period of 1939 to 1942, but recalled happenings and imagined episodes reach decades back into the past. In spite of the scenic simplicity, the action is not narrowly encapsulated. There are frequent suggestions of the physical world outside—nostalgically recalled in the scene in which the elder Franco and three of his children look out toward the ocean from the harbor of El Ferrol, but menacingly actual when the father closes the apartment windows against the sounds of martial music accompanying the Nationalists' victory march through Madrid. The play is, to be sure, also rich in emotional nuance, as Salom explores a range of complex human relationships with psychological insight.

The notoriety that surrounded the opening of *The Cock's Short Flight* in 1980 distracted from an appreciation of the fundamental dramatic values of Salom's study of the effects of conflicting ideologies and conservative sexual mores on both private and public life. In addition to personal threats and attempts at intimidation of all concerned with the play, the unfavorable reviews of most Spanish critics impugned the playwright's motives with undisguised hostility. Only when the play was restaged in Mexico City in 1981 was there a truly objective (and unreservedly favorable) evaluation of the work on its own merits. There, where the late Spanish dictator had been viewed from a safe distance, reactions were unclouded by personal trauma or political ambivalence.

## CORONADA AND THE BULL

When Fernando Arrabal first attracted international attention with his Panic Theatre, his young fellow-expatriate, Francisco Nieva, was existing as an artist in Paris, and the highly unorthodox plays that he had begun to write seemed to him beyond hope of production. Only after a widely successful career as a set designer in Madrid and Berlin did playwriting become his major creative activity. Nieva himself dates the moment of renewed dedication to the occasion of his first contact with the Living Theatre through their production in Venice, in 1965, of *Frankenstein*, which gave him new confidence that the theatre could eventually accommodate his special talents.

Nieva has divided his dramatic writing into two basic groups: "Theatre of Farce and Calamity" and "Furious Theatre," and it is to the second group—the works he once considered least performable in the period of censorship—that *Coronada and the Bull* belongs. A fundamental characteristic of Furious Theatre is the use of characters who are strictly prototypic, devoid of psychology, and moved by some urgency that causes them to become theatrical incarnations of an idea or a passion. There is also a conscious distortion of language and a compression of action and event akin to an opera libretto which is not slowed down by its musical accompaniment. As exemplified in *Coronada*, it is not a form of political theatre that takes an ideological stance before a particular circumstance at a specific time and place but a theatre of conscience that satirizes the insular, ritualized image of Spain—an image the rest of Europe and America have frequently adopted as a convenience, rejecting the very nonconformity that is so frequently a distinctive attribute of Iberian creative art.

*Coronada* is in its way a morality play drawing from a variety of dramatic forms familiar to Spanish audiences. In the program notes for the Madrid production in 1982, Nieva maintained that the work begins as a *zarzuela* and ends as an *auto sacramental*, having passed through the *sainete* and other "fantastic genres." Whatever the Iberian bases touched in the course of the action, there is in Nieva's gleeful, irreverent exploitation of traditional forms an obvious spiritual kinship with Christopher Durang's wildly hilarious parody of the traditional Nativity and Passion plays in *Sister Mary Ignatius Explains It All For you*, in spite of pronounced differences in national sensibilities.

The script of *Coronada and the Bull* may suggest the play's staging to some extent, but it cannot provide the reader with an adequate visual impression of Nieva's scenic design—inspired by the paintings of Zuloaga—or the aural effect of the dialogue's verbal pyrotechnics. Music and dance figured prominently in the performance, with choreographed interludes and deliberately distorted electronic versions of Spanish compositions. The Town Voice declaimed his verses and proclamations to the accompaniment of ominous music, while piano and percussion underscored the dramatic junctions of the play. Scenically, Nieva brings a sense of magic to his works with costumes, sets, and visual surprises that reflect their mysterious or surreal aspects. To signal the resurrection of the Nun Man, a ball of fire appeared in his hand and was thrown into the stage trap from which Coronada emerged to continue her ascent toward heaven on a suspended rope. While accomplished with all the technology of the modern theatre, the magical effects recall the spectacle employed in Spain's *autos sacramentales* in the sixteenth and seventeenth centuries.

Nieva can no doubt be considered one of the most cosmopolitan of Spanish playwrights through his extensive contacts with many of the leading writers, directors, and designers of Europe, and his influence on scenic values of theatre production in Spain has been considerable. At the same time, his plays remain the most resolutely Iberian of any of his contemporaries, including Arrabal. His works of Furious Theatre and his provocative adaptations of Aristophanes, Larra, and Galdós represent the most individualistic dramatic statement of the Spanish theatre of transition.

## About the Translations

The playscripts included in this collection follow closely the versions of the plays seen at their respective premieres in Madrid, with the exception of *The Inmates of the Convent of Saint Mary Egyptian*, which is a terser version of the published play prepared by translator Robert Lima and director Manuel Duque, in close collaboration with the playwright, for its United States premiere by the resident company of the Pennsylvania State University. In the published versions of his plays, Antonio Buero-Vallejo customarily indicates by brackets the cuts made during the rehearsal process; most of these textually insignificant cuts have been observed in the English version of *The Foundation* to provide a concise playing script. The Signes version of Nieva's *Coronada and the Bull* follows the expanded script of the Madrid production of 1982 and not an earlier published edition of the play.

# The Foundation

## Fable in Two Parts

## Antonio Buero-Vallejo

THE FOUNDATION [Teatro Figaro, Madrid, 1974]
Directed by José Osuna

CHARACTERS:

Thomas
The Man
Berta
Tulio
Max
Asel
Linus
The Superintendent
The Aide
First Waiter
Second Waiter
Voices

*In a country whose name is unknown.*

Note: *The stage setting and the physical changes that occur on it are described in the stage directions with an eye to the greatest technical simplicity. Directors can elaborate as their means permit and according to their own inventiveness.*

# PART ONE

## Scene 1

*The room could be a part of almost any modern residential complex. It is not spacious or luxurious. The building has been designed for the maximum utilization of space. The walls are gray and bare; no baseboards or cornices. Simple but tasteful furnishings: those of a functional living space where comfort is of prime importance. But the relative crowding of the details that distinguish it curiously increases the sensation of being closed in. However, the ceiling is totally out of view of the audience. The floor, of a neutral color and without tiles or fissures of any kind, appears to be of polished cement. The corner between the right and the upstage walls is not visible: the folds of a long curtain hanging at an angle from above hide it, creating a kind of alcove. Open metal shelves which serve as a cupboard are fastened to the right wall near this curtain, and their appearance contrasts with that of the other furnishings. Fine glassware, china, silver trays, white tablecloths and napkins are arranged on the two shelves. Underneath, there is the white porcelain door of a small refrigerator that is built into the wall; further downstage on the same wall, a simple metal rack from which hang six small duffel bags, each different from the others. Under them and against the wall is a folding bed which forms an upright piece of furniture. In the upstage wall, near the alcove curtain, the only door, which is narrow, low, and paneled. It cannot be seen now because it is open offstage from the right of the frame. The door is set deep into the walls to suggest their great thickness. Over the door there is a light fixture and, higher up, the round grill of a loudspeaker. Next to the door and extending the width of the upstage wall to the extreme left, an enormous glass window of great height, with a sill that is only a little lower than the lintel of the door. Its frame is also set deep into the wall. The window does not appear capable of being opened: two simple vertical stringers without bolts support the glass. Under the window and with the head against the left wall is a simple, light bed of modern design. Aligned under it are three bundles covered by burlap or canvas whose use is not apparent for the moment. Fastened to the wall over the bed, a small conical metal light shade. Almost all of the remaining space on the left wall is taken up by a built-in wall unit of fine wood, with spaces and shelves of varying dimensions. On a lower shelf, a television set; another section contains several buttons or knobs. Numerous beautiful and expensively-bound books and fine porcelain figurines stand out on some of the shelves. Under the wall unit and near the bed, the top of a small table extends from the wall. It is apparently metal too: a plain surface on which books, magazines, and a white telephone are placed. Downstage left there is a small rectangular table of light wood polished to a semi-gloss. On it are newspapers and an illustrated magazine or two; around it, five inviting armchairs of shining metal and gleaming leather. At left, hanging from a long rod that disappears from view above, a huge lighting fixture with a multicolored shade. The door opens out onto what seems to be a narrow exterior gallery, with a metal railing that extends in both directions to create the impression of leading into emptiness. Behind the large window, in the distance, the extensive view of a marvelous landscape: clear sky, majestic mountains, the gleaming silver of a lake, the delicate green of meadows and copses, the clean lines of attractive buildings somewhat nearer. The same panorama extends beyond the gallery railing and into the distance. With its contradictory mixture of modernity and overcrowding, the room suggests an efficiency apartment urgently and provisionally put into the service of some important activity that is in progress. Bright spring light floods the landscape; an iridescent brightness, slightly unreal, sifts into the room.*

*Soft music in the background: the pastorale from Rossini's overture to* William Tell, *a fragment which, in spite of its brevity, is repeated without interruption until the action cuts it off. A motionless man is lying face to the wall on the bed, under flowered sheets and an expensive coverlet. With a shiny new broom, Thomas is sweeping bits of trash toward the door. He is a young man about twenty-five, who is wearing dark pants, a gray shirt, and soft shoes. On his chest there is a small black rectangle where the inscription C-72 stands out in white. He moves the broom lazily and whistles softly some of the music he is hearing; then he stops, accompanying himself with a light movement of his head.*

THOMAS: Rossini . . . (*He turns toward the bed.*) Do you like it? (*There is no reply. He makes a couple of sweeping motions.*) You and I haven't talked much since we came to the Foundation. I don't even know if you like music. (*He stops again.*) It has a soothing effect on sick people. But if it bothers you . . . (*No reply.*) It's a melody as serene as the morning air when the sun comes up. It's good to hear it on a day like this. (*He faces the window.*) I wish you could see how clear it is. (*He goes back*

to his sweeping; he pushes the trash through the door and leaves it outside at left. Then he leans on the railing to look at the landscape. The
sun bathes his face. He comes back into the room and pushes the alcove
curtain aside slightly to put the broom behind it.) Would you like to see
the view? The air's warm. If you want to, I'll help you get up. How
about it? (No reply. He goes closer to the bed and lowers his voice.) Are
you asleep?

(The sick man does not move. Thomas moves away on tiptoe. We hear the
Man's voice, tired and weak.)

MAN: Talk all you want. But don't ask me any questions . . . I'm tired.
THOMAS: (He goes to the table and picks up a magazine.) Of course. You
    don't eat enough. (He laughs and sits down.) Asel has told you that it's
    bad for you not to take any solid food, and Asel's a doctor. (He puts the
    magazine down.) But I never see you drink anything either. (Pointing
    toward the curtain.) Or go to the bathroom. (He gets up and goes
    closer.) Do you get up while we're sleeping? (He leans over him.) Huh?

(Berta has appeared through the left gallery corridor and enters in time to
hear Thomas's last words. She looks at him smiling. She is a girl of gentle
and serious expression, with a shiny mane of hair. The white shorts she is
wearing reveal her exquisite legs; on her immaculate open-neck shirt, a
blue rectangle with the inscription A-72. She is holding something tiny
and white in her hands.)

BERTA: He won't answer you. He's fallen asleep.
THOMAS: (Turning around.) Berta! (He crosses to embrace her.)
BERTA: (Evading him, smiling.) Careful! (She comes downstage.)
THOMAS: (Behind her.) Don't try to escape!
BERTA: (Showing what she has in her hands.) You'll crush it.
THOMAS: A white mouse?
BERTA: From the laboratory. We've become friends. (She shows it to him.)
    He's very tame. He hardly moves.
THOMAS: They've probably inoculated him with something.
BERTA: No. We haven't begun work yet. How about you?
THOMAS: (Putting his arm around her shoulders.) We haven't either.
BERTA: (Holding up the mouse.) He's looking at you. He likes you.
THOMAS: You're imagining things.
BERTA: Don't you see the affection?
THOMAS: Where?
BERTA: In those little drops of wine he has for eyes. Kiss it. (Thomas kisses
    her neck.) Him!
THOMAS: No thanks!

BERTA: Try to ignore him, Tommy. He's my boyfriend.

THOMAS: (*Releasing her.*) You've given him my name? (*Berta nods. Thomas goes toward the table, thinking.*)

BERTA: (*To the mouse.*) Thomas Long Tail, the gentleman is angry. He's selfish.

THOMAS: (*With a half-smile.*) Jealous is a better word.

BERTA: (*Walking toward him.*) Don't you feel sorry for him? I wish you would save him from his fate. You could keep him in the bathroom . . . he could be your mascot. (*He shakes his head.*) You won't?

THOMAS: Put him back in his cage, Berta. They need him.

BERTA: (*After a moment.*) I hate the Foundation.

THOMAS: Thanks to its generosity you're able to go on with your studies, and I'm writing my novel . . . (*He moves closer. Berta pets the rodent without looking at Thomas.*) The Foundation is admirable, and you know it.

BERTA: It sacrifices mice.

THOMAS: And dogs, and monkeys . . . Heroes of science. A sweet martyrdom: they don't know that it's happening to them. And they're treated well to the very end. What better destiny? If I were a mouse I'd accept it.

BERTA: (*She looks at him enigmatically.*) No. (*Brief pause.*) You are a mouse, and you don't accept it.

THOMAS: (*Looking uneasy.*) Sometimes I don't understand you.

BERTA: Yes you do.

THOMAS: (*Walking about.*) But what's with these belated scruples! It's your work!

BERTA: I'd like to save my little friend.

THOMAS: All mice are the same! (*He puts his arms around her waist.*)

BERTA: This one's name is Thomas . . . like yours. (*She pulls away and turns to face him.*) And I'll save him! (*Thomas looks at her perplexed.*) Goodbye. (*She goes toward the door.*)

THOMAS: Wait! (*He takes her by the arm.*) My friends will be back soon. And they want to meet you. (*He leads her to a chair. She sits down, petting the mouse.*) They don't quite believe that you've come to the Foundation too.

BERTA: Why not?

THOMAS: They say it's too much of a coincidence. (*He sits on the table beside her.*) They have a blind spot when it comes to chance happenings. (*He points to the number on her shirt.*) Yesterday I told them about that. (*She smiles.*) Is it so hard to believe that my girl is at the Foundation too?—I said—Well, besides that, they've given her the same number as mine: seventy-two.

BERTA: They didn't believe that either?

THOMAS: Even less! They all laughed . . . except Asel. He's the puzzling one.

BERTA: (*Without looking at him.*) Did you know him before?

THOMAS: No . . . no. Why do you ask?

BERTA: No reason.

THOMAS: He didn't laugh. He said: That would be more than a coincidence; it would be a miracle. You'll meet them now. They'll see your number for themselves, and they'll be convinced that everything that happens to you and me is miraculous. Right?

BERTA: Right. (*He bends over and gives her a prolonged kiss. She laughs.*) Tommy is going to get away. (*She gets up and grasps the mouse firmly.*) Be still, Long Tail. Don't be jealous. (*She holds him up.*) Look, he's telling me something.

THOMAS: I don't hear anything.

BERTA: It's another miracle. (*She puts the mouse close to her ear.*) He says it's time for lunch. He's probably only jealous, but he's right. I can't stay any longer.

THOMAS: (*Standing up.*) Just a minute more! They'll be back soon . . . (*He takes her by the arm.*) How did you know that I didn't go out for a walk today?

BERTA: Isn't it your turn to clean the room?

THOMAS: How do you know that? We haven't talked since day before yesterday.

BERTA: (*She looks at him intensely.*) You must have told me.

THOMAS: (*Intrigued.*) No.

BERTA: (*Turning away and looking up.*) I smell a bad odor.

THOMAS: It's coming from the bathroom. The toilet doesn't flush properly. I've notified the orderly. Even a research center like this has some deficiencies . . . They were in such a hurry to get it built and opened that there are still no eating facilities, no dining rooms . . .

BERTA: And the overcrowding.

THOMAS: Of course. Until they complete the new wings. Do the women have better service?

BERTA: It's the same. No services at all. And that's why I have to go now. Shall we go, Long Tail? (*She starts to exit.*)

THOMAS: (*Restraining her timidly.*) They'll be here any minute . . . They're interesting people. You'll like them. Even Tulio. He's a bit vulgar and hates music . . . But he's an exceptional photographer who's close to an important optical discovery. A real brain, although a bit unbalanced. And Max, another brain. An eminent mathematician. But very nice and accommodating. Linus is an engineer . . . he's experimenting with a new technique for pre-stressing building materials. He doesn't talk a lot but he's a great person.

BERTA: And Asel?

THOMAS: Asel. He's the finest of them all.

BERTA: (*Referring to the man in the bed.*) What about him?

THOMAS: (*After a moment.*) You probably won't believe it, but I still don't know what field he's in. (*He goes closer to the bed.*) Since he's sick, we don't bother him with questions.

BERTA: Do you think he's listening to us?

THOMAS: He sleeps very soundly. (*He motions to her to come over.*) Look. (*Brief pause.*)

BERTA: It's late, dearest. I do have to go now.

THOMAS: (*He embraces her; his voice becomes husky.*) Come back tonight.

BERTA: (*Surprised.*) Here?

THOMAS: They're very understanding. If we go into the bathroom, they won't say anything.

BERTA: (*To the mouse.*) He's crazy, Tommy.

THOMAS: Crazy about you. Will you come?

BERTA: (*After a moment.*) I hate the Foundation.

THOMAS: (*Kissing her.*) But not me . . . Come back tonight.

BERTA: Stop . . . (*She pulls away from him.*) Stop. (*She goes toward the door.*)

THOMAS: Will you come?

BERTA: (*From the door, holding up the mouse.*) I have to protect my other boyfriend . . . (*Indicating the curtain.*) And it smells bad in the bathroom.

THOMAS: We'll go somewhere else!

BERTA: (*With a little laugh.*) Where? (*He doesn't know what to answer.*) Goodbye! (*She disappears left. Thomas runs out to the gallery and calls to her.*)

THOMAS: I know you'll come! (*Berta's silvery laugh comes from further off. Thomas watches her leave. Then he looks at the landscape and breathes the fragrant air. He comes back into the room and glances toward the sick man with a smile.*) Dear God, what a morning! As clear and pure as Rossini's. Sleep, sleep. (*He crosses.*) I'll turn down the music a little.

MAN: I'm awake.

THOMAS: (*Hesitating.*) We thought you were asleep . . . I guess we bothered you.

MAN: I dozed a little . . . (*Groggy.*) No bother. (*Thomas continues to the wall unit, turns a knob, and the music becomes softer.*) There's an unpleasant odor.

THOMAS: (*Turning to him, disturbed.*) It's from the bathroom. They'll fix it soon . . . Do you prefer the music this way? (*There is no reply. Thomas crosses to the table noiselessly and picks up a magazine. When he is about to sit down, four men appear from the right gallery corridor. They look to the left for a moment. As soon as he sees them, Thomas runs to the wall unit to turn off the music. The first to come* onstage is Tulio—*gaunt and in his forties, with sharp, severe features. Like the others, he is wearing a gray shirt; on his black rectangle is the inscription C-81. All are wearing pants which differ somewhat.*) How was your walk?

TULIO: (*Gruffly.*) Fine.

(*The others enter immediately: Max, about thirty-five and attractive, C-96 on his shirt, crosses to sit at the table and leafs through the magazine that Thomas has left.*)

MAX: It was splendid! We even played leapfrog. Can you imagine, grown men playing leapfrog? And Tulio turned out to be an expert! (*Tulio throws him a scowl.*) In falling down, of course. But an expert!

(*He laughs and Thomas laughs with him. Meanwhile, Linus crosses and sits at the extreme left of the table. Very vigorous and tight-lipped, he appears to be about thirty. C-46 on his shirt.*)

TULIO: (*Sourly.*) I'm going to get a drink of water.

(*He goes toward the curtain. Almost immediately Asel has gone over to the bed and observed the man in it. Then he reclines against the foot of the bed and watches Thomas. Asel is the oldest: about fifty, maybe more. Gray hair, reflective expression. On his rectangle, C-73.*)

THOMAS: They're only teasing you, Tulio. Can I get you a beer?

TULIO: (*Curtly.*) I prefer water.

ASEL: And you, Thomas, what have you been doing?

THOMAS: Killing time. I listened to Rossini, I read . . . When do we begin our projects?

MAX: You can start whenever you wish. A writer doesn't need an office or a laboratory. (*Tulio reappears wiping his mouth with his sleeve.*)

THOMAS: I've already been taking notes. But I also need isolation.

ASEL: So you had a quiet morning to yourself. No visitors?

THOMAS: (*Smiling.*) One.

(*The others look at him; there is a tension in their faces. With a snort of disgust, Tulio goes over to one of the bags hanging at right, opens it slightly without taking it down, and takes out a handkerchief, which he puts in his pocket. Linus gets up, glances at Thomas, and goes over to lean against the edge of the door.*)

ASEL: Who?

THOMAS: (*With a look of amusement.*) Can't you guess?

ASEL: (*Suddenly sitting up.*) Be quiet. Someone's coming.

(*He goes over near the door. Max gets up and stations himself beside him. Tulio turns to face the door. The superintendent and his young aide appear, all smiles, from the right gallery. Both are dressed impeccably in black jacket, tailored trousers, and silk tie, in the style of head waiters. The superintendent is a middle-aged man of distinguished bearing. Thomas goes to meet him.*)

THOMAS: Good morning, sir!
SUPERINTENDENT: (*Turning on his smile.*) Good day, gentlemen. Is everything satisfactory?
THOMAS: Yes, sir. A few trifles . . . When will the dining room open?
SUPERINTENDENT: (*With a quiet laugh.*) Very soon. The Foundation hopes you'll forgive these temporary deficiencies. If I may . . . (*He comes in and observes the man in bed.*) He hasn't gotten up today either?
ASEL: He's still weak. But it's not serious.
SUPERINTENDENT: Fine. (*He sniffs the air discreetly without saying anything and gives the room the once-over.*) I'm glad you gentlemen are comfortable. (*He returns to the door.*)
THOMAS: Thank you very much.
SUPERINTENDENT: (*From the gallery, he flashes a subtle smile.*) I'm always at your disposal, gentlemen. (*He exits left. The aide bows, all smiles, and disappears in turn.*)
THOMAS: They're very thoughtful.

(*With a scornful grunt, Tulio crosses and picks up a small, tattered book from the table, which he leans against to leaf through the book. Linus peers out the door. Asel sits again at the end of the bed.*)

LINUS: The slop will be here soon.
MAX: (*Crossing to sit at the table.*) That's no way to talk about our catered dinners.
THOMAS: The food's delicious.
LINUS: I'm sorry, Thomas. It's the way I talk.
THOMAS: You have no reason to be. Who wants a beer?

(*Without looking up from his book, Tulio lets out another of his contemptuous grunts. Thomas looks at him. Max makes a motion to him not to pay any attention to Tulio.*)

MAX: I prefer whiskey. I'll pour my own. (*Still reading, Tulio laughs sarcastically. Asel reprimands him with a movement of his head.*) And a tranquilizer for him.

THOMAS: (*With a laugh.*) He certainly needs it.

TULIO: (*Without looking up from the book.*) I was laughing at something . . . that's written here.

(*Thomas goes to the refrigerator and opens it. We get a glimpse of bottles and containers. Linus absent-mindedly hums an absurd and discordant tune: improvised tones that become grating at times. Thomas, who is deciding what to take from the refrigerator, looks at him uneasily.*)

THOMAS: If you wish, I'll turn on the music. (*Linus looks at him, says nothing, and shrugs.*) Would you like a beer? (*Linus looks at Asel, who gives him a faint nod of assent.*)

LINUS: Fine.

ASEL: (*Looking at Tulio.*) Another for me.

(*Tulio gives him a look of contempt. Thomas takes an opener from the shelf and opens a bottle of beer. Max takes down two tall glasses and holds them out to Thomas, who fills them. Max goes over to Linus and hands him one.*)

MAX: Here.

LINUS: Thanks. (*But he doesn't take it. Thomas is opening another bottle. He takes another glass from the shelf and serves himself.*)

MAX: (*To Linus.*) Here, man . . . (*Thomas looks at them.*)

LINUS: (*Reluctantly.*) Give it to me. (*He takes the glass. Max goes over to Asel.*)

ASEL: Who visited you this morning, Thomas? You haven't told us.

(*Linus, about to take a swallow, stops. Tulio closes his book and looks at them. Max pauses.*)

THOMAS: (*Laughing.*) I don't know if I should tell you. (*He starts to drink, pauses, and holds his glass toward Tulio.*) I'm sorry, Tulio. Would you like one? (*Tulio looks at him angrily.*)

MAX: Shall I put in some strychnine to make it taste better? (*He and Thomas laugh. Tulio slams the book on the table.*)

THOMAS: Really now, don't get so excited! (*He takes a swallow.*)

MAX: Your beer, Asel. (*He hands him the glass.*)

ASEL: (*Taking it.*) Thank you.

(*Linus crosses to the table with his eyes lowered and quietly leaves the drink which he has not touched. He sits down and begins to tap on the arm of his chair with his fingers.*)

THOMAS: And your whiskey, Max?

(*Max goes to the shelf and takes down a glass that already contains a few jiggers of whiskey.*)

MAX: Here it is. Will you put some ice in it for me?

(*Thomas looks at him with surprise and takes a metal container from the refrigerator.*)

THOMAS: When did you pour the whiskey?
MAX: (*With a quick glance at the others.*) A moment ago. Didn't you see me?
THOMAS: No.

(*He takes out a few ice cubes with tongs and puts them in the glass. Max stirs his drink. Thomas puts everything away and closes the refrigerator.*)

ASEL: (*Softly.*) Thomas, tell us who came.

(*Linus interrupts his strumming and waits for the answer. Tulio crosses his arms and looks at Thomas. Max drinks, keeping his eyes on him.*)

THOMAS: Well . . . it was that lovely little creature whose presence at the Foundation you persist in denying. (*They exchange glances.*)
ASEL: Your girlfriend?
THOMAS: (*Boastful.*) And with the number seventy-two on her blouse! You just missed bumping into the miracle, Asel! It hasn't been five minutes since she left. (*Tulio sits down with a snort.*) They don't believe me, Max. They think I like to invent things. (*He paces and drinks.*) Let them ask the sick man. He was awake when she came.
TULIO: (*Irate.*) Oh, shut up!
ASEL: Tulio!
TULIO: I can't stand any more of this. (*He gets up and crosses to look out from the doorway.*)
ASEL: What is it you can't stand? (*Tulio gives him an angry look.*) Try to control yourself. Your nerves have been on edge . . .
THOMAS: (*Smiling at Tulio, he goes toward him.*) If it bothers Tulio, I won't mention her again.
TULIO: Talk about anything you wish.
THOMAS: (*Reflecting.*) We've been rather isolated here . . . That may be the reason.
ASEL: The reason for what?
THOMAS: Asel, you get news of your wife and children. You had a letter

yesterday.

ASEL: That's right.

THOMAS: Max's mother visits him, and Linus also gets letters, from his parents . . . Are you married, Tulio? (*Silence.*)

ASEL: He doesn't have anyone.

THOMAS: I hope you'll forgive me. I'll tell Berta . . .

TULIO: (*He paces; excitedly.*) Not to come here? Thank you, thank you! Let them all come! I wish the whole world would come! (*To the others.*) The reason my nerves are on edge is not what Thomas supposes, and you all know that quite well!

ASEL: Don't shout, Tulio.

TULIO: Isn't shouting permitted either?

THOMAS: What are you talking about? (*Linus strums on the table again.*)

ASEL: Please, let's keep control of ourselves. Thomas, ask Berta, for all of us, to pay us a visit at the earliest opportunity.

TULIO: That's a mistake!

ASEL: (*Slowly.*) What are you saying? . . .

MAX: (*Smiling.*) It's not a mistake, and you should offer Thomas an apology.

THOMAS: That's not necessary.

MAX: But it is. To you and to us. (*He laughs.*) Why don't you make one of your marvelous photographs of us? The good friends at the Foundation having a friendly drink together. How does that sound?

TULIO: (*In a low voice.*) You're all off your rocker.

MAX: If you give me the camera, I'll take it, with you in the middle. On condition that you watch the birdie and smile. It will be a historic smile! (*They all laugh except Tulio; even the absorbed Linus laughs in spite of himself.*)

TULIO: (*With a distorted smile.*) Agreed. Provided that Berta stands beside me for the picture. (*Thomas's annoyance shows through.*)

ASEL: That's a crude thing to say, Tulio. (*Tulio shrugs. The telephone begins to ring softly. No one acknowledges it.*)

THOMAS: (*Coldly.*) You can take a picture of Berta, if you wish. But not now since she's not here.

TULIO: Right you are. She's not here.

(*Angered, Thomas takes a step toward him; he regains control and manages to smile.*)

THOMAS: Tulio, I give up on you! (*He finishes off his beer.*) Isn't anyone going to answer the phone? (*The others exchange glances.*) It's been ringing for quite a while now. It could be your wife, Asel. Or maybe your mother, Max . . .

MAX: I'll get it.

TULIO: (*Through his teeth.*) And so you will.

(*Max picks up the phone; all except Linus watch.*)

MAX: Hello . . . No, no. This is not Thomas . . . (*He winks at Thomas, who smiles.*) This is Max . . . How nice of you! We'd all like to meet you too . . . (*With a long face, Tulio crosses and disappears behind the alcove curtain. Thomas gives him a look of triumph.*) Well, almost all of us . . . (*Thomas is beside him, nervous.*) Thanks very much. I'll put Thomas on. He's standing here biting his nails . . .

THOMAS: Don't be silly. (*Asel goes to the table and sits down as he observes Thomas.*)

MAX: (*Laughing.*) He's already eaten his little finger. Be careful with him. He's capable of chewing up the phone!

THOMAS: Give it here, you fool! (*He snatches the telephone from him. Max goes over to the curtain and, as if he were seeing Tulio through it, points to Thomas with a gesture that asks: "What do you have to say now?" Afterwards he goes to the bed, observes the sick man an instant, and then leans against the foot of the bed.*) Berta, you got back so quickly! . . . In your car? I thought you had walked . . . (*Putting his hand over the mouthpiece.*) It runs, but I've promised her something better after we're married. (*He removes his hand.*) Since we saw each other? Oh, I can still see you! . . . Of course I can! . . . (*He turns toward the window.*) From here I can see you in your lodge. Listen, is Thomas still alive?

ASEL: Thomas?

THOMAS: (*Covering the mouthpiece.*) A mouse from the laboratory. She gave him my name. (*Removing his hand.*) Tell him we'll see about that! I'll hang him up by his tail. They hate that most of all . . . On the contrary! You called at a perfect time. Certain people who were denying your existence have had to bite the dust. Tonight they'll offer you their apologies . . . No, no! I don't want to hear it! You're coming tonight . . . So that my friends can see how beautiful you are! (*The roar of a toilet being flushed behind the curtain interrupts him.*) No, I can't hear very well right now . . . (*Bothered by the prolonged noise, he covers his free ear. Tulio reappears fastening his trousers.*) Listen! . . . You come tonight! . . . (*Upset, he hangs up the phone.*) She's hung up on me. Or the connection was broken. I don't know which . . . I expect she'll come. Tonight or tomorrow at latest.

TULIO: Or day after tomorrow.

THOMAS: (*Dryly.*) Thanks for the kind thoughts. At least you can't say she's not here.

TULIO: (*He crosses to sit at the table.*) I didn't speak to her on the phone.

THOMAS: But Max did! And he talked with her! And if it weren't for that damn noise you made, probably on purpose! . . . You could have decided to relieve yourself at some other moment, I believe . . .

ASEL: Not again! Please . . .

TULIO: Don't worry. I'll keep my mouth shut.

THOMAS: So will I.

(*He paces. Linus resumes his strange humming. Thomas stops in front of the window and contemplates the countryside.*)

LINUS: How long is it till lunch?

ASEL: Ten minutes or so. (*He takes out a short pipe, old and scorched, and sucks on it intently.*)

LINUS: That long?

MAX: No. Less than five minutes. (*Pause.*)

LINUS: (*To Asel, in a low voice, pointing to the sick man.*) Is it your turn to get his ration? (*Thomas turns around slowly, listening to them with a vague uneasiness.*)

ASEL: (*Sighing.*) Well . . . yes. I'm sorry.

(*Thomas starts to say something but holds back when he hears Linus. Max leafs through a magazine.*)

LINUS: If we at least had something to smoke in the meantime . . . (*Asel takes the pipe from his mouth and smells it with pleasure. Tulio takes out his handkerchief and passes it over his lips.*) You don't have any left, do you, Max? (*Max shakes his head.*)

ASEL: Patience. It's another flaw in this admirable Foundation. I don't think the cooperative store will be opening for a few days yet.

THOMAS: (*Stepping forward happily.*) I can solve the problem for you right now!

LINUS: (*Hopeful.*) You've got some cigarettes left?

THOMAS: Of course I have! I don't smoke very often. (*He goes to the duffel bags at right.*) And drink your beer, man! You haven't even tasted it! (*Linus picks up his glass and takes a sip, keeping an eye on Thomas. Tulio buries himself in his book. Max takes another sip of whiskey. Asel watches Thomas, who takes a pack of cigarettes from one of the bags and holds it up to view. Nevertheless, something disappoints Linus keenly, for he bows his head.*) Have a smoke! (*Thomas opens the pack and offers it around.*)

ASEL: Take your cigarette, Linus. (*Linus takes a cigarette from the pack with clumsy fingers and holds it in his hand.*)

THOMAS: (*To Asel.*) None for you?

ASEL: (*Putting his pipe in his mouth.*) You know that I'm trying to give up the habit.

MAX: I'm a hopeless addict. Let me have one. (*He accepts a cigarette and takes a box of matches from his pocket.*)

THOMAS: (*Timidly.*) Tulio . . . (*Without looking up, Tulio refuses with a movement of his finger.*) But you smoke . . . (*Angry, Tulio shakes his head. Thomas looks at the others and makes a gesture of dismay.*)

ASEL: (*Gently.*) You also refused his beer. Don't slight him a second time. He thinks a lot of you.

TULIO: (*He strikes the table with his fist, and with a grimace of impotence, he strikes it again and again.*) Enough sermons! Fine. I offer my apologies! (*Flushed with anger.*) And I'll prove to him that I also think a lot of him! I'll prove it to all of you! (*Calmer.*) Forgive me, I have a quick temper. (*Thomas offers him the pack of cigarettes.*) No. I said I don't want to, and I don't. (*He gets up and crosses. He turns back toward Thomas.*) Thank you. (*He stations himself in front of the door and looks out. Max lights his cigarette and offers a light to Linus, who hesitates. Max insists; Linus puts the cigarette in his mouth and lights it. But after two or three draws, he lets it burn away on an ashtray. Thomas takes out a cigarette and puts the pack away.*)

THOMAS: Will you give me a light? (*Max lights the cigarette for him.*) Thank you. Shall I turn on the television?

MAX: It's all too insipid at this time of day.

THOMAS: With all the silliness going on I forgot to set the table. I'll do it in a flash.

MAX: And how! If literature fails you, you can become a waiter in a resort hotel. They earn more than novelists . . .

THOMAS: (*Laughing.*) I'll give it some thought.

(*He has gone to the table and gathered up all the newspapers and magazines, which he leaves on the small table. Tulio turns and looks at him with sad eyes.*)

TULIO: (*Humbly.*) Can I help you?

ASEL: Bravo, Tulio! (*Tulio manages an embarrassed smile.*)

THOMAS: (*Touched.*) If you wish. I could use some help. Collect the glasses, please. Have you all finished?

MAX: (*Hurrying to drain his glass.*) Finished.

(*Tulio approaches the table with uncertainty. Thomas picks up the ashtray where Linus's cigarette is still sending up its column of smoke.*)

THOMAS: Don't you like this brand, Linus? (*He snubs out the butt.*)

LINUS: What? Yes. I like any brand.

THOMAS: (*He leaves the ashtray on the small table.*) You let it burn away in the ashtray.

LINUS: (*Disconcerted, he looks at the others.*) I wasn't thinking.

THOMAS: Ask me for another whenever you wish. (*He has hardly put down the ashtray when he stops in amazement at the incredible performance of Tulio who, after miming the collecting and arranging of the glasses, starts toward the shelves with his imaginary load. He has not even touched the glasses which are visible on the table. The others do not seem to find anything irregular in his actions. Max stands up, taking a final draw from his cigarette and leaving the butt in the ashtray. He then goes to the bed and takes a discreet look at the man in it. Linus strums absent-mindedly on the table with both hands. Smiling and savoring his empty pipe, Asel watches Tulio. Thomas controls his anger.*) You shouldn't offer to help just to make fun of me.

(*They all look at him in suprise. Unnerved, Tulio stops and turns around. Asel, paying close attention, walks toward them.*)

TULIO: Were you speaking to me?

THOMAS: (*Coldly.*) Who else? (*He goes to the table.*)

TULIO: And why . . . are you saying that?

THOMAS: What are you doing?

TULIO: Carrying the glasses . . . to the cabinet.

THOMAS: What glasses?

TULIO: (*Hardly daring to lift his hands.*) These.

THOMAS: I don't know what to think about you. (*He collects the glasses on the table with distinct clinking sounds.*)

TULIO: But . . . I . . .

MAX: (*Quickly.*) It was a joke, Thomas.

THOMAS: In very bad taste! (*He crosses with the glasses to the shelves.*)

ASEL: No doubt, but don't let it upset you . . .

THOMAS: (*Taking a print tablecloth from the shelf.*) He offered to help just to make fun of me.

TULIO: No!

THOMAS: (*Going to the table and laying the cloth.*) I'll ask the superintendent to move him to another room.

MAX: (*Helping him spread the tablecloth.*) Don't you understand? You have to excuse him . . .

TULIO: (*To Asel.*) I wanted to please him!

THOMAS: And he still insists! (*He goes to the shelves to get napkins.*) I don't want to hear another word! The matter is closed. (*With an angry look at Tulio.*) Forever.

ASEL: No, Thomas . . .

THOMAS: Are you going to take his side?

MAX: Give me the napkins. (*He takes the napkins and starts placing them.*)

ASEL: It wasn't a joke, Thomas. (*Thomas goes to look for knives and forks.*)

TULIO: (*With a grunt of sarcasm, he points to Max.*) Well, now! It seems that I'm the only one who doesn't know how to help.

MAX: (*To Thomas.*) I'll set the wine glasses. (*He goes to the shelves and takes down some wine glasses which he carries to the table.*)

TULIO: (*With contempt.*) Wine glasses!

ASEL: (*Going to Thomas.*) You've got to understand. He didn't know what he was doing.

MAX: I'll get the wine.

TULIO: Asel, if you're going to explain it that way, I prefer to do it myself!

ASEL: Don't be so easily offended. (*To Thomas.*) And you, come here.

(*Max carries a bottle of wine to the table. Thomas leaves the knives and forks on the table.*)

THOMAS: I have to set the table. (*He gets the plates.*)

ASEL: (*Following him.*) Listen to me, please. (*He takes Thomas by the arm.*)

THOMAS: Leave me alone.

ASEL: (*Leading him downstage.*) Come.

TULIO: (*Following them.*) I tell you not that way! I've had enough.

ASEL: (*Sharply.*) Just be quiet! (*Brief pause.*)

TULIO: (*With a deep sigh.*) Do it your way! I'll go on being patient. (*He withdraws to the table and sits at the left end of it, folding his arms.*)

ASEL: (*In a low voice.*) Thomas, you know that Tulio . . .

THOMAS: I don't know anything.

ASEL: You know that he's . . . an unusual person. (*Brief pause.*) You have to be patient too. And understanding.

THOMAS: All right, all right! If you say so. (*He goes to the table and puts down the plates; then he returns to get more. Max helps him place them.*) Thanks. (*Tulio is angered by Max's participation and the abruptness with which Thomas has set a plate in front of him. He pushes himself up from the table and, with eyes averted, pounds on it with his hands.*)

MAX: (*Trying to relieve the tension.*) What kind of car do you intend to buy when you get married, Thomas? (*Asel sits.*)

THOMAS: I don't know . . . What do you recommend? (*To Linus.*) Or you, engineer. You must know a lot about such things. What make do you recommend?

LINUS: I don't really know much about cars. I'm an engineer.

THOMAS: That's why I asked! What make do you drive?

LINUS: (*Laughing softly.* ) It's . . . the best.

THOMAS: (*Setting the final plate and laughing.*) I don't doubt it! (*He surveys the table and rubs his hands together.*) It's all ready. (*He stands *near the bed and looks through the window.*) What a beautiful day! (*They look at one another behind his back.*)

LINUS: And what a long one! It's been five hours now since breakfast. (*He puts his head down on the table between his folded arms and resumes his curious humming.*)

TULIO: Damn it, that smell keeps getting worse!

THOMAS: (*To Asel.*) Oh! . . . that's been taken care of too. (*They all look at him.*)

MAX: Taken care of?

THOMAS: I reported it this morning. (*Linus toys with the plate in front of him. Tulio clenches his fists.*)

ASEL: (*Getting up slowly.*) To whom?

THOMAS: To the superintendent. He came by earlier.

(*Linus gets up and, without putting down his plate, goes to the door and peers out cautiously. Then he turns around to listen, turning the plate nervously in his hands.*)

ASEL: (*At the same time.*) You said that there was only one visitor.

THOMAS: Berta. But the superintendent came earlier. You'd hardly left.

MAX: Aren't you confusing this with another day?

THOMAS: Why should I confuse it? He noticed the smell, and I explained to him what the problem was. He promised to call the plumber at once. (*Tulio turns his back and props himself against the table.*)

ASEL: Did he have anything else to say? (*Without turning around, Tulio stiffens.*)

THOMAS: The usual courtesies. Are we satisfied . . . all that.

ASEL: (*Smiling.*) You must have had something else to say to him, novelist. You like to talk.

THOMAS: (*Laughing.*) I told him about Berta, and about how nice you all are . . . (*Looking at Tulio.*) All of you.

ASEL: (*After a moment.*) Did he also talk with the sick man?

THOMAS: I . . . don't believe so. He was sleeping, just as he is now.

MAN: (*Without moving.*) I'm not asleep. I hear what you're saying.

THOMAS: (*To Asel.*) Well, he was asleep then. (*The others look at him strangely.*) Why are you looking at me that way? Don't you believe me now either? Ask him when he comes with lunch.

ASEL: It's not necessary, Thomas.

MAX: No one doubts your word.

THOMAS: (*Pacing.*) They're taking their time today . . . I'm beginning to have an appetite too. (*He's facing Linus.*) It must be the fresh air. We'll all be fat when we leave here. (*He laughs.*) It'll look good on you . . . You're muscular but a bit skinny.

(*Meanwhile, Asel goes over to Tulio and, in a way that Thomas will not notice, says something in an amiable manner and shakes his head in resignation. Tulio nods in agreement.*)

ASEL: You don't have so much weight on you either, Thomas.

THOMAS: (*Turning to face him.*) I don't need it!

ASEL: Come here, please. (*He steps forward. Thomas comes closer.*) You're pale.

THOMAS: I was always pale.

ASEL: (*He examines the mucous membrane of one of his eyelids.*) You're still quite anemic.

THOMAS: That's not possible!

ASEL: (*Smiling.*) Am I a doctor or am I not?

THOMAS: You are, but . . .

ASEL: I've already told you that you need extra nourishment. Let's do something. Apart from all the incursions you wish to make to the refrigerator, today you eat the sick man's ration.

LINUS: (*Annoyed.*) Why?

ASEL: If it's my turn today, I can give it to whomever I wish, can't I?

TULIO: To whoever needs it. And you need it, Asel.

ASEL: No. I cede it to Thomas.

THOMAS: You've done that before . . . And I can't eat everything I fancy! What about the others?

ASEL: Your appetite is greater. (*He looks at him hard.*) You said so yourself. It's the fresh air . . . Admit that you're dying to stuff yourself for just one day. And that you never do.

THOMAS: It's true. I don't understand it.

ASEL: Today you'll eat your fill.

THOMAS: Asel, I shouldn't accept it.

ASEL: Don't say any more about it. (*He puts his hand on Thomas's shoulder.*) A prescription from your doctor!

THOMAS: (*Looking down.*) Thank you. (*Silence.*)

TULIO: If I don't say something, I'll explode.

ASEL: If it's not something foolish. (*He sits and plays with his pipe.*)

TULIO: You are the most admirable man I've ever known.

ASEL: (*Smiling.*) That's foolish. (*Brief pause.*) Yesterday you also gave Thomas part of your food . . .

TULIO: Because you asked me to.

ASEL: Nonsense. You did it of your own free will.

TULIO: You may believe that. (*Silence.*)

MAN: I'm hungry too. Why have you got me on a diet?

(*No one acknowledges these words. Thomas, very perplexed, casts a glance at the sick man.*)

THOMAS: I, too, am going to explode if I don't say something, Asel.

ASEL: Well, say it.

THOMAS: I don't understand what you're doing . . . as a doctor.

ASEL: Because you aren't a doctor.

THOMAS: Shouldn't the sick man eat something? (*The others exchange glances without Thomas noticing.*)

ASEL: Absolute restriction of food.

MAN: Why?

THOMAS: Why?

ASEL: It would take a long time to explain.

THOMAS: He doesn't even drink.

ASEL: He drinks. Every night I give him the liquid that he needs.

THOMAS: (*Confused.*) And during the day . . . nothing?

ASEL: Nothing.

THOMAS: He'll die of thirst.

ASEL: No.

THOMAS: (*Timidly.*) Are you going to examine him today?

ASEL: There's no need. His condition is stabilized.

THOMAS: (*Suspicious.*) I suppose you know what you're doing.

ASEL: Rest assured.

THOMAS: But tell me, Asel . . (*He presses his shoulder.*) If we have more food than we need, why do we take his ration every day and eat it by turns? (*Asel falters.*)

MAX: And why not?

LINUS: You admitted that you were hungry.

THOMAS: (*Pacing.*) Yes. We all are . . . And I can't figure it out!

MAX: It's the air.

(*Silence. Thomas looks at them one by one and gets an innocent look in return. Then he goes to the bed and leans over the Man in it.*)

THOMAS: Are you all right? Do you want something? (*There is no reply. Thomas straightens up and turns to Asel.*) You don't suppose something's happened to him . . . do you, Asel?

ASEL: No.

THOMAS: (*Taking a few hesitant steps, he turns to look at the landscape.*) It's beautiful living here. We'd always dreamed of a world like the one we finally have. (*Silence.*)

MAX: Don't mention the toilet to the superintendent again. He might get annoyed.

TULIO: (*Dryly.*) It's certain the superintendent won't forget.

THOMAS: Don't worry. (*He goes to the wall unit.*) A little music?

ASEL: Whatever you wish. (*Thomas starts to press a button.*)

MAX: Wait. I think lunch is here. (*He goes toward the door with a plate in*

*his hand.)*
LINUS: Yes. They're bringing it.

*(Tulio takes a plate and crosses in turn, lining up behind Linus and Max. Thomas goes to the table.)*

ASEL: *(With indifference, he puts away his pipe, takes a plate, and stands up.)* You take the sick man's plate.
THOMAS: I was going to.

*(He picks up two plates and goes toward the door. Asel places himself behind Tulio. Guided by two waiters attired in tails, a chrome, double-leveled serving cart appears along the right gallery corridor. The upper level is heaped with platters of delicious foods, and the lower one with succulent desserts. The superintendent appears, all smiles, between the cart and the railing.)*

SUPERINTENDENT: Good day, gentlemen.
ALL: Good day.

*(The first waiter hands Linus a small basket of golden rolls, which Linus quickly passes to Max and he to Tulio, who passes it to Asel. Asel steps out of line for a moment and places the basket on the table.)*

SUPERINTENDENT: *(At the same time.)* Today's menu is excellent and varied. *(The waiters smile.)* You have a good selection. *(To Thomas, who is approaching with the two plates.)* Is one for the sick man?
THOMAS: Yes. What do you suggest? *(A giggle from the first waiter.)*
SUPERINTENDENT: Can he eat everything?
THOMAS: Everything.
SUPERINTENDENT: *(With a faint little laugh.)* Then allow me to recommend these delicious appetizers, the pâté de foie-gras, and sirloin with mushrooms. *(The waiters stiffle their giggles of amusement. Thomas holds out a plate and one of them starts filling it.)* And for dessert . . . I suggest the apple tart. It's delicious.
THOMAS: Perfect. I'll have the same.
SUPERINTENDENT: Thank you. *(The second waiter asks Thomas for the other plate and starts to serve him.)* Does that little odor bother you much? *(Thomas looks at his companions and hesitates.)* Forgive me for asking at such an inappropriate moment . . . *(A short burst of laughter escapes from one of the waiters. The superintendent gives him a quick look but smiles too.)*
TULIO: *(From the line.)* We hardly notice it.
SUPERINTENDENT: *(Very serious.)* Nevertheless, it will be fixed as quickly

as possible . . . have no doubts about that.

(*The curtain falls for a few brief moments or fade-out.*)

## Scene 2

*The same iridescent brightness in the room; the upstage landscape, unchanged and radiant. The door is still open. Although nothing seems different, three changes can be noted if we look closely. Of the five elegant chairs, the two situated at the right of the table have disappeared, and two of the three bundles that were under the bed have replaced them. It can now be seen that each of them consists of an old mattress, thin and narrow, whose rolled up spiral is exposed through the edges of their sack covering. The third change affects the bedclothes: the sheets and coverlet have been replaced by a drab cover, and the pillow no longer has a case.*

*The man remains in the same position. Seated on the floor downstage right, Tulio is reading his tattered book; he puts his handkerchief to his nose from time to time. Linus, absorbed in thought, is seated in profile on one of the rolls at the right of the table. Facing forward and seated near the left end of the table, Thomas comments on a large book of art reproductions to Asel and Max, who are standing on either side of him. A few moments of silence.*

THOMAS: I never get tired of looking at them.

MAX: Is it a small painting?

THOMAS: It's probably no more than a meter wide.

MAX: That's incredible. (*Tulio grunts contemptuously without looking up.*)

THOMAS: Notice the gold lamp. Such details! And see how clearly the map stands out in the background.

TULIO: (*Without interrupting his reading.*) The map in the background, with its old creases . . . (*The others exchange glances.*)

THOMAS: Exactly. Like a piece of oilcloth that's cracked. (*He points to the page.*) Do you see? It must be very difficult to paint those effects. But Terborch was a master.

TULIO: Terborch was a master, but that painting isn't by Terborch.

ASEL: Tulio, why don't you come over and look at it with us? Why do you need to sit on the floor?

TULIO: (*Curtly.*) For variety.

THOMAS: (*Bending over the book to read.*) It says Gerard Terborch here.

TULIO: A painter is seated with his back to the viewer, sketching a girl crowned with laurel and holding a trumpet. Is that the one?

THOMAS: The same!

TULIO: (*With a sigh.*) I'm sorry, but I can't help getting into the discussion. That painting is by Vermeer.

THOMAS: It says here! . . .

TULIO: I don't care what it says!

THOMAS: (*Bending over the reading closely.*) It said . . . (*straightening up, puzzled*) Vermeer. How could I have read Terborch?

ASEL: (*Laughing.*) These Dutch painters are all alike. The window, the curtain, the glass of wine, the map . . .

MAX: You simply confused them.

THOMAS: (*Incredulous.*) The names? Besides, I knew that the painting was by Vermeer . . . (*He bends over the book again.*) It says so here. Thank you, Tulio. (*Tulio gives him a scornful look and says nothing.*) Do you want to come see? Obviously you like the painting.

TULIO: I don't feel like getting up.

THOMAS: (*Warmly.*) Not even to look at art books? You have around you the most beautiful works created by man, and you never look at them.

ASEL: Everyone has the right to be himself.

THOMAS: But it's absurd for him to spend hours with his nose in that beaten-up old book! A manual on cabinet making! Who would think it? (*He points to the bookshelves.*) He could be enjoying a great novel . . . Do you want me to pick one for you? (*Tulio looks at him coldly.*)

MAX: Let's look at some more pictures.

THOMAS: (*Perplexed by Tulio's silence.*) Yes . . . yes. (*He looks at the book.*) Vermeer . . . (*His enthusiasm is rekindled.*) For certain, there's something curious in this painting. The lamp is almost identical to the one in an earlier work. (*He searches through the book.*) A small painting by Van Eyck . . . The portrait of a couple.

TULIO: (*Between his teeth.*) Arnolfini.

MAX: It's not Italian, Tulio. It's Flemish.

TULIO: *Arnolfini and His Wife!* It's in the National Gallery in London. But I'll keep my mouth shut. (*He appears to bury himself in his book.*)

THOMAS: Yes. That's the one. Here it is. Look! (*He compares the two pages.*) One would say that it was the same lamp.

MAX: And if it were the same?

THOMAS: No. Vermeer copies Van Eyck . . . or it's a mysterious coincidence. It's very improbable that he knew this painting.

TULIO: All that imagination! Those two lamps are like you and me.

THOMAS: They're almost the same. Look at them.

TULIO: I don't need to. In Vermeer's, the lamp has slender arms, a spherical body; in the Flemish work, wide arms with fretwork, a cylindrical body . . .

THOMAS: Slight differences . . .

TULIO: And a large metal eagle crowns Vermeer's. Or am I wrong? (*Silence.*)

THOMAS: I think . . . you're right.

TULIO: So, there goes your mysterious coincidence.

ASEL: Your memory is remarkable, Tulio. (*Tulio shrugs.*)

THOMAS: I'll grant you that. It's natural: a photographer as good as you had to know a lot about painting. What's the word for that technique you want to perfect?

TULIO: (*He lays down his book but doesn't look at them.*) Holography. (*He sighs.*) Yes . . . Images that walk among us . . . three-dimensional. And yet they're only projections in the air: holograms.

MAX: Haven't they discovered how to do that already?

TULIO: It can be improved. It's an immense field. (*Brief pause.*) I . . . was doing some research in it, yes. With another person. I wanted . . . (*He hides his face in his hands.*) My God! I wanted.

ASEL: (*Going to his side.*) You will, Tulio . . . Don't lose hope.

THOMAS: That's why you've come to the Foundation . . . You'll see when you get down to work. We'll do all the great things we've dreamed of here! Max will solve the problem of N Functions, Linus will perfect his technique for pre-stressing, Asel will systematize the science of acupuncture . . .

ASEL: I've never spoken to you about acupuncture.

THOMAS: That is your research; someone told me. The microcurrents of the skin and their relation to illnesses . . .

ASEL: (*Smiling.*) If you say so . . .

THOMAS: And Tulio will fill the world with images undreamed of, and I . . . will write my novel. Come over to the table, Tulio. You comment on the paintings. (*He turns the pages of the book.*) Look, Botticelli . . . El Greco . . . Rembrandt . . . Velazquez . . . Goya . . . Chardin . . . Won't you? (*Silence.*)

ASEL: You continue. (*He sits at the table.*)

THOMAS: (*Distressed.*) Something is wrong.

MAX: Go on!

THOMAS: Watteau . . . Turner . . . (*He stops.*) Turner! It's like a diamond of light. (*He turns toward the window.*) Almost as splendid as that view. Another rainbow of clouds, or rocks, of fresh water, of radiant places . . . (*He has been searching nervously for something in his pockets. Brief silence.*) Where did I leave my cigarettes? I put the pack in my pocket and it's not there. (*Tulio uncovers his face. They all look at Thomas.*)

ASEL: Are you sure you put them there?

THOMAS: What? . . .

MAX: (*Laughing.*) Do you suppose it was a holographic pack?

THOMAS: Don't joke.

MAX: You probably put them down someplace and forgot.

THOMAS: I haven't taken them out of my pocket! We couldn't have smoked them all.

ASEL: (*Looking into his eyes.*) Then think.

THOMAS (*Smiling in spite of himself.*) Is this a guessing game?

ASEL: Maybe.

THOMAS: You've hidden them.

ASEL: I swear to you that no one has touched your cigarettes.

THOMAS: (*Doubtful.*) It can't be . . .

ASEL: (*Pointedly.*) And nevertheless, it is.

MAX: Don't worry. They'll turn up.

THOMAS: (*Still suspicious.*) I hope so . . . (*He turns the pages of the book again.*) Manet . . . Van Gogh . . . I hope so . . . (*He lapses into silence. Asel observes him closely.*) I don't know this painter. Do you like him?

ASEL: Do you?

THOMAS: Solid line but weak color . . . (*Tulio is attentive to what he is saying.*) Must be a nineteenth-century animalist.

MAX: An animalist?

THOMAS: You can see for yourself. Mice in a cage. A sordid theme. (*As he speaks these words, Berta appears inconspicuously in the doorway. She is smiling.*) There's something repellent in those creatures. (*Unnoticed, Berta takes a few steps into the room. Thomas is still bent over the book.*) Tom Murray. I don't know who he is. (*Absorbed in himself, Linus is making his warbling sounds.*)

ASEL: Do you know his work, Tulio?

TULIO: No.

(*Thomas sits up slowly. Without turning around, he seems to realize intuitively that Berta is standing behind him.*)

ASEL: And what are those poor mice doing? (*Berta frowns and steps back in silence.*)

THOMAS: (*Entranced.*) What are they doing?

ASEL: They're doing something or waiting for something. Right? (*Berta observes them from the gallery with a grave expression and then disappears left. Thomas stands up and suddenly turns around. He goes to the door and looks out in both directions. He turns around, deep in thought.*) What's wrong with you?

THOMAS: Nothing.

(*A pause, in which the only sound is Linus's humming. Suddenly this stops. Thomas looks at his companions with misgiving; then at the motionless man on the bed. Alarm and doubt show in his eyes.*)

LINUS: How long until dinner?

ASEL: About four hours.

LINUS: (*He takes a deep breath, covering his mouth and nose. He gets up and goes downstage, taking in air eagerly.*) It's hard to breathe here now.

ASEL: It'll all be over soon.

LINUS: And will it be better?

ASEL: We'll see.

THOMAS: (*Uncertain.*) They'll fix the commode right away . . . (*To Linus.*) If you can't breathe at that window, come to the door. You can smell the countryside from here.

LINUS: Then smell to your heart's content!

THOMAS: (*Murmuring.*) Sometimes it's hard to please you. (*He starts to return to the table but stops when he notices Linus's bedroll.*)

ASEL: (*Getting up and going to Linus.*) A little calm for a while yet, Linus. You know it's necessary.

(*Thomas listens to him and looks at the bedroll again. He goes on to the table and stops beside the book. He looks inquisitively at Max.*)

MAX: You haven't told us yet what those mice represent.

THOMAS: (*Curtly.*) No more paintings for today. I can see that I'm boring you.

ASEL: No, not at all! (*Thomas closes the book and returns it to the shelf.*)

MAX: On the contrary! . . .

THOMAS: (*With finality.*) Yes. (*He examines the book spines and decides to take another one. Max clicks his tongue and shakes his head.*) What?

MAX: (*Smiling.*) If the devotion has ended, the obligation will begin.

THOMAS: What are you talking about?

MAX: Guess the riddle. Who's the shirker in charge of cleaning today?

THOMAS: (*With a look of annoyance.*) I'm sorry. I'll take out the trash now.

(*He crosses and stops near one of the small armchairs and caresses its back; then near the two mattress rolls which he studies furtively. Asel observes him with keen interest. Thomas leans over and touches the covering of the one at right.*)

ASEL: What are you looking at?

THOMAS: (*Straightening up quickly.*) Nothing. (*He goes upstage and disappears for some seconds behind the alcove curtain; he reappears looking with amazement at the broom he has in his hand. It is not the one he used during the morning but an old, dirty broom with a very short handle. He looks at his companions and hesitates.*)

ASEL: Is something wrong?

THOMAS: No . . . but I'd like to know . . . (*Lowering his voice.*) I don't understand.

ASEL: What is it you don't understand?

THOMAS: (*He laughs suddenly.*) What's the point of all these jokes?

MAX: (*Good-humoredly.*) What jokes?

THOMAS: Don't pretend. I'm not a fool. You're changing things, or hiding them.

ASEL: What things? Where?

THOMAS: (*Seriously.*) Are you going to deny it?

ASEL: I, at least, am not playing jokes. (*They look at each other intently.*)

THOMAS: (*Morose.*) Let's drop it. (*He considers the broom in his hand again. He bends over and sweeps out a small pile of trash, which he leaves in the gallery at left of the door. When he straightens up, he looks out toward the right.*) They're making their pickups now. I almost forgot. (*He enters at the same time that the two waiters arrive by the right corridor. They are carrying a dark box with handles. They are no longer wearing their dress coats but long aprons over gray shirts and old trousers. They place the box at left of the door, and the second waiter, the only one visible now, takes a small broom and a dustpan from it. He collects the trash, dumps it in the box, and places his equipment back in it. He lifts the box by a handle—it is assumed that the first waiter has lifted the other side—and exits left. Thomas starts to look out but steps back: the door is being closed slowly by the smiling Superintendent who bows obsequiously and quietly completes his action. The surface of the door is of light, finely-varnished wood; on its left side there is a bronze knob and, in the center, a peephole. Thomas reacts with a start.*) Why has he closed the door without asking permission?

MAX: He smiled at you. He fixed everything with smiles. (*Suspicious, Thomas puts the broom behind the curtain.*)

THOMAS: But why did he close it?

LINUS: (*Annoyed.*) They do it every evening.

THOMAS: Every evening?

TULIO: (*Getting up and going to the table to put down his book.*) If it bothers you so much, open it.

ASEL: Don't tell him that.

TULIO: Why not? (*To Thomas.*) Open it, and call it to his attention so that he won't do it again.

ASEL: Are you crazy, Tulio?

TULIO: You're the one who's crazy! Where is all this getting us?

MAX: We're going to have to send you to the infirmary, Tulio.

LINUS: No, not Tulio! (*He points to Thomas, who watches them anxiously.*) Him!

ASEL: You just keep your mouth shut.

LINUS: I'm always keeping my mouth shut! But it's time to stop. Let him go to the infirmary, and us . . . wherever.

ASEL: What if they talk with him?

TULIO: (*Sitting on the edge of the table.*) Open the door, Thomas!

ASEL: (*Shaking his head vehemently.*) Please!

TULIO: Open it, boy! (*Asel stands aside in dismay.*) What difference does it make to you, Asel. Ending this is part of your plan.

ASEL: If you could just keep quiet . . .

MAX: (*Laughs.*) Ah! So there's a plan? I trust you'll keep me informed . . .

ASEL: Don't pay any attention to him. But if you could all be a little more understanding . . . without any more talk. Try to keep calm, think . . . and then, please, let's proceed.

(*Max looks at him inquisitively. Linus sighs and sits in an armchair. Tulio hangs his head. Silence.*)

THOMAS: (*Full of mistrust.*) What . . . are you talking about?

TULIO: (*To himself.*) This is what they call co-existence . . . and it's maddening.

THOMAS: (*With his hand on the door knob.*) Shall I open it, Asel? (*Asel hesitates.*)

TULIO: It's not going to hurt anything . . . Tell him to open it. Open it, novelist.

THOMAS: (*He thinks about it. Trembling.*) I don't dare . . . What are you doing to me?

TULIO: Nothing. Nothing harmful to you. (*Standing up.*) It's not important, Thomas. Really. Let's try to amuse ourselves . . . What game can we play?

MAX: (*With a giggle.*) Taking pictures.

ASEL: Now?

TULIO: Why not? It's a good idea. Shall I take them, Thomas. When they're developed, you can give them to your parents.

ASEL: (*Severely.*) No more of that, Tulio.

THOMAS: (*Cheerfully.*) Yes, Asel! Tulio wants to prove his friendship, and I appreciate that. I'll give the pictures to Berta. I can't, of course, to my parents. I no longer have any. Get your camera ready, Tulio. (*He steps forward.*) The rest of you, form a group around the table. Come on. (*They begin to place themselves.*) Is there enough light?

TULIO: Certainly.

THOMAS: (*Crossing.*) I'll turn on the chandelier. It's very strong.

LINUS: (*With sarcasm, to himself.*) The chandelier. (*Thomas presses the switch of the large fixture but it doesn't light. He tries again without results.*)

ASEL: (*In a low voice.*) I wouldn't do it, Tulio.

TULIO: (*In a low voice.*) Let me give him the satisfaction.

THOMAS: It doesn't turn on.

TULIO: It's all the same. We don't need it.

MAX: The current's probably off.

THOMAS: Do you think so? I'll try the television. (*He pushes a button.*) Or the stereo speakers! Do you want to hear some music?

ASEL: If you're in the mood for it . . . (*Thomas presses another button and waits a few seconds.*)

THOMAS: That's odd. It doesn't work either.

ASEL: (*To the others.*) Which is . . . very interesting!

THOMAS: And the television won't turn on . . . I'll leave all the switches on so we'll know how long it lasts. (*To Tulio.*) Is your camera ready? (*He laughs.*) That will work.

TULIO: In a jiffy. (*He goes to the shelf and takes down an ordinary aluminum tumbler, while Thomas finds himself a place with the group.*)

THOMAS: (*Sitting.*) I'll get here.

MAX: Attention! Smile, everyone. Watch the birdie!

TULIO: One moment. (*He simulates preparing his camera.*) Ready! (*He turns toward them and pretends to focus on them with the tumbler. Asel does not conceal his uneasiness.*) Look this way! (*He strikes the tumbler with his fingernail.*) Another?

THOMAS: (*Standing up angrily.*) No. And I don't want that one either.

TULIO: But it's already made!

THOMAS: I appeal to you! Because now he's played a joke on all of you, not just me!

ASEL: (*In a low voice.*) I was expecting it.

TULIO: I wanted . . .

THOMAS: To make a fool of me again.

TULIO: Asel, I wanted to please him! (*Asel sighs.*)

THOMAS: (*Rushing at Tulio and snatching the tumbler from his hand.*) With this? (*Holding it up.*) You tell me whether it's madness or a calculated trick! I'm beginning to think the latter!

TULIO: I never do the right thing. (*Asel takes out his old pipe and caresses it.*)

THOMAS: (*To Tulio.*) Who did you think you were, you dunce?

ASEL: What do you have in your hand, Thomas?

THOMAS: A metal tumbler!

ASEL: (*To all of them.*) Take a good look. The reactions are becoming encouraging.

THOMAS: I don't understand your jargon! (*He grabs Tulio by the shirt.*) And you, you miserable clown, crazy piece of shit, get out of here. Go live in another room!

TULIO: (*Jerking free.*) Go yourself and leave us in peace!

THOMAS: I'm going to! . . . (*He tries to attack him, but the others in-*

*tercede and subdue them.*)

ASEL: No, Thomas!

LINUS: (*To Thomas.*) Leave him alone! You're the one at fault!

THOMAS: Shut up, engineer! (*They struggle. Thomas throws himself at Tulio again and is repelled. The others subdue him again.*)

ASEL: (*Forcefully.*) Let me speak! All of you listen! Please! . . . I beg you, Thomas . . . (*They calm down little by little.*)

LINUS: (*He goes to sit down.*) Let him go. Let's end this once and for all.

ASEL: It'll end soon for all of us. And it's ending for him too. Don't you realize? Just bear with me for a while longer, please.

LINUS: For what? If it's all ending for him too, leave him in peace. He'll be better off.

ASEL: No! I assure you it's not the best way. (*Morose, Tulio crosses, grabs his old book, and sits down as far away from the others as he can.*) Thomas, explain to me, if you can, where that tumbler came from.

MAX: From the shelf.

ASEL: Will you let him talk?

MAX: (*Sarcastically.*) At your orders, chief.

THOMAS: Tulio took it from the shelf.

ASEL: And it was there? (*Thomas doesn't reply.*) Had you seen it there before?

THOMAS: That's what I've been asking myself . . . (*He goes to the shelves, takes down a crystal glass, and compares the two.*) Because here there are only wine goblets and crystal, like this one.

LINUS: Bad.

ASEL: (*With a smile.*) No. Not completely bad. Where do you suppose that tumbler came from, Thomas?

THOMAS: This tumbler . . . and other things.

ASEL: Can't you say?

THOMAS: You and the others will have to say.

ASEL: Return the glass and the tumbler to their places, please. (*Thomas does so with a brusque motion and turns around to face him.*)

THOMAS: You explain it!

ASEL: Stay beside the shelves. If his camera is still there, Tulio will take your picture.

TULIO: What are you saying?

ASEL: (*Firmly.*) If your camera is there, you will take the picture! (*To Thomas.*) But is it there?

THOMAS: It always has been . . .

ASEL: Then bring it.

THOMAS: (*He searches in vain on the shelves. He turns around.*) It's not there!

ASEL: How curious! As far as I know, no one has hidden it.

THOMAS: But it has disappeared too.

ASEL: And in its place, an unexpected metal tumbler. (*Silence. Thomas looks at them and thinks hard.*)

THOMAS: Max, this morning you didn't pour your drink.

MAX: I assure you I . . .

THOMAS: I assure you that you took it from here already served. The broom that we had has been transformed. Suddenly neither the television nor the speakers work . . .

MAX: The current is off.

THOMAS: Two of the chairs have disappeared.

ASEL: (*Very interested.*) Oh, really?

THOMAS: Yes. And in their place, two bedrolls. And now, a filthy tumbler in place of a camera.

MAX: (*With his little laugh.*) What did I tell you! They must be holograms.

ASEL: Forget about your holograms! (*To Thomas.*) There are no devices here, no laser beam projectors. (*To the others.*) There's only . . . a little more to eat. I hardly dared to believe that there would be any result, but it's happening. With a rapidity that amazes me, and delights me.

THOMAS: No, please! I've had enough puzzles. The way you're talking proves that you know something I don't. And all these strange things that are happening are a surprise to me but not to you! I insist on an explanation.

TULIO: Why not speak, Asel?

ASEL: I've told you many times. It would be dangerous.

LINUS: For whom?

ASEL: For him, although he doesn't matter to you. But also for us.

LINUS: (*After a moment.*) You aren't a doctor.

THOMAS: (*Astounded.*) Did he say you aren't. . . ?

ASEL: (*To Linus.*) Careful what you say.

LINUS: You're not a doctor. And you don't know what's advisable and what isn't.

ASEL: I know, unfortunately, quite a few things more about life than you.

THOMAS: Is it true, Asel? Aren't you a doctor?

ASEL: What do you think?

THOMAS: I'd like to believe that you are . . . (*He lowers his voice.*) But . . . if you aren't . . . what are we doing to that poor man? (*He points to the man in the bed and his expression suddenly changes when he sees the bedclothes.*) No! Why? What have you done with the sheets and the spread?

TULIO: Nobody's done anything.

THOMAS: There's only a blanket left, and a filthy pillow.

ASEL: (*To the others.*) The most difficult moments are coming now! Not a word too much or a word too little. If you help me, I expect that we'll deal with the case successfully. (*Max looks at the other two and nods his approval. Tulio and Linus look away.*)

THOMAS: I don't understand what's going on!

ASEL: Are you sure? (*Silence. Thomas doesn't know what to answer. Asel goes to him and puts his arm around his shoulders.*) Come with me. (*He leads him toward the bed.*)

THOMAS: Are you going to examine him?

ASEL: There's no need. (*Very confused, Thomas touches the blanket lightly.*) Leave him in peace. (*He points over the bed with his index finger.*) And tell me what you see there. (*Thomas looks without comprehending.*)

THOMAS: Beyond the window?

ASEL: (*After exchanging a glance with the others.*) Beyond the window.

THOMAS: The landscape.

ASEL: (*He places his pipe in his mouth and sits down.*) Like a Turner. That's what you said.

THOMAS: But . . . more beautiful. Because it's real. (*He turns to face the landscape.*) Real! (*To Asel.*) Isn't that so?

ASEL: Go on.

THOMAS: Words get in the way. Seeing it is enough. It's our finest evidence.

MAN: (*Motionless.*) They've taken my covers. I'm cold.

THOMAS: (*Perturbed.*) Dazzling evidence. Now the world is like a garden. Men have finally brought it about, with suffering and tears . . .

ASEL: (*Very softly.*) That still exist . . .

THOMAS: What?

ASEL: They still exist . . . don't they? And in abundance.

THOMAS: (*Hesitating.*) Still, yes. But . . .

MAN: I'm hungry.

THOMAS: (*To Asel.*) . . . but you know it too: what we see is the future we used to dream of . . .

MAN: Give me some water!

THOMAS: (*Pointing to the landscape.*) And now it's ours!

MAN: (*Raising his voice.*) Why don't you give me something to eat and drink?

THOMAS: The Foundation builds and improves . . . I can see its people from here . . . laughing in the morning sunlight.

MAN: (*Louder.*) Tell Asel to give me something to eat!

THOMAS: (*Nervous.*) Do you hear it, Asel?

ASEL: People laughing in the sunlight?

THOMAS: Yes.

ASEL: Are you certain? Don't you notice sadness in some of the faces?

THOMAS: They're so far away . . .

MAN: Why do you eat my ration?

THOMAS: Answer, Asel! If you don't the nightmare of the anthropoids has not ended yet!

ASEL: Answer whom? That man?

MAN: (*Strongly.*) This is the nightmare of the anthropoids!

THOMAS: (*Very nervous, he points to the landscape.*) No! Men are beginning to be human! Don't prevent it, Asel! And answer!

MAN: (*Shouting.*) Animals! Hypocrites!

THOMAS: Asel, give him something to eat!

ASEL: He doesn't need it. You spoke of the morning sunlight. Do you know what time it is?

MAN: You're devouring me, you're killing me!

THOMAS: Asel, for pity's sake!

ASEL: At least you know it's evening and not morning. From which direction is the sun shining on that landscape?

THOMAS: From the east . . .

ASEL: And this morning?

THOMAS: (*Puzzled.*) From . . . the same.

ASEL: Doesn't it seem strange that you don't notice the slightest difference? Or do you?

MAN: Sing and dance for joy . . . I have good news for you . . . I'm dying.

THOMAS: (*Pointing to the man.*) Asel, he's dying!

MAN: (*Shouting.*) Murderers!

THOMAS: Murderers! We're helping to kill him! (*He rushes at Asel, who stands up. The others, tense, step closer.*)

MAN: I can't endure any more.

THOMAS: (*He puts his fists against his head and lets out a scream.*) Murderers!

LINUS: Don't shout!

ASEL: (*Restraining him.*) Calm down, Thomas. It's only a crisis and it will pass!

MAN: Water!

THOMAS: Give him water!

MAN: I'm dying. . . !

THOMAS: (*He slips out of Asel's grasp. He shakes the man's shoulders.*) I'll give you water!

MAN: Like a hungry rat!

THOMAS: (*Shouting.*) I won't stand for it! . . .

TULIO: Shut up! They're going to come check! (*Thomas runs toward the alcove curtain. Asel catches him.*)

ASEL: Quiet!

THOMAS: Turn loose! (*They struggle.*) I'm going to give him a drink! (*They all attempt to restrain him.*)

LINUS: Shut your mouth!

ASEL: Silence! All of you!

MAN: (*In a very weak voice.*) It's too late . . . now. (*Thomas struggles. Aided by Asel, Linus subdues him with a wristlock.*)

ASEL: Do you hear them? They're at the door.

(*Thomas works loose. Motionless, they all fix their eyes on the door. A few seconds of absolute silence. Suddenly we hear a harsh metallic sound, and the door opens very rapidly toward the right. The interior light changes instantaneously. A gray, oppressive glow replaces the bright iridescence. The Superintendent bursts in, followed by his aide who remains in the doorway with his hand suspiciously hidden in his jacket pocket. The Superintendent surveys the scene, runs to the bed, and jerks the cover from the man who is revealed in poor and worn underclothes. He shakes the body a bit and turns around.*)

SUPERINTENDENT: How long has this man been dead?

(*The lights suddenly change, becoming brighter and harsher. Only the corners of the room and the overhead fixture remain in a dull, indistinct half-light.*)

THOMAS: Dead? . . . Why, he just spoke.
SUPERINTENDENT: You be quiet! (*To the others.*) Answer!
ASEL: Six days.
THOMAS: (*Mumbling.*) It's not possible.
SUPERINTENDENT: Why didn't you report it? (*Silence. An evil smile comes over the Superintendent's face.*) You wanted to keep his ration. Right? (*Silence. He directs his words toward the door.*) Get this carrion out of here! (*The waiters, now dressed in white hospital jackets, appear with a stretcher which they put down just outside the door. Without disguising their revulsion, they enter, take the rigid body out, place it on the stretcher and exit with it.*) His personal effects. (*To the aide.*) And you, roll up the mattress. (*Max hastens to take one of the duffel bags from its hook. The Superintendent takes it from him. The aide puts the pillow and blanket on the mattress, rolls it all up, puts it on his shoulder, and takes it into the corridor.*) Plate, cup, and spoon. (*Tulio goes to the shelves and, to Thomas's surprise, takes down a plate, a metal tumbler and a crude metal spoon, which he hands over to the Superintendent. The Superintendent points downstage.*) Keep the window open! (*From the doorway, in an icy voice.*) And depend on the consequences.

(*He exits. The door closes with a loud clank. Its surface has changed. It is no longer of wood but of studded metal plate, and the knob has disappeared. Silence. Thomas rushes to the door, which he pushes to no effect. He looks in vain for the brass knob. His face distorted, he caresses the cold sheet of metal. He turns around and stands with his back glued to the door, looking aghast at his companions. Asel watches his every move-*

*ment. The others wearily find a place to sit down.)*

TULIO: It finally happened. I'm almost glad.
LINUS: I'm not. Six days aren't very much.
TULIO: Better than nothing.
MAX: Now they'll take us downstairs to the hole.
ASEL: *(Fervently.)* That's what I'm hoping for.
MAX: Do you mean . . . you wanted this?
ASEL: I didn't say that.
LINUS: Will it be long before they move us?
TULIO: Within a couple of hours. Or maybe tonight.

*(Silence again. Thomas slowly moves away from the door, shaking his head.)*

THOMAS: *(In a veiled voice.)* He wasn't dead. *(Taking a few more steps.)* We all heard him speak. He asked for something to eat.
LINUS: *(Hostile.)* No one heard him. Except you.
THOMAS: *(Frightened.)* Are you insinuating that . . . I'm sick?
LINUS: *(After a moment.)* He's been dead for six days.
THOMAS: But it can't be . . .
LINUS: Of course it can! Why do you suppose it smelled so bad in here? *(With a mordant laugh.)* They've fixed the plumbing for you!

*(A new and instantaneous increase in the harsh illumination, except in the corners.)*

ASEL: Be sensible, Linus.
LINUS: What does it matter now? It's all finished now.
ASEL: Not for him.
THOMAS: Is that true, Asel? Was I the only one who heard him? *(Asel bows his head.)* You didn't hear him? Tell me the truth . . .
ASEL: *(Sad, he goes and sits on the bed.)* No, Thomas. I didn't hear him. *(Thomas goes to the foot of the bed and leans against it.)*
THOMAS: Why did you kill him?

*(Linus represses a retort.)*

ASEL: Nobody killed him. He died of starvation.

*(Thomas straightens up. Perplexed, he runs his fingers over the bedframe. He studies the room, the overhead fixture, the harsh new light. He goes over to the bedrolls and touches one of them.)*

THOMAS: It's stifling in here . . . I think I'll have a beer. (*He has hardly dared to say this. Unsteadily, he goes to the refrigerator. When he gets close, he stops in amazement and steps back. The light suddenly becomes even harsher and stronger. At the same moment, a panel the same color as the wall descends and completely hides the porcelain door. Thomas turns around.*) It's not . . . possible. (*He goes to the wall unit and holds out an unsure hand. The light makes its final leap and remains fixed in a hard and almost unbearable whiteness that only respects the shadows in the corners. A panel descends, gradually hiding the bookshelves until they disappear completely. With increasing anxiety, Thomas goes to the telephone and stands looking at it. Undecided whether to pick up the receiver or not, he puts his hand on it. Then he withdraws his hand very slowly and places it against his other hand. Suddenly he turns toward the window and toward the sundrenched landscape. He then goes downstage and takes a deep breath as he looks through the invisible window. Without turning around, he appeals to Asel.*) Am I sick, Asel?

ASEL: No more than the rest of us. (*He gets up and goes to his side. They look through the invisible window together. Asel points with his pipe to the exterior.*) The afternoon is beautiful.

THOMAS: Yes. (*Tulio, Linus, and Max watch them.*)

ASEL: Look. A band of swallows.

THOMAS: They're playing.

ASEL: The world is marvelous. And that is our strength. We can recognize its beauty even from here. These bars can't destroy it. (*Thomas reacts with a start. His hands sieze two invisible bars.*)

THOMAS: Where are we, Asel?

ASEL: (*Gently.*) You know where we are.

THOMAS: (*Unconvinced.*) No . . .

ASEL: Yes. You do know. And you'll remember. (*They stand looking through the window.*)

(*Curtain.*)

# PART TWO

## Scene 1

*The light has stabilized—harsh and garish, although less intense than before. The strange gray half-light persists in the curtained area and downstage left. The dazzling panorama still glows behind the large window. All of the smaller armchairs have disappeared; around the table, only three bedrolls which serve as seats. The folding bed at right is still in its place. The table is no longer of fine wood but of cast iron similar to the wall shelves, and it is fixed into the floor. The bed has also been transformed: a simple cot of the same cast iron, built into the left wall, with two wide metal legs at the foot. On the small table, only the telephone. No expensive dishes, no fine crystal or linens on the shelves; only the dull shine of metal tumblers and a stack of spoons. In the doorway, a small pile of trash.*

*Thomas is still wearing his dark trousers, but his four companions are dressed in wrinkled pants of the same color as their numbered shirts, which they now wear loose like blouses. On the bare bed and propped against the head, another bedroll on which Asel is seated savoring his old pipe. Tulio, seated on the bedroll nearest to the left wall, is reading, bored, in his eternal old book. Linus is drying, with a greasy cloth, five dented metal plates which are stacked on the table. Max is not visible. Leaning against his folding bed, Thomas watches Linus, who smiles and shows him the plate he is drying. Their faces are all more emaciated now.*

LINUS: Fine china! Worthy of the exquisite meal we've just bolted down.
   (*Thomas lowers his head.*)
MAX'S VOICE: (*From behind the curtain.*) I've got the runs!
LINUS: You too?
MAX'S VOICE: A minor complaint.

(*Linus goes on with his task and becomes immersed in his peculiar hum-*

*ming. Without turning to look at it, Thomas touches the piece of furniture he is leaning against like a blind man trying to identify its shape. Afterwards, he goes to the table and studies its metal form. He looks at Linus and then at the others.)*

THOMAS: Have you always worn those pants?
TULIO: (*Without looking up from his book.*) Ever since we came here. (*Thomas sneaks a look at his own to compare. He then walks slowly behind Linus to the small table. Doubtful, he places his hands on it.*)
ASEL: The ration was worse than ever today.
MAX'S VOICE: Little more than slop.
ASEL: I wish I knew if it was punishment for us or if everybody got the same.
MAX'S VOICE: I don't think they're giving us any special treatment . . . They haven't even shaved our heads.
ASEL: No, and it's odd. (*Brief pause.*)
THOMAS: (*To himself.*) The magazines were here. (*Asel looks at him.*)
TULIO: (*Offering his book to Thomas.*) If you want to read, this is all there is.
THOMAS: No, thanks. (*Tulio goes back to his reading. Thomas turns his head and contemplates the radiant light of the landscape outside. The light in the room is dimming very slowly.*)
LINUS: (*Carrying the plates and the cloth to the shelves.*) Now you can sweep under the table. We're due for a room inspection.
TULIO: They opened the doors a minute ago.
LINUS: All except ours, of course. (*He looks for the broom behind the curtain and glances at the floor under the table.*) It's not worth the bother to sweep. Nobody ever drops a crumb around here. (*He goes to the door, sweeps the trash into a more compact pile and, still holding the broom, leans against the wall with his arms crossed.*)
THOMAS: (*Facing forward.*) It's growing dark. (*He turns back toward the landscape, where the glorious morning still gleams.*)
TULIO: You can't see a thing. They're taking their time to turn on the light . . .
LINUS: (*Toward the curtain.*) Finish up, Max. They'll be coming soon.
MAX'S VOICE: I'll be right there.

*(There is the sound of a toilet flushing. Thomas notices it. Then he goes to the bed and sits at Asel's feet. He runs his fingers over the metal work of the bedframe. The light suddenly comes on over the bed.)*

TULIO: Speaking of the devil . . . (*He tries to go on reading.*)
THOMAS: This metal is strong.
ASEL: Very strong.

THOMAS: And the bed is fastened into the wall.

TULIO: What a pitiful light! (*He drops the book on the table with a dull thud.*)

THOMAS: (*Standing up hurriedly.*) Maybe if I turn on . . . (*He starts to the left to turn on the overhead lamp. Silently the great glass shade rises and disappears; the light in the area that it occupied is not the same as in the room.*)

TULIO: The what? (*Thomas watches the shade disappear without too much surprise and passes his hand over his forehead. He then goes to the head of the bed to turn on the reading lamp attached to the wall. He extends his hand only to see the little lamp sink into the wall. Max comes out of the curtained alcove fastening his trousers under his loose shirt. Thomas returns to downstage left.*)

THOMAS: Asel . . . weren't any of those things ever here? (*Max sits on his bedroll.*)

ASEL: Did you see something?

LINUS: (*Caustically.*) Of course he did. He even turned it on sometimes. A lamp.

THOMAS: It's hard for me to think . . . that they only existed in my imagination.

TULIO: You're to be congratulated, Asel. The mental confusion is clearing up. And a bit of extra food was all it took. You were right.

ASEL: (*Gravely.*) I'm not so sure.

TULIO: The boy's better and it seems there've been no relapses.

ASEL: (*Hesitating.*) Yes . . . unless . . . something else is involved.

THOMAS: Are you talking about me? (*Asel does not answer him.*)

TULIO: I don't understand what you mean.

MAX: Neither do I. What are you talking about?

ASEL: (*Measuring his words.*) Yesterday . . . Thomas had a visit from his girlfriend. Not here, but in the visiting room. At least that's what they said when they summoned him.

THOMAS: (*Surprised.*) And what about it? (*They all look at him. We begin to hear doors slamming consecutively; each time the sound is closer.*)

LINUS: The inspection! (*He takes a position against the wall beside the door. Max and Tulio get up quickly and go to the door, stationing themselves at attention on the other side. Asel puts away his pipe, leaps from the bed and lines up next to Linus. Thomas moves more slowly and takes a place, facing the door.*)

THOMAS: The doors slamming . . .

MAX: You hear them every day.

THOMAS: Yes . . . I know that. (*The sound of the slamming doors grows louder, recedes, and becomes louder again until it can be heard very near. Suddenly it ceases.*)

LINUS: Attention. (*He stiffens. We hear the noise of a heavy key, and the door opens. The Superintendent and his aide, in their elegant attire, are in the doorway. The fragment of remote countryside that could still be seen through the doorway has been eclipsed; now we glimpse another long gallery, several yards away and parallel to the familiar one, with a railing identical to the other. It projects over a gray wall in which the dark steel rectangles of numerous identical doors are visible.)*

SUPERINTENDENT: The garbage.

LINUS: Yes, sir. *(He quickly sweeps out the little pile and leaves it at left of the door, returning immediately to his rigid position. The Superintendent enters and brushes Thomas aside. With quick fingers, he inspects the utensils on the shelves; he pokes a bit at the duffel bags, runs his hands over the table, the bed . . . His eyes investigate every corner of the room. Thomas is struck by anxiety when he notices the new panorama through the door.)*

THOMAS: *(To the Superintendent.)* Why don't they let us go out?

*(The Superintendent turns around like a flash and studies him for a moment. From the gallery, the aide lets out a faint guffaw.)*

SUPERINTENDENT: *(Opting to smile.)* The Foundation offers you once more its apologies, Mr. Novelist. It is necessary to open an investigation into what has happened here. And in the meantime . . . *(His hands complete his apology. He goes out into the corridor and speaks over the stifled laughter of the aide.)* We wish you gentlemen a peaceful repose. *(He exits left. The aide closes the door with a dull thud. Immediately the sounds of successive doors closing resume. The noise gradually diminishes for a few moments. Linus leaves the broom behind the curtain. Tulio starts toward the most distant bedroll; Max sits again where he was; Asel walks slowly downstage and looks through the invisible window.)*

ASEL: It's night now.

TULIO: I'm going to unfold my sumptuous divan and lie down.

MAX: We have to conserve our strength.

*(Linus sits on another bedroll and starts to hum absentmindedly. Thomas hasn't moved. Suddenly he goes to the door and pushes in vain. Then he studies the brilliant landscape. Asel notices what he is doing, moves back to the table and sits on its edge with his arms folded. Tulio unrolls the bedroll at left and extends it along the wall after spreading the wrapping on the floor. He pounds the mattress without much effect and also softens up the pillow, which he puts in its place. He then tosses the narrow blanket over it all.)*

THOMAS: *(Mumbling.)* I can't believe it.

MAX: (*Softly.*) Can't believe what?

THOMAS: When they opened the door . . . you couldn't see the countryside.

MAX: What did you see?

THOMAS: A lot of doors . . . like ours.

TULIO: (*Sitting on his thin mattress.*) And you heard them open and close.

THOMAS: Yes.

TULIO: (*To Asel.*) You must surely recognize that the process continues.

MAX: You believe you're seeing odd things, right? The Superintendent was probably dressed differently. In a uniform, for example . . .

THOMAS: No, no. He was dressed the same as always. But those doors . . . are incomprehensible. (*Tulio stretches out with a sigh of relief.*)

ASEL: Something else is incomprehensible. And I wonder if you've all noticed how incomprehensible it is.

TULIO: I know.

ASEL: So what's your opinion?

TULIO: Perhaps they're thinking it over.

ASEL: There's nothing to think over. It's been three days since they discovered the dead man. They should have transferred us to the hole immediately. And we're still here. (*Linus stops humming.*)

MAX: (*Justifying it.*) But we're cut off from the rest and denied the right to take exercise.

ASEL: The transferral hasn't happened, and it always does, even for the slightest infraction. They haven't even searched us for weapons. (*Thomas hears these words with amazement. Asel turns to look at him.*) And even our isolation isn't complete. (*Tulio sits up and looks at him.*)

MAX: Are you referring to what happened before the inspection?

ASEL: Thomas was called to the visiting room yesterday. Yesterday: two days after they discovered what we had done.

THOMAS: It was Berta . . . You heard him say so.

ASEL: (*Without looking at him.*) Isn't that unusual? Max, your mother has moved to a town nearby to see about you better, and she visits you frequently. It's certain that she must have tried to see you during these three days of isolation, and they haven't called you.

MAX: Special treatment . . .

TULIO: Like we've given him.

MAX: It's the only thing that they are in agreement with us about.

ASEL: You don't understand what I'm saying. Let's suppose for a moment that his mysterious girlfriend . . . didn't come, as she never came here.

THOMAS: But she did visit me! And she's here!

ASEL: (*Without looking at him.*) She doesn't come, and they call him. And when he returns, he tells us about her visit. (*They all look at Thomas and he, astounded, at Asel.*)

TULIO: What are you thinking?

ASEL: (*Twisting his hands.*) The worst part of our situation is that we can't even speak frankly. I'm thinking what you are.

TULIO: (*After casting a glance at Thomas, he murmurs.*) It's hard for me to believe.

MAX: (*Calmly.*) And me.

ASEL: But you are thinking it.

MAX: Even if it were true, how can you explain that they don't move us?

THOMAS: (*Disturbed.*) You're leaving me out of things again!

MAX: (*To Asel.*) You seem to be sorry that they haven't taken us to the hole. (*Asel and Tulio exchange looks.*) We wouldn't be better off down there than here. Or would we?

TULIO: We'd be worse off.

LINUS: Then what does it matter?

ASEL: (*Irritated.*) It matters because it's not logical! And I don't like that at all.

MAX: Given our situation, maybe they haven't considered the infraction so serious.

ASEL: With Thomas, at least, they've acted differently.

LINUS: (*Laughing.*) Are you losing your confidence in him? You've changed in a hurry. (*Thomas sits on Asel's bedroll and hides his face in his hands.*)

ASEL: I just wonder why they called him. That's all.

LINUS: That I don't know. (*He gets up and disappears behind the alcove curtain.*)

MAX: He must have had a visitor . . .

ASEL: (*Sharply.*) We're not allowed visitors.

MAX: Maybe they're making exceptions.

ASEL: And what about your mother? (*Silence. The toilet is flushed. Asel turns around slowly and faces Thomas.*)

MAX: Thomas, tell us about your visit with Berta.

THOMAS: (*Uncovering his somber face.*) I've already told you.

ASEL: But not in detail.

THOMAS: What difference does it make? (*Linus reappears and leans against the wall.*)

ASEL: (*Holding back his anger.*) Please.

THOMAS: You think I'm lying.

ASEL: Then tell us and don't lie.

THOMAS: I've never lied!

TULIO: (*Mildly.*) Thomas, tell us about your visit . . . I believe you.

THOMAS: (*Sighing.*) They called me over that speaker. (*He points over the door.*) All of you heard it.

TULIO: And then?

THOMAS: Berta was waiting for me in the visiting room.

ASEL: Behind a metal screen?

THOMAS: No.

ASEL: What do you mean no?

THOMAS: Didn't you want details? Behind two screens. Our fingers couldn't even touch. They apologized for that.

LINUS: What did they say?

THOMAS: That they were doing it to avoid possible contagion. Because of the work she does in the laboratory and because of what had happened here.

TULIO: What did your girlfriend say to you?

THOMAS: She asked me how I was. I said fine. I reproached her for not coming to see me more often, or hardly ever phoning me.

MAX: And she? . . .

THOMAS: (*Bowing his head.*) She started to cry. She wouldn't tell me why. I told her she couldn't fool me, that something was wrong. Because . . . she was not wearing the clothes of the Foundation . . . but an old suit, without a number. She said that she was dressed that way because . . . she had gone into town to do some shopping . . . and she promised to visit me soon, or call me. But she hasn't come . . . And she left in tears . . . really sobbing. And now you . . . I don't know what you suspect or what you're up to. And I don't understand anything about what's going on! (*Asel goes to the bed and sits at its foot.*)

ASEL: And what did you say to them?

THOMAS: A half-dozen words. They insisted on escorting me back.

MAX: Perhaps they asked you about your novel . . .

THOMAS: And about your work . . . They expressed regret for the atrocity we had committed; they asked me if some medical experiment had been involved . . .

ASEL: Medical?

THOMAS: They know that you're a doctor. (*Asel looks at the others.*)

ASEL: Did you tell them?

THOMAS: They already knew, didn't they? And they asked if it was a medical experiment.

ASEL: Mine?

THOMAS: (*Thinking.*) I don't recall that they mentioned you specifically. They only asked me what our purpose was in doing it. (*Asel gets up and takes a few steps. He turns around.*)

ASEL: And what did you answer them?

THOMAS: That I wasn't well and that I didn't remember a lot of things . . . that, in my judgment, the absurd thing had been done to have something more to eat. Then they apologized again for the shortage of supplies and assured me that it would get better very soon.

LINUS: They spend their lives promising.

TULIO: But it hasn't gotten better.

THOMAS: No.

(*Silence. Thomas looks at the landscape and notices that it is fading. It frightens him but he says nothing.*)

LINUS: I'm going to make my bed. They'll be turning off the lights soon.

ASEL: Wait. (*He goes very close to Thomas and speaks to him.*) What else did you tell them?

THOMAS: (*Intimidated by the hardness of his tone.*) I think . . . that's all.

ASEL: You think. But your head doesn't always work so well . . . you admit that yourself. You see things the rest of us don't see, you speak of people we don't know . . . Let's suppose for a moment that your memory is false . . . A false memory that conceals the real one.

THOMAS: She was in the visiting room. And she was crying.

ASEL: Let's suppose . . . you didn't go to the visiting room; they take you to an office. And they ask you why we concealed the death of our companion.

THOMAS: I told them on the way back!

ASEL: (*Forcefully.*) What else did you tell them?

THOMAS: (*Sitting up.*) You have no right to suspect me like this! (*He leaps from the bed and Asel grabs him by the arm.*)

ASEL: Berta didn't come! Why did they call you?

TULIO: (*Intervening.*) Asel, you're going too far . . .

THOMAS: Let go of me!

ASEL: What did you talk to them about?

THOMAS: (*Struggling.*) Let me go! . . .

ASEL: (*Angrily.*) Why don't they transfer us? (*Thomas pulls free and goes downstage angrily.*)

MAX: An interesting question.

THOMAS: Let someone answer that who knows. The Foundation is very strange, I do know that. But the Superintendent has just apologized! That was real! (*He points upstage.*) As real as that landscape!

ASEL: Which never changes!

THOMAS: (*With his finger extended toward the window.*) It's growing dark! Night's falling and it's growing dark! Don't you see it?

TULIO: The relapse.

ASEL: Or a stupid lie.

THOMAS: (*Making an effort to remain calm as he speaks.*) I'm not lying. And Berta is here. She'll come tonight. Because I'm going to tell her to right now.

ASEL: (*Ironically.*) By telephone?

THOMAS: Yes! Before someone makes it vanish too. (*He goes slowly to the phone and puts his hand on it; he watches the others suspiciously. With an angry movement, Asel extends his bedroll on the bed; without ar-*

*ranging it further, he observes Thomas with deep distrust.*)

MAX: (*Meanwhile, being conciliatory.*) We all lose our calm sometimes, and today it was Asel's turn.

LINUS: (*Looking at him.*) Not everyone.

MAX: Everyone! You included. Asel's a very rational man, and if something seems to him incomprehensible, he loses patience . . . Maybe your call will explain things. Pick up the phone. (*Max makes a pleading gesture to Asel to keep calm. Asel then lies back against the edge of the bed and folds his arms. Tulio sits on his mattress. Thomas glances around and picks up the telephone. He dials. A long pause. He jiggles the phone several times and continues to listen nervously.*)

THOMAS: Nobody answers. (*The others watch him suspiciously. He hangs up slowly, with a look of puzzlement. He withdraws his hand and stands contemplating the telephone. Then he moves away without looking at anyone.*)

ASEL: (*Softly.*) I don't know what to think.

TULIO: (*Sitting on the bed beside Asel.*) Now I'm the one who tells you: keep quiet and give it some thought.

ASEL: (*Keeping an eye on Thomas.*) I'll try.

TULIO: Maybe he is sincere and the process is still going on. It appears that the telephone is still here, but it no longer works.

LINUS: (*Softly.*) And it's possible that his girlfriend really did visit him.

(*Unhappy with himself, Asel arranges his mattress on the bed. Tulio goes closer to Thomas, who notices him and proceeds to the folding bed and begins to open it up. Once his meager bed is ready, Asel stretches out and enjoys his pipe.*)

TULIO: (*To Thomas.*) You'll see your girl again, just as I'll see mine. At least I hope so. (*Asel shows interest in what Tulio has said.*)

MAX: Yours?

TULIO: I've never mentioned her to you. Why? I don't know. But tonight I can't get her out of my mind. I'm almost twenty years older than she is. I adored her and couldn't tell her so. Just imagine: I felt so ridiculous before that girl . . . (*He laughs.*) She had to propose to me. (*Max smiles. Linus sits on his bedroll.*)

ASEL: (*Putting his pipe away.*) Where is she now?

TULIO: Abroad. We decided that she should take advantage of the fellowship she'd won . . . (*Thomas listens as he finishes arranging his bed.*) That was a real fellowship! When she came home, we were going to get married. I don't know where she is now. Her trip saved her.

THOMAS: (*Timidly.*) From what?

TULIO: (*Looking at him and smiling.*) From me . . . (*He sits.*) You don't know how much it means to me that she's safe and able to use her time productively. She has a doctorate in Physics; she knows a lot more than I do. She came to me to find out what all the fuss about holograms meant . . . because I am a good technician. (*Thomas is leery of this topic.*) If we were together again, there's an excellent universtiy that would hire us . . . in another country. We spent a year there: the best year of our lives. We had all the equipment we needed, they built whatever we requested . . . and we approached it like a game . . . For us, the most fascinating of games.

ASEL: Holographics? (*He goes toward them.*)

TULIO: Yes. We played jokes on each other. We would project three-dimensional objects to fool the other . . . We had achieved enormous perfection in the images and in disguising the projection source. (*Thomas stops what he is doing. He feels nauseated.*) I fell for it more often than she; I've always been a little naive. And she would burst into laughter, with that laugh of hers . . . that I'll hear always.

THOMAS: (*Very softly.*) Stop talking.

TULIO: One day she was waiting for me in the laboratory, sitting very quietly in a chair reading. I started to kiss her . . . (*He laughs.*) It was a hologram!

MAX: (*Astonished and amused.*) A hologram?

TULIO: From top to bottom! Even the chair! She had hidden behind a table, she began to laugh like crazy. (*He laughs.*) And I . . .

THOMAS: (*Shouting.*) Shut up! (*They all look at him. Silence.*)

TULIO: Patience, boy. You'll have Berta in your arms again.

ASEL: Don't tell him that.

TULIO: Let's dream a little, Asel! (*Standing.*) He'll be reunited with his girl and I'll be with mine! Life would have no meaning if that didn't happen. I understand you very well, Thomas. (*Thomas shakes his head without turning around.*) One day we'll have them in our arms! And they won't be illusions, they won't be holograms! (*Thomas buries his face in his clenched fists.*) It will be a reality we can touch . . . of flesh and blood. (*He goes toward Asel.*) That's why I'll do all that you say, Asel. It must happen!

LINUS: What?

ASEL: (*Quickly.*) His reunion with her, man. (*He and Tulio exchange looks.*) You'll invite us to the wedding, won't you?

MAX: (*Looking at Asel curiously.*) Now you're starting to dream.

ASEL: (*Laughing.*) Just a little unburdening, before the lights go out.

LINUS: They're taking their time tonight.

ASEL: Then what's wrong in using the time that's left to dream a little? Yes. Maybe one day we will toast the health of the happy couple.

TULIO: We'll drink a lot of toasts on a lot of occasions. (*He paces.*)

MAX: What occasions?

TULIO: (*Very seriously.*) When they give my girl and me the Nobel Prize.

(*Max laughs broadly. Thomas manages a smile and turns toward them slowly. The others laugh too; and Tulio laughs in turn.*) Well, here we are in a madhouse and all happy. But I warn you that it was already being talked around the university . . . when we had the bright idea of coming back here.

MAX: Homesickness.

TULIO: Stupidity.

MAX: (*Laughing.*) I swear I'd like to have a beer now. (*Thomas looks instinctively at the place where the refrigerator had been.*)

LINUS: So would I!

MAX: To toast your Nobel Prize and the one that Thomas will get for his novel!

THOMAS: (*Smiling, he goes to the table and sits on the end.*) Don't talk like children.

TULIO: (*Slapping him on the shoulder.*) Why not! We're all children, like you! Dream, Thomas. I'm sorry I criticized you for it. It's our right. To dream with our eyes open! And you're opening yours now. If we dream that way, we'll get somewhere.

ASEL: If they give us time. (*He sits on Thomas's bed.*)

LINUS: Sentences can be commuted, Asel! They could commute ours!

ASEL: I prefer not to hope for that.

MAX: What else can we hope for?

ASEL: (*He and Tulio exchange looks again.*) True.

THOMAS: What would they have to commute for us? (*A burst of laughter from the others.*)

TULIO: Asel, that is the voice of innocence!

ASEL: (*Coldly.*) Perhaps.

THOMAS: (*He gets up; his manner is more outgoing.*) I'm glad you said all that, Tulio. We've had our disagreements, but I am your friend. You'll be with your girl again! (*With strength and seriousness.*) Life, the happiness of creating, awaits us all.

TULIO: That's how it will be, Thomas. They won't destroy us. One day we'll remember all this, over a beer. (*He puts his arm around his shoulders.*) We'll say: it seemed impossible then. But we dared to imagine it, and here we are.

ASEL: (*Gravely.*) You said it. Here we are.

TULIO: No, no! We shall be, we shall say: here we are. (*He presses Thomas's shoulder affectionately.*) And you, with your fantasies, have made me understand that. You're not so crazy. You're alive. Like me.

THOMAS: (*Moved.*) But . . . do you understand, Tulio. If we believe in that future it's because, in some way, it already exists. Time is another illusion. We don't hope for anything. We remember what is going to happen.

ASEL: (*With a melancholy smile.*) We remember that time does not exist

. . . if they give us time to.

TULIO: (*Laughing.*) Don't ruin this night for us, Asel. Not tonight!

THOMAS: (*Almost like a child.*) Not tonight, Asel. (*And he laughs too.*)

ASEL: Agreed, agreed. Long live the eternal present! (*He takes out his pipe.*)

MAX: Bravo! Smoke your pipe filled with air, Asel! (*Asel laughs and puts the pipe back in his mouth. But he puts it away at once and sits up, tense.*)

ASEL: Shhh. Be quiet. (*Brief pause.*) Don't you hear footsteps?

TULIO: Footsteps? (*Asel gets up and looks toward the door. Linus rushes to the door and listens with his ear against the metal. Tulio becomes tense.*)

LINUS: They're coming closer.

MAX: Maybe they're only passing by. (*Absolute silence. A few seconds pass.*)

LINUS: They're not going by. (*He steps back toward the right wall. The sound of a key. The door opens quickly. On the threshold, the Superintendent and his aide. Behind them the gallery full of closed doors. Both men have their right hand in their jacket pocket; the Superintendent has a piece of paper in his other hand. He enters.*)

SUPERINTENDENT: C-81.

TULIO: (*His hand touches the inscription on his breast.*) That's my number.

SUPERINTENDENT: (*Reading.*) Tulio. . . ?

TULIO: (*Interrupting him.*) That's me.

SUPERINTENDENT: Come with us and bring all your possessions.

ASEL: No one else?

SUPERINTENDENT: (*Irritated by the question.*) From here, no one else. (*Tulio gives a deep sigh and crosses to take his bag from its hook.*)

LINUS: I'll help you. (*He turns around and takes a plate, a tumbler, and a spoon from the shelf. Tulio crosses with his duffel bag and leaves it on his mattress. Asel goes to his side and bends over to help him. Linus starts to cross; he hesitates and looks at the Superintendent.*)

SUPERINTENDENT: (*Sharply.*) What's wrong with you?

LINUS: Are they taking him below?

SUPERINTENDENT: Why below?

LINUS: Because of what happened here . . .

SUPERINTENDENT: No.

(*Linus goes on to Tulio's mattress, opens the duffel bag, and puts the utensils in it. He immediately goes to the foot of the mattress and looks at Asel, who is at the other end.*)

TULIO: (*In a weak voice.*) Let me do it.

LINUS: No. Not you. (*With Asel's help, he rolls up the mattress and ties it *with some cords attached to the cover.*)

THOMAS: (*At the same time, to the Superintendent.*) Are they transferring him to another room? (*Linus gives him a hard look; Tulio is motionless, with his eyes down; the Superintendent smiles.*)

SUPERINTENDENT: To another place.

THOMAS: I never went so far as to request it, Tulio . . .

TULIO: I know. Don't worry.

THOMAS: (*Puzzled.*) Come back to see us . . .

SUPERINTENDENT: (*To Asel and Linus.*) Get a move on you!

ASEL: It's ready. (*He and Linus stand at attention.*)

SUPERINTENDENT: (*To Tulio.*) Pick it up.

TULIO: (*Disdainfully.*) Not without saying goodbye first. (*The Superintendent shows him impatience but he says nothing.*) Thomas, we'll always be friends. (*He embraces him.*)

THOMAS: (*Smilingly.*) I swear we'll not have any more arguments. I'll see you soon.

TULIO: In case we don't see each other, just a word of advice . . . Wake up from your dreams. It's a mistake to dream. (*He releases Thomas.*)

THOMAS: (*Surprised.*) But . . . I thought we . . .

TULIO: (*He cuts him off with an affectionate pat on the shoulder.*) Good luck. (*Turning to Max.*) Max . . .

MAX: (*Embracing him.*) Keep your courage.

TULIO: I will. Thanks for your help, Linus.

LINUS: (*Embracing him.*) We won't be any luckier than you.

TULIO: Who knows? (*To Asel.*) Who knows, Asel? They haven't given me enough time, but it can all still work out. (*They embrace warmly.*)

ASEL: (*His voice breaking.*) Tulio . . . Tulio.

TULIO: No. Don't weaken now. (*They separate. Their hands are still firmly clasped.*)

SUPERINTENDENT: Come along! (*Linus and Asel hoist the bedroll onto Tulio's shoulder. He walks to the door and turns around.*)

TULIO: Luck to all of you!

THOMAS: (*Affected in spite of himself.*) I hope you see your girl soon, Tulio! (*For Tulio, this is like a stab in the back, and a look of desperation comes over his face. But he grits his teeth and exits rapidly, disappearing at left. The Superintendent exits behind him and the door is closed. Silence. Asel throws himself down on his bedroll.*)

LINUS: (*Striking his hand with his fist.*) That's why they didn't turn off the light!

MAX: (*Mumbling.*) I'll make my bed. (*He goes to his bedroll.*)

LINUS: Do you prefer his place? It's more private.

MAX: You take it. (*Linus takes his bedroll and begins to spread it out in the place that Tulio's had occupied. Max extends his between the bed and the table. Asel begins to undress very slowly: first, his shoes, which he* places under the bed. Then his shirt, which he puts at the foot of the bed. He is deep in thought.) We'll try to sleep. (*Max takes off his shoes and unbuttons his blouse.*)

LINUS: Will they deprive Tulio of light also?

ASEL: At dawn.

LINUS: You didn't understand me.

ASEL: You didn't understand *me*.

LINUS: (*Taking off his shoes.*) We'd better hurry. They're going to turn it off. (*He continues undressing. Thomas sits on his bed and takes off his shoes.*)

THOMAS: We're all sorry to see Tulio leave . . . He was a good companion in spite of his moods. (*He starts placing his clothing on the bed. Linus watches him closely.*)

ASEL: Just be quiet, please!

MAX: Don't pay any attention to him.

ASEL: None of you can understand how alone I feel.

THOMAS: (*Fondly.*) You're not alone, Asel. And it won't be long before we see Tulio again. (*He has finished undressing and remains in immaculate underwear, which contrasts with the tattered and not very clean underclothes of his companions.*)

ASEL: (*Harshly.*) If you were pretending, you would not be forgiven.

LINUS: I don't think he's pretending. He just doesn't want to wake up.

THOMAS: Wake up?

LINUS: (*Bitterly.*) The last thing Tulio said to you . . . don't forget it, because you won't see him again.

THOMAS: What do you know about it?

LINUS: They're going to kill him. (*Thomas's expression suddenly changes and he stands up. The light over the door goes out. The only illumination is the pale moonlight that penetrates through the invisible window.*)

MAX: At least there's a moon. (*He finishes undressing hurriedly.*)

THOMAS: (*To Linus.*) What did you say?

LINUS: They're going to kill him, you fool! Like all of us! (*To Asel.*) He has to be told, Asel, even if you don't wish it!

ASEL: (*Seated on his bed, he looks at Thomas.*) I have nothing more to say.

THOMAS: Are we all losing our minds? (*Suddenly he runs to the telephone.*)

LINUS: Where are you going? (*Thomas starts to pick up the phone as the instrument slides across the table and disappears through an opening in the wall which then closes.*)

THOMAS: Are you all trying to destroy me? . . . Asel, can't I even trust in you? (*In the face of Asel's silence, he returns to his bed and sits down, trembling.*)

ASEL: (*In a voice like ice.*) What else did you tell them when they called you? (*With a desperate gasp, Thomas hurriedly climbs between his clean sheets. He contracts his body and pulls the sheets up until only his staring eyes are visible over the edge. Asel lifts up his legs, props them on the bed and hides his face in his hands. Max, seated on his bedroll, can hardly be seen behind the table; his arms crossed over his knees, he rests his head on them. Linus sighs and crawls under his blanket; half sitting up on one elbow, he stares straight ahead. A long pause.*)

LINUS: What else could he have told them? And what can it matter to you?

ASEL: (*Without lifting his head.*) Very little now. This is the end.

LINUS: You shouldn't think the worst . . .

ASEL: You're young . . . Is this the first time?

LINUS: Yes. And you?

ASEL: The third. The second was very long. This one won't be so long. And there won't be a fourth time.

LINUS: You can never say that.

ASEL: Even if I escaped from this one, there wouldn't be another. I've used up my strength. For some time now I've been asking myself if it wouldn't be preferable to hear music, to see television sets, cars, refrigerators, all around me . . . If Thomas wasn't pretending, his world was real for him, and a lot more bearable than this horror in which we insist that he live too. If life is so short and so poor, and he enriched it this way, perhaps there is no other wealth, and we're the crazy ones for not imitating him . . . (*With sad humor.*) It's curious. I would like for all that I've fought against, because it's a lie, to be true. (*He laughs feebly.*) These are the things you think when you know it's all over.

LINUS: Only when you're tired. Tomorrow you'll see things differently.

MAX: Shall we try to rest then? It's all we can do. (*He crawls into bed and covers up.*)

LINUS: Are you asleep, Thomas? . . . (*Thomas's eyes are wide open but he doesn't answer.*)

MAX: At least there won't be any more visits tonight.

LINUS: I hope you all get some rest. (*He stretches out, turns toward the wall and covers himself up.*)

ASEL: Poor Tulio. (*He lies down. Without changing his position, Thomas closes his eyes. A long pause. Very soft, almost inaudible, a faint melody begins: Rossini's "Pastorale." At the same time, and with no change in the spectral moonlight inside the room, the gentle light of dawn brightens the landscape behind the window. Thomas opens his eyes and listens, ecstatic, to the soft notes. A silent silhouette appears slowly from behind the bathroom curtain. Thomas sits up suddenly and sees Berta, dressed in the white outfit of her first appearance.*)

THOMAS: (*Very softly.*) Berta.

*(She motions to him to be silent and advances cautiously, looking at the sleeping men. Then she sits on the edge of Thomas's bed.)*

BERTA: Keep your voice down.
THOMAS: How did you get in? The door is locked.
BERTA: Not for me.
THOMAS: You certainly took your time.
BERTA: *(Ironically.)* If you wish, I'll leave.
THOMAS: *(Grabbing one of her hands.)* No. You're my only certainty.
BERTA: Certainty?
THOMAS: I'm going to wake them up. I want them to see you.
BERTA: They're tired. Let them sleep.
THOMAS: They've moved Tulio.
BERTA: I know that.
THOMAS: The others told me that they're going to kill him. But it's not true. If you're here, it's not true.
BERTA: I suppose you know.
THOMAS: I don't know anything, Berta. Why is the Foundation so unfriendly to us? Do you know?
BERTA: Yes. And so do you.
THOMAS: I don't.
BERTA: Well, then you don't.
THOMAS: *(He embraces her and she allows it passively.)* Won't you answer me? Have you come to tease me? . . . You used to love me. It's not the same now.
BERTA: *(With a little laugh.)* No?
THOMAS: Please don't laugh.
BERTA: *(Serious.)* As you wish. *(She looks into the void.)*
THOMAS: Why were you crying in the visiting room?
BERTA: For Thomas.
THOMAS: For the mouse?
BERTA: He's very sick.
THOMAS: Is he going to die? *(Silence.)* He'll be a martyr.
BERTA: For science.
THOMAS: If you've inoculated him with something . . .
BERTA: No, nothing. I don't even know if there'll be any research. *(They look into each other's eyes.)*
THOMAS: Then what is Thomas going to die of?
BERTA: *(Sharply.)* I don't know if he's going to die.
THOMAS: He's alive, so he'll die. He'll die, Berta. And we don't even know if there will be any research. Come here. *(He pulls her toward him.)*
BERTA: What do you want?
THOMAS: *(He lifts the bed covers.)* Lie down beside me.
BERTA: *(She lies back.)* What about them?

THOMAS: What does it matter? Let's devour each other. Consume me, kill me.

BERTA: (*With a little laugh.*) Is that all you want me for?

THOMAS: What difference does it make? You're not Berta anymore. (*They look at each other. She throws herself on him and bites his lips. As they kiss, his hands become bolder. They fall back together on the bed; he lifts the covers so that she can get under them. The kiss goes on; he moans softly. The music suddenly stops and Asel's voice is heard.*)

ASEL: What's wrong with you, Thomas?

BERTA: (*Sitting up quickly and whispering.*) I told you so!

THOMAS: (*Whispering.*) Go into the bathroom. (*Berta gets up and steps back toward the curtained alcove. She disappears. Asel sits up on the side of his bed.*)

ASEL: Whom were you talking to?

THOMAS: (*Not sitting up.*) Nobody.

ASEL: You're not going to tell me that you thought we were asleep. No one could sleep after what happened to Tulio. Not even you.

THOMAS: I wasn't asleep. (*Max sits up in his bed.*)

ASEL: Then were you trying to fool us? (*Thomas sits up, sullen.*) To show us that Berta, in spite of everything, had come. Was that it?

MAX: Even if he wasn't asleep, maybe he was imagining it.

ASEL: That's what I say.

MAX: You don't get my meaning. I'm talking about . . . the compensations of loneliness. Relieving the senses by imagining a pleasant intimate encouter . . .

THOMAS: (*Unsure.*) I wasn't imagining.

ASEL: (*Bitterly.*) He wasn't imagining. Berta has come . . . and gone.

THOMAS: (*Unsure.*) . . . She hasn't gone.

LINUS: What?

THOMAS: She's . . . in the bathroom. (*A loud laugh from Linus. Exasperated, Thomas puts his hands to his head.*) Yes, and you're going to see her! I won't let her leave until you see her. It's time to put an end to all this secrecy.

ASEL: If they took Tulio because of something you said . . .

MAX: What could he say to them?

THOMAS: (*Putting on his pants quickly, he gets up.*) Berta is listening to every word you say! You're going to see her now!

ASEL: (*Getting up too.*) Fine! Have her come out! (*Linus gets up, intrigued.*) Call her!

THOMAS: (*Stammering.*) You want me to call her?

LINUS: Yes! Call her!

THOMAS: Berta! Come out, Berta! Now! (*He waits a few moments; he runs toward the curtain. Angry, Asel stops him.*)

ASEL: Is it your fault that they haven't transferred us?

THOMAS: Let me go!

ASEL: Answer! (*Thomas evades him and runs to the curtain, lifts up a portion of it and looks behind it. Demoralized, he looks again. He turns around.*)

THOMAS: (*Very softly.*) She's not here.

MAX: (*Calmly.*) But the door hasn't been opened. (*Thomas rushes to the door and pushes it in vain. Then he beats on it in a frenzy.*)

THOMAS: I want to get out! . . I want to get out! (*They all run to subdue him.*)

LINUS: Quiet, you lunatic! They'll hear you!

THOMAS: (*Sobbing.*) . . . get out! (*Linus gives him a slap. Thomas falls to his knees as they release him. He cries silently. Max withdraws and sits on the table.*)

MAX: He's beginning to disgust me. (*The landscape is growing darker, almost to total blackness.*)

THOMAS: She . . . hasn't come. (*He looks toward the window.*)

ASEL: Do you admit that?

THOMAS: She never came. (*Absorbed in the night that inundates the landscape.*) I've been delirious.

MAX: Spare us your play-acting. You're not going to fool us any longer. (*Thomas hides his face in his hands. Linus walks away and sits on his bedroll. Silence.*)

ASEL: (*Who has been watching Thomas with the keenest attention.*) It's not play-acting.

MAX: Please, Asel! It's impossible to believe him now.

ASEL: On the contrary. Now is when he can be believed. And I'm sorry for all I've said to him.

MAX: Don't defend him anymore!

ASEL: If his hallucinations were invented, he would have maintained that Berta was in our presence, even when we didn't see her. Or that the door was being opened and she was running away, even if the door remained closed. A liar who was caught in the act would have done that. The disappearance of Berta is the reality that overtakes him in spite of himself. . . . That meeting may have been the last attempt to escape into his delusions and the final crisis.

LINUS: Why final?

ASEL: He said himself that she never came here . . . Believe him. He can't be lying. (*Silence. Perplexed, Linus gets up and looks at Thomas, who has been listening to Asel with increasing emotion. Asel goes to Thomas.*) Thomas, do you know where you are?

THOMAS: (*Humbly, his head down.*) You tell me.

ASEL: No. You say it. (*A short pause.*)

THOMAS: We're in . . . jail.

ASEL: Why?

THOMAS: You say it.

ASEL: No. You.

THOMAS: I . . . don't remember very well . . . yet.

ASEL: Then go to bed. Rest. (*Thomas stands up and walks toward his bed. For a second, he looks at the landscape, now dark and faint. He unfastens his pants, sits on the bed, and takes them off. Linus stretches out again on his bed.*)

THOMAS: Is it true . . . that they're going to kill Tulio?

ASEL: Yes. (*He sits down on his bed.*)

THOMAS: Was he . . . condemned to death?

LINUS: Yes. (*Thomas crawls into bed. Silence.*)

THOMAS: Couldn't it be just a transfer?

ASEL: Those who are condemned to death are no longer taken to another prison.

LINUS: If they take only one, it's because they're going to carry out an order of execution.

MAX: (*Returning to his bed.*) And besides, they ordered him to leave with all his belongings.

THOMAS: I don't understand . . .

ASEL: In every prison they have their own way of doing things. In this one, when you go to be executed, you have to take all your possessions . . and leave them in the office.

LINUS: If they transfer you to the special punishment cells, they also tell you: "With all your possessions." When you hear that, it won't be too difficult for you to figure out what's in store for you.

MAX: If they order you to leave and bring nothing with you, either it's for a visitor or for business.

THOMAS: Business?

ASEL: Interrogation . . . very hard . . . unbearable. (*Thomas sits up and looks at him. A brief pause.*)

THOMAS: Are we condemned to death? (*Asel hesitates.*)

LINUS: All of us. (*Silence.*)

THOMAS: Yes . . . I seem to remember. You explain it to me, Asel.

ASEL: (*Enigmatically.*) Why me?

THOMAS: I don't know. (*Asel goes to his side.*)

ASEL: Our individual cases matter little. You'll remember yours, but that's the least of it. We live in a civilized world that still finds the very old practice of killing the most intoxicating sport of all. They murder you for fighting established injustice, for belonging to a detested race: they let you starve to death if you're a prisoner of war, or they shoot you for supposed attempts to incite revolt; secret tribunals condemn you for the crime of resisting in your own occupied nation . . . They hang you because you don't smile at the one who decrees smiles, or because your God is not theirs, or because your atheism is not theirs . . . Throughout time, rivers of blood. Millions of men and women . . .

THOMAS: Women?

ASEL: And children . . . The children pay too. We've burned them, suffocating their terrified cries to their mothers, for forty centuries. Yesterday the god Moloch devoured them in a brazier in his belly; today napalm eats at their flesh. And the survivors can't congratulate themselves either: children who are crippled or blind . . . Their parents have destined them for that. Because we are all their parents. (*Short silence.*) Am I supposed to remind you where we are and which of those killings we face? You'll remember.

THOMAS: (*Somberly.*) I already remember.

ASEL: Then, now you know . . . (*He lowers his voice.*) This time it has been our turn to be victims, my poor Thomas. But I'm going to tell you something . . . I prefer it. If I saved my life, perhaps one day it would be my turn to play the role of executioner.

THOMAS: You no longer want to live?

ASEL: We must live! To put an end to all the atrocities and all the outrages against humanity. But . . . in so many terrible years, I've seen how difficult it is. It's the hardest struggle: the struggle against oneself. Combatants sworn to carry out a violence without cruelty . . . and incapable of distinguishing, because the enemy doesn't separate them either. That's why a strange calm comes over me at times . . . almost a kind of happiness. The happiness of ending up as the victim. The truth is, I'm tired. (*Silence.*)

THOMAS: Why . . . everything?

ASEL: The world is not the landscape you envision. It's in the grip of plunder, of lies, of oppression. It's one long calamity. But we do not resign ourselves to endless calamity, and we must abolish it.

THOMAS: We?

ASEL: Yes. Even though we're exhausted. (*He lowers his voice.*) Even though we may fear to dirty our hands and lie.

THOMAS: (*Thinking.*) Was I fighting too?

ASEL: Yes.

THOMAS: With you?

ASEL: In a sense.

THOMAS: Yes. I'm beginning to remember. (*He rubs his hand over his forehead.*) But I don't remember you.

ASEL: You never saw me before coming here. But we had a certain relationship.

THOMAS: What kind?

ASEL: (*Pressing his shoulder.*) If you remember it, I'll help you understand what happened.

THOMAS: (*After a moment.*) Victims . . .

ASEL: That's how it is.

THOMAS: Poor Tulio. (*The light begins to dim.*)

LINUS: The moon has gone behind a cloud. Let's try to sleep. (*He covers up with his blanket.*)

ASEL: Rest, my boy. (*He goes upstage and gets into bed. Almost complete darkness. Distant and faint, the monotonous chant of a sentry is heard: "Station One, all is well." A few seconds later, a second voice, closer, responds: "Station Two, all is well.")*

THOMAS: The sentries.

ASEL: Like every night.

THOMAS: But I refused to hear them.

(*Another voice, still closer: "Station Three, all is well." On the dark background behind the window, a faint figure emerges little by little. It is Berta, and she seems to be holding something in her hands. Very tall, almost floating, the apparition captures Thomas's attention. He doesn't need to turn his head to see it. A fourth voice, very close, is heard: "All is well, Station Four." The arms of Berta's image separate and her right hand is extended. From it, a motionless white mouse hangs suspended by the tail. Another voice, farther away: "Station Five, all is well." With a sorrowful expression, the image releases the mouse and it falls. The feminine head turns toward Thomas and looks at him with the deepest pain. The light that illuminates the figure fades completely and darkness prevails, while the calls of the sixth, seventh, and eighth sentries are heard, each more distant than the last. The curtain falls for a few moments or fade-out.*)

## Scene 2

*Harsh daylight. The large window has disappeared behind a flat identical to the other walls. At right, in the space the folding bed occupied, there is now another bedroll. The only thing that remains from Thomas's imagination is the curtain over the alcove, which is still in an indistinct half-light.*

*Thomas is seated on his bedroll, deep in thought. His gray pants are identical to those of the others; his blouse hangs loose. Asel, seated at the head of the bed on his bedroll, sucks on his empty pipe. Seated on his bedroll at the left end of the table, Linus strums on the metal frame. Max is similarly seated near the right end, with his hands folded on the table. A few seconds of silence. Thomas touches his bedroll pensively; then he takes a pinch of his pants and examines the cloth.*

THOMAS: My mind has been full of amazingly clear images. And they were all false. And others, which according to you are the real ones, were simply erased. (*Max looks at him with mistrust; Asel watches him with interest.*) Am I crazy, Asel?

ASEL: I suppose you've suffered what doctors would call an episode of schizophrenia. Still, I can't tell you for certain because . . . (*he smiles*) I'm not a doctor.

THOMAS: (*Astonished.*) It's not the first time I've heard someone say that. Who said it before? . . . (*He points to Linus.*) Yes. The engineer.

LINUS: I'm not an engineer, Thomas.

THOMAS: You aren't?

LINUS: I'm a lathe operator.

THOMAS: A lathe operator? (*Linus nods.*)

ASEL: You always thought of him as an engineer. You changed our professions for us . . . Because I really am an engineer.

THOMAS: You?

MAX: Don't look like that. You've always known it.

THOMAS: I assure you I didn't . . .

MAX: (*To the others.*) I can't believe him.

THOMAS: And you aren't a mathematician either?

MAX: (*Ironically.*) It depends on how you look at it. Numbers everywhere, yes . . . But as for integral calculus, not a bit. I'm an ordinary accountant, as you well know.

LINUS: You believed him before.

MAX: Well, I don't any longer. (*Brief pause.*)

THOMAS: (*To Asel.*) Why would I insist that you were a doctor?

ASEL: I suspect that you invented a doctor because you needed to. (*Smiling.*) And I tried not to be too bad a doctor for you.

LINUS: Did Berta really come to the visiting room?

THOMAS: (*He stands up anxiously; he takes a few steps.*) Yes. It was hard for me to recognize her. Poorly dressed . . . she looked unwell. (*Holding back his emotion.*) She was studying to be a laboratory technician. But there was no fellowship from any Foundation . . . She had just lost her job when they arrested me.

ASEL: Do you remember that?

THOMAS: (*He looks through the invisible window.*) She's all I have in the world. I lost my parents when I was a child, and there was no one to pay for my education. I took all sorts of jobs and I read everything I could. I wanted to write. And she encouraged me. I didn't dare involve her in anything. They would have questioned her and even abused her physically. I may never see her again. (*A pause. Linus starts humming. A metallic voice comes from the grill over the door.*)

VOICE: Attention. Number C-96, prepare for the visiting room. (*Linus stops humming. Thomas looks up.*)

MAX: (*Standing up.*) It's for me!

VOICE: Attention. Prepare for the visiting room, C-96.

MAX: (*Smoothing down his hair with his hands to make himself more presentable.*) I have a visitor!

THOMAS: (*To the others.*) It must be his mother . . .

MAX: Of course! My mother! (*He runs to the door to listen.*)

LINUS: (*Thinking.*) Then we're not forbidden contact with the outside.

MAX: Well, no! Thomas had a visitor, and now mine proves it. Maybe your parents will come tomorrow, Linus!

LINUS: How I wish.

MAX: (*Listening.*) Be quiet.

ASEL: (*To himself.*) It still doesn't seem logical.

MAX: I think it is. They've limited our isolation to a few days in view of the fact that we're under the death penalty. (*Asel looks at him dubiously.*)

LINUS: Maybe she's bringing you some food . . .

MAX: It would certainly be welcome, but I don't know. The poor thing hardly has enough for herself.

LINUS: (*Pessimistic.*) Or maybe she brought it and they won't let her give it to you.

MAX: They're here!

(*Sound of a key. The door opens halfway. The panorama of cells can be glimpsed in the background. The aide is in the doorway and is wearing a black uniform, visored cap, and a holster belt with pistol.*)

AIDE: C-96, to the visiting room.

MAX: Yes, sir. (*He exits and the door closes. A pause.*)

THOMAS: (*Sitting on Max's bedroll.*) In a uniform.

LINUS: The aide?

THOMAS: Yes.

LINUS: He always came in a uniform. (*He gets up and walks about, still skeptical.*)

ASEL: Now you see that your episode was temporary. (*Linus jumps onto the iron bed in a single leap and sits at Asel's feet.*)

LINUS: Asel . . . (*Asel motions to him to keep quiet.*)

THOMAS: (*Continuing the thread of his reflection.*) Was it because of my weakness?

LINUS: Listen, Asel . . .

ASEL: Afterwards. (*To Thomas.*) Because of weakness and wanting to escape from a reality that seemed unacceptable to you.

THOMAS: Don't continue . . .

LINUS: (*Impatiently.*) You tried to kill yourself. Everyone in the prison knows it.

ASEL: No, Linus! Not that way.

LINUS: Yes, man!

THOMAS: (*Standing up.*) It's true! I tried to throw myself over the railing.

(*He points toward the door.*)

ASEL: (*Leaping to the floor and going to him.*) And I stopped you! (*Very affected, Thomas looks at him and steps back. Asel follows him and takes him by the arm.*) Easy. If you remember everything, stay calm.

THOMAS: (*Pulling away, in great distress.*) I informed on you!

LINUS: (*He sits on Asel's bedroll.*) What? . . .

ASEL: Yes, you informed on us. And you were closer to the head of our group than you realized.

THOMAS: And you were arrested because of me, Asel!

ASEL: I and the others, yes.

THOMAS: (*Choking.*) And they condemned you to death!

ASEL: (*Holding him by his arms.*) I told you I'd help you to understand! Get control of yourself!

THOMAS: (*Bowing his head.*) I have understood!

ASEL: You haven't understood anything! You need twenty more years to understand. (*Thomas leans on the table for support, and his face is convulsed with pain.*) What's wrong with you?

THOMAS: I feel sick . . . I hurt . . .

ASEL: It'll pass.

THOMAS: My stomach. (*His face contorted, he looks toward the alcove curtain. He staggers over to it as if drunk and hides behind it. Asel shakes his head sadly and leans on the table.*)

ASEL: Don't go to pieces, boy. They caught you handing out leaflets, you told who gave them to you; he in turn informed on us, and they captured us all. Do you hear what I'm saying, Thomas?

THOMAS'S VOICE: (*From behind the curtain.*) Yes.

ASEL: You talked because you couldn't endure the pain.

THOMAS'S VOICE: I'm a despicable person.

ASEL: (*Shaking his head.*) You're a human being. Strong sometimes; weak at other times. Like almost everyone.

LINUS: But he did inform on us.

ASEL: (*Sharply.*) And what about it? (*Linus shrugs; he has already passed judgment.*)

THOMAS'S VOICE: A traitor.

ASEL: We're close to death. Words like that no longer have any meaning to me.

THOMAS'S VOICE: I can't forgive myself!

ASEL: That's why you tried to kill yourself. And that's why, when I prevented it, your mind created the immense fantasy of the Foundation: from the beautiful landscape you saw on the wall to the shiny bathroom.

(*The alcove curtain rises and disappears. At the same time, the light in the area becomes identical to that in the rest of the room. In the dirty corner, crusty with dampness, there is only a lidless commode with its high water tank, a button to flush it and, waist-high, a faucet over a metal drain, At one side, the old broom; on the other, crumpled pieces of paper on the floor. Very pale, Thomas is sitting on the toilet, with a piece of paper in his hand. No sooner has the alcove curtain risen than he sees his companions and jumps up in embarrassment. He throws the paper in the toilet and pulls up his pants.)*

THOMAS: *(Fastening his pants clumsily.)* You saw me . . .

LINUS: And you saw us. We're all tired of seeing each other's butt around here.

ASEL: You believed that you were hidden by a door or some kind of curtain . . . *(Thomas nods.)* Until now?

THOMAS: Yes.

LINUS: Modesty . . . what a luxury!

ASEL: You've just lost your last refuge. Now you're cured.

LINUS: Flush the toilet. *(Thomas pushes the button. The water is released. Not daring to look at Asel, Thomas faces Linus with humble eyes and Linus gives him a severe look in return. Then he crosses and sits on the bedroll at left, with his back to the others.)*

ASEL: No one can be strong if he doesn't first know how weak he is.

THOMAS: You were captured because of me.

ASEL: I and the best who remained. *(He goes over to him. Thomas hides his face in his hands.)* A catastrophe. *(He moves a little closer.)* But you couldn't endure the pain.

LINUS: It was his duty to endure it!

ASEL: Duty? *(He smiles.)* Categorical positions, solemn words: betrayal, duty, informer . . . You throw them around and he picks them up. In the final analysis, you're both alike: two youngsters. Have they ever tortured you?

LINUS: They gave me a good working over when they brought me here.

ASEL: Then keep quiet, because that's nothing. *(He sits at the table.)* And listen to what I say to Thomas. *(To Thomas.)* They tortured me. The first time, many years ago . . . Like you, I knew my duty was to keep silent. *(Brief pause.)* But I talked, and my accusations cost at least one life. *(Thomas looks up without turning around. Linus does not miss a word.)* Are you surprised? A steadfast man like Asel confessing under physical pain? Hard to believe! But Asel informed. His flesh informed, after screaming like a tormented mouse. And now, you tell me what Asel is: a lion or a mouse? *(Brief pause.)* The courtyard of this jail fills up every day with naive souls who consider him a lion. But he knows that he can always be dangled like a mouse. It all depends on what they do to him. *(He sits a bit closer to Thomas.)* His greatest fear is still that.

Year after year, he lies awake knowing that he's like some soft-shelled mollusk between steel pincers. He's toughened a bit, to be sure. But he knows he can't resist indefinitely. And so he lives a half-life . . . afraid . . . feeling remorse for the poor man his words killed. (*To Linus.*) I know what you're thinking, my young friend. (*He goes to his side.*) I've been like you as well as like Thomas . . . You think that a man who is so afraid is incapable of action. (*Linus looks away.*) Of course. You have to believe that you can keep silent even under torture. But we're all afraid, and we all carry within us an informer and, still, we must act. I know very well I shouldn't be saying it, and I shouldn't demoralize you! But on a very special occasion, like this . . . it's a time to be humble and sincere. (*He paces a bit and turns toward Thomas.*) I saw it in you and I wanted to save you. I did my part and you must do yours. (*He puts his hand on Thomas's shoulder.*) Don't be ashamed of your weakness in front of me. You're no weaker than I am. (*Linus looks at him suspiciously; he jumps out of bed and turns on the faucet in the corner to get a drink of water. Thomas breaks into quick sobs. Without turning around, he clasps the hand that Asel has placed on his shoulder.*) No man! None of that! (*Asel steps away. Linus turns off the faucet, turns around to look at them, and wipes his mouth with his sleeve. Then he goes downstage and looks through the invisible window. As Asel passes behind him, he reaches out and grasps his arm for an instant without turning around.*)

LINUS: You'd make a great legislator. (*Asel gives him a pat on the shoulder and stands beside him looking out.*)

ASEL: Not very likely now. What did you want to tell me before?

LINUS: A little thought that was bothering me . . . But I got sidetracked. It's evident that Thomas told the guards something. If he informed before, he must have also been the informer this time. (*Thomas looks up with surprise.*)

ASEL: (*Slowly.*) Informed about what?

LINUS: You must know . . . I'm not in on the game. (*Thomas stands shaking his head. Asel siezes Linus by the arm and pulls him back.*)

ASEL: What are you referring to?

LINUS: You asked him several times if he was the reason they hadn't transferred us to the isolation block. If he had told them something . . . that worries you and I don't know about . . .

THOMAS: (*Stepping forward.*) No! Asel, my head is clear. I remember the plan. But I never told them anything.

LINUS: A plan?

THOMAS: That you don't know about. Tulio did, and I remember it too. (*To Asel.*) I swear I didn't say anything.

LINUS: Who knows about that . . .

ASEL: He's telling the truth.

LINUS: (*Going to the table and sitting on the bedroll at right.*) Possibly. But what I was thinking was not so farfetched.

ASEL: (*He sits on the edge of the table.*) Explain yourself.

LINUS: You wanted them to move us to the punishment cells in the basement. (*Thomas sits at the other side of the table.*)

ASEL: It was just that the lack of logic troubled me . . .

LINUS: Do you think I'm a fool? It troubled you because they didn't move us. You were nervous, irritable, and you let some suspicious words slip out.

ASEL: (*He looks at him uneasily, smiles and sighs.*) Well . . . let's say that I proposed the scheme of passing off the dead man as sick for two reasons: the first, to help us out a little with his food, and, the second . . . yes, to get us moved to the hole.

LINUS: And they didn't move us, so you think that someone put them on guard.

ASEL: It couldn't have been Tulio. Nor Thomas . . .

LINUS: That leaves only two of us.

ASEL: (*Shaking his head and thinking.*) It wasn't you either, that's evident . . . (*Murmuring.*) Could it be possible? . . .

LINUS: There's no doubt in my mind: Max. I've suspected him for several days.

ASEL: (*With a gesture of concern.*) Why?

LINUS: Why is a squealer a squealer? (*Asel looks at him with suspicion. Linus lowers his voice.*) One day I saw him talking with a guard. They were laughing. They had called him, like today. But he wasn't in the visiting room. I saw him pass by from the courtyard door, not going in the direction of the visiting room but toward the prison headquarters.

THOMAS: They could have called him for a number of reasons . . .

ASEL: But he didn't tell us.

LINUS: No. He only said that he'd come from seeing his mother.

ASEL: Are you sure that's who it was?

LINUS: Absolutely. But there's more.

ASEL: Well, out with it!

LINUS: Pegleg, the cripple fellow who's in one of the cells opposite us . . . he's a wizard at opening the peep hole from inside. About ten days ago he told me something in the courtyard. And he's not one to make things up.

ASEL: He's a sensible man.

LINUS: Well, the day before, Max had had one of his visitors. And Pegleg saw him come back to his cell . . . very slowly . . . stuffing himself with food from his package . . . while the guard waited for him to finish, very amused by it all.

ASEL: Any hungry man could have done that.

LINUS: And what about the guard? He wouldn't have waited for any of us.

ASEL: That's for certain . . .

LINUS: He's the one who squealed. All of us have lost control here at one time or another. Including you, Asel! But never Max. Always calm, joking . .. He had a sureness about him that we lacked.

ASEL: Why didn't you tell us about this before?

LINUS: (*Muttering angrily.*) I never trusted anyone. (*He lowers his voice.*) Not even you. (*Pause.*)

ASEL: He's going to return.

LINUS: And soon. (*He goes to the door to listen.*)

ASEL: (*Nervously.*) We don't have much time left. (*Standing.*) You have to be in on the plan, Linus. If they had moved us, I would have explained it down there. But they obviously suspect something. They suspect me. You were the last to come, Linus; and as for Thomas . . . they think he's crazy. Max has probably told them that I want to go to the hole. I've been imprudent, and they won't let me set foot there now. But they may let the rest of you, later, if you can figure out some way to get them to punish you. If you manage it, you have a possiblity of escaping. (*He stops to listen beside the door.*)

LINUS: (*Excited.*) To get away? Now you're talking!

ASEL: (*He brings them together.*) My profession gave me the chance to become familiar with the construction plans for this entire zone. And for this building. The isolation block is not near the outside wall; there's no worry about thick concrete. The cells are at basement level, with tiny windows that face one of the courtyards. Only three meters below and some two meters behind the wall opposite the window . . . do you follow me? . . . (*he sketches in the air with his hand*) . . . a sewer crosses. If a tunnel is burrowed from the edge of that wall, with a twenty-seven degree slope . . . (*his hands trace the triangle in the air*) at two meters and twenty-five centimeters, more or less, it will reach the sewer wall. If that is bored through, you must follow it to the right. Twenty meters further, it's almost certain there's a grating. It will be necessary to file through it. Once you're on the other side, you enter the northern collector. The best thing would be to walk left and try one of the exit shafts. It's a spot that's not closely guarded.

LINUS: (*Astounded.*) Are you out of your mind?

ASEL: No.

LINUS: What would you do it with? Your fingernails?

ASEL: (*Leaning on the table between the two of them.*) Do you remember the angle, the direction?

THOMAS: The hole, half in the floor and half in the wall opposite the small window, so that it can be covered with a bedroll. Is that right?

ASEL: Exactly.

THOMAS: Twenty-seven degree slope and some two meters and twenty-five centimeters to the sewer line.

ASEL: One other point: it can only work from cells 14 or 15. If they take you to any other, it will be impossible.

LINUS: Why?

ASEL: They are the only two with windows that face the same courtyard as the latrine windows of the second block.

LINUS: What has that . . .

ASEL: (*Lowering his voice.*) In that block there are two prisoners we can trust. There's no need for you to know their names. They have managed to smuggle in and hide a file, a cord, and a wicker basket. The bar is for excavating the tunnel. Spoons can be used too. Every night, after the final check, one of them goes to the latrine and stays there half an hour. If he hears on the floor three blows and one more, like this: pam-pam-pam; pam. . . , he'll determine which of the two cells they're coming from and lower the basket with the tools to the little window.

LINUS: What about the noise?

ASEL: You'll have to work all night and nap whenever you can during the day. All that subsoil is very cloddy; once you're on the other side of the wall and the floor, the sound will be negligible.

THOMAS: And the rubble?

ASEL: The basket will take up all the loads it can during the night. The others won't be sleeping either.

LINUS: What if they search?

ASEL: They usually don't in those cells. They think they're very secure.

THOMAS: Where will they put all the dirt and rocks?

ASEL: All that can be gotten rid of in the latrine and through the outside windows, which will be put in the trash containers. They're building a new wing, so there's always debris in the common collection.

LINUS: How many days will it take to dig the tunnel?

ASEL: With two people working . . . six nights maybe.

THOMAS: We'll be in constant danger of being discovered, our friends in the cell block being caught . . .

ASEL: There's one greater danger: being executed before the transfer is carried out.

LINUS: We can at least try! And if we succeed, I know where to go.

THOMAS: (*Standing up and pacing anxiously.*) It's absurd, Asel! That's not freedom; it's a hell! To dig into the earth only to die smothered in darkness, or under a cave-in. It's incredible . . . an illusion.

ASEL: As incredible as freedom! That tunnel will be hell only if you don't believe in it.

THOMAS: They'll hear us, they'll catch us!

ASEL: Do you prefer the firing squad? (*Thomas stops, altered.*)

LINUS: Get it into your head, novelist. If something can be thought, it can be done.

THOMAS: We can't even get them to transfer us.

LINUS: We'll see about that. (*His energy exhausted, Thomas sits down on the iron bed.*)

THOMAS: (*To Asel.*) If you could come with us . . .

ASEL: I suspect I've lost this game. But you two can win it. Try! (*Silence.*)

LINUS: What do we do with Max?

THOMAS: We have to make sure . . . If we were wrong . . .

LINUS: After what I told you?

ASEL: And Berta's visit to Thomas confirms it.

THOMAS: Why?

ASEL: He was informing on us when they called him to the visiting room. So that they could keep on calling him without arousing our suspicions, they first auhorized your girlfriend's visit.

LINUS: And he's informing this very minute . . . although he knows nothing concrete, fortunately.

ASEL: Both of you, listen carefully: we have to pretend. Being at a disadvantage, we have to use our wits. If we show our hand . . . (*a slight smile to Thomas*) the Foundation will eliminate us without a second thought.

LINUS: Asel, we have to neutralize the informers! If they are an arm of the Foundation . . . (*He interrupts himself.*) Fine! Now I'm talking about the Foundation too!

ASEL: Go on.

LINUS: Exactly because we are at a disadvantage, we must deal relentlessly with any arm of the enemy!

ASEL: Not here! The reprisals are always more severe!

LINUS: But don't you understand?

ASEL: You don't understand! You're young and you're impatient for action. I've been at this for years, and I know that in this case we have to be cautious . . . to protect our comrades in the cell block, to avoid detection.

LINUS: But it makes sense to unmask him and give him a scare! If they find out that we've discovered one of their stoolies, they'll eliminate him, because he's of no use to them anymore. And we diminish their strength!

ASEL: We double it! We incite them to take away the little breathing space we have left. (*He smiles sadly.*) Linus, I've lived through many defeats that were the result of not having measured well the poverty of our means . . . But no one learns from another's mistakes. You're very quiet, Thomas. What do you think?

THOMAS: I don't know what to say. It's all so complicated.

LINUS: We must confront him now! As soon as he returns from that supposed visit with his mother.

THOMAS: Why?

LINUS: I think I've hit on a way to trap him.

ASEL: How?

LINUS: Let me think it out! (*He sits, wary of Asel's reaction.*)

THOMAS: We don't have much time . . .

ASEL: Linus, listen to me! Don't do it!

LINUS: Just let me think!

ASEL: Then think. . . but think hard. (*Pause.*)

THOMAS: It won't be long before he comes back.

ASEL: No. (*He sucks on his pipe. Linus hums very softly.*)

THOMAS: Asel . . .

ASEL: What?

THOMAS: Have you ever wondered if all this is . . . real?

ASEL: The jail?

THOMAS: Yes.

ASEL: Do you want to go back to the Foundation?

THOMAS: I know that wasn't real. But I wonder if the rest of the world is any more so . . . It happens to those outside too: a television set suddenly vanishes, or a glass that they're holding in their hand . . . or a beloved person . . . And they keep on believing, nevertheless, in their comfortable Foundation . . . And sometime, from afar, they'll see this building and they won't say: it's a prison. They'll say: it looks like a great research center, a Foundation . . . and they'll pass on by.

ASEL: Quite true.

THOMAS: Then, isn't the prison perhaps equally an illusion? Our sufferings, our death penalty . . .

ASEL: And we ourselves?

THOMAS: (*Avoiding his eyes.*) Yes, even that.

ASEL: Everything, inside and out, like a gigantic hologram displayed before our perceptions, not knowing if they're our own, or what they are. And you, a hologram for me, and I, another one for you . . . Something like that?

THOMAS: Something like that.

ASEL: It had occurred to me before. (*Linus has listened to them in astonishment. He brushes off their speculations with a gesture of his hand to follow his own train of thought. Asel smiles.*) It seems silly to Linus . . . But I have indeed thought that.

THOMAS: And if it were true, why escape from here to find freedom or a prison that are equally illusory? The only freedom would be in destroying the hologram, to find the authentic reality . . . which is here too, if it does exist . . . or in us, wherever we are . . .

ASEL: No.

THOMAS: Why not? (*A long silence.*) Why not, Asel?

ASEL: Maybe everything is one immense illusion. Who knows? But we won't find the hidden truth by turning our backs on it. We must immerse ourselves in it. (*With a penetrating look.*) I know what your problem is at this moment.

THOMAS: What is it?

ASEL: It's not that you scorn escape as another fantasy, but you're cowered by the risks.

THOMAS: My Foundation still has me entrapped. (*He sits down.*)

ASEL: No, you've left it now. And you've discovered a great truth, even though it still may not be the definitive truth. Once you've been in jail, you come to understand that no matter where you go, you are in jail. You've come to that realizatin without escaping.

THOMAS: Then . . .

ASEL: Then you must exit into the other jail! (*Walking about.*) And when you're in it, go into another, and from it, to still another. Truth awaits you in all of them, not in inaction. You found it here, but only by making yourself see the lie of the Foundation you imagined. And it waits for you in the effort of that dark tunnel in the basement . . . in the hologram of that escape.

THOMAS: I'm ashamed that what I imagined was so absurd.

ASEL: You were afraid . . you invented a rose-colored world. And not so absurd at that . . . One day they'll build better prisons of metal and bars. The cells will have a television set, a refrigerator, books, and background music . . . To the inmates it will seem like freedom itself. Then you'll have to be very intelligent indeed not to forget that you're a prisoner. (*Pause.*)

THOMAS: We have to think up some way to get the three of us to the punishment cells. With you beside me, I'll prefer the tunnel to the landscape.

ASEL: (*Putting his hand on Thomas's shoulder.*) Never forget what I'm going to say. You dreamed some foolish things, but the landscape you saw . . . is real.

THOMAS: (*Not understanding.*) It has been erased too . . .

ASEL: I know. It doesn't matter. The landscape was truly real. (*Thomas looks at him in astonishment. Linus looks up and listens; he gets up and runs to the door.*)

LINUS: They're coming! And I have my trap set. You must tell him that they also called me to the visiting room and . . .

ASEL: (*He runs to him and grabs him by the arm.*) That's too flimsy to work.

LINUS: (*Pulling free.*) Just let me do it!

THOMAS: I won't be able to look him in the eye. (*He searches on the small table for the old book and sits at the left of the table, opening the book in front of him.*)

LINUS: They're here! (*He moves back from the door and leans on the edge of the table. The sound of a key. With a gesture of disapproval, Asel gets on the bed and sits on his bedroll. The door opens halfway, and Max enters smiling. The door closes.*)

MAX: Hello!

ASEL: How was your mother?

MAX: Weak and exhausted. But her spirits are good. (*Sadly.*) She's convinced that she'll get my sentence commuted.

LINUS: Did you bring you anything to eat?

MAX: (*He laughs, steps forward and pats him on the shoulder.*) You had to ask that, you hungry fellow! (*Sighing.*) They wouldn't let her bring the package in. (*He crosses and leans on Thomas's shoulder.*) Are you reading that?

THOMAS: (*Without looking up.*) What do you expect? I'm bored.

MAX: (*Sitting beside him.*) The art books were prettier, weren't they?

THOMAS: (*Embarrassed.*) Please . . .

MAX: Did you really see them?

THOMAS: I thought I did.

MAX: (*Sarcastically.*) You thought you did . . . Well, have it your way. (*He looks skeptically at Asel. He walks toward the right. Behind him, Linus sits up; he starts to speak. Asel gives him a warning look, leaps from the bed, and grabs him. But Linus pulls free.*)

LINUS: Have you been in the visiting room all this time, Max?

MAX: Of course. Where else?

LINUS: That's strange.

MAX: Why?

LINUS: Because I didn't see you.

MAX: You?

LINUS: They called me right after you. My parents came. And you weren't there. Or your mother either. (*Brief pause. Asel pretends to be arranging something on his bedroll.*)

MAX: What kind of game is this, Asel?

ASEL: Why, I don't know, Max . . . Linus just got back too.

MAX: (*He crosses and puts his hand on Thomas's shoulder.*) Thomas, did Linus have visitors?

THOMAS: (*With difficulty.*) Yes.

MAX: (*He no longer doubts that they suspect; he tries to throw them off the track.*) Fine. Now you can explain to me.

LINUS: (*Curtly.*) What?

MAX: The joke. Obviously all three of you are in on it. (*Laughing.*) Even our fantastic novelist. (*He gives Thomas a pat on the shoulder.*) Because I was in the visiting room. And the one who wasn't there was you, Linus.

LINUS: (*Turning to face him, he leans on the table.*) Then one of us must be lying.

MAX: You weren't there, Linus! (*He starts walking nervously.*) And I don't like your joke anymore, if it is a joke! Because it strikes me more like some . . . foul suspicion, that I can't explain!

ASEL: But if he didn't see you there . . .

MAX: (*Facing him.*) You're lying too! He hasn't left this cell.

LINUS: And you went to the visiting room.

MAX: Yes! (*He stops, breathing hard. Linus approaches him with a smile and puts his hands on his shoulders.*)

LINUS: It's all right, Max. It was stupid of me to think you'd bite the bait. My parents didn't come. Now, what about your mother?

MAX: (*Pale.*) Take your hands off me.

LINUS: (*He gives him a shove.*) Go on, sit down. We're going to talk frankly. (*He forces him to sit on the bedroll.*) A few days ago we were in the courtyard, and they called you. An unexpected visitor! Do you remember? (*He sits on the table.*)

MAX: (*Coolly.*) Yes.

LINUS: But you were in the office.

MAX: That's a lie!

LINUS: The guard with the mustache was with you. Both of you were laughing your heads off . . . You looked like two lovers.

MAX: I won't put up with any more of your lies! (*He tries to stand up.*)

LINUS: (*Shoving him back down.*) Sit down!

MAX: It's not true! Who saw me? Another madman like Thomas? Maybe it was Thomas himself. (*To Thomas.*) Did you see me? Or did you tell them you saw me so that they wouldn't suspect you?

THOMAS: What are you making up?

LINUS: (*Seizing his arm tightly.*) Shut up, squealer! That tactic won't work. You're only getting yourself in deeper . . . I saw you!

MAX: You?

LINUS: From the door to the courtyard. (*He gets up.*)

MAX: You mistook someone else for me!

LINUS: My sight's good. And others saw you too. Ten days ago they saw you from one of the peepholes on the opposite side . . . (*he places himself behind Max and puts his hand on his shoulders*) . . . returning to the cell. You were carrying the package you had received, and we shared it.

MAX: At least you remember that. I did share my package!

LINUS: After you'd stuffed yourself outside before you came in. And they saw the guard with the mustache too, laughing and waiting for you to get your fill. (*He laughs softly.*) Has the cat got your tongue?

MAX: (*Bowing his head.*) It was weakness on my part, and I beg your forgiveness. We're all hungry, and the package was mine . . . But I'm not an informer!

LINUS: Then you just like to chat with the guards. Now you can tell me what you talk about.

MAX: No . . . you're mistaken. That guard . . . he must be queer. He smiles at me and takes me aside to tell me a lot of pointless things . . . You can understand why I didn't tell you about all the attention he was showing me . . . because I was embarrassed.

LINUS: (*Sitting on the table beside him.*) No, you're not a fool. But if you're not an informer, who is? They didn't transfer us to the hole, they allow us to have visitors . . . Someone from this cell is giving them information. Asel is a very important prisoner, and they've put a spy in his cell. (*Asel makes a warning gesture.*) Who squealed? Thomas?

MAX: I have nothing more to say. You're all crazy.

LINUS: Because there's nothing you can say. A Judas like you has a difficult job. There are thousands of eyes watching you. Sooner or later they find you out.

MAX: You haven't found out or proven anything.

LINUS: No? . . . All right. Then we agree that your mother visited you.

MAX: That's the truth; all there is!

LINUS: And they didn't let her give you the package.

MAX: No . . . not this time.

LINUS: (*He leans toward him.*) Let me smell your breath.

MAX: What?

LINUS: (*Seizing him by the hair and twisting his head back.*) Open your mouth!

MAX: Turn loose, you fool! If you think I'm going to put up with any more of your dirty tricks . . . (*He tries to get up, to get loose, but Linus grabs his jaw and forces him to open his mouth. Max lets out a groan. Linus smells his breath.*)

LINUS: (*Still holding on to Max, he looks up at the others.*) Get a whiff, Asel. And you, Thomas. (*Thomas gets up.*) He reeks of wine. He gave them his report and got his customary payment in food and drink. (*Max flails his arms and moans. Linus gives him a knee thrust in the stomach, causing him to scream in pain and become motionless. Thomas goes over and sniffs Max's breath. Asel nods without making the test.*)

THOMAS: You're right. (*He steps back. Linus releases Max, who doubles up.*)

MAX: The guard with the mustache gave me a glass of wine . . . that's all.

LINUS: Listen, you clown: this isn't a trial. We've had enough proof already. (*Silence.*)

THOMAS: Did they beat you . . . to make you talk? (*Max looks at him askance and doesn't reply. Thomas steps back, observing him; then he goes to the invisible window and takes a deep breath.*)

ASEL: It's not the same thing, Thomas. He's only a small-time spy. They tell him that he may save his life, they offer him a few scraps, some cigarettes . . . Above all, they provide him with the reassuring feeling that the ones in power are counting on him, that he's going to be a person again instead of a worm. I don't hate you, Max. You're a frightened child and you've sold yourself. No one would be a spy in a human world.

LINUS: But now our little friend is going to tell us, willingly or by force, what he told them. And what they said to him. (*He sits down beside Max again. Max looks at him with fright. Worried, Thomas goes back to sit on his bedroll.*) I also know how to make people talk.

ASEL: No, Linus. No more violence.

LINUS: You leave him to me. (*He leans over him.*) Come on sweetie, loosen your tongue. (*Max gets up, his eyes staring.*) Where're you going? (*Max steps back toward the right. Linus stands up in a threatening manner. Asel restrains him.*)

ASEL: Leave him alone! It would only make matters worse!

LINUS: You bet it's going to be worse! (*Max runs to the door and starts pounding on it frenziedly. Thomas gets up. Asel rushes over and tries to pull Max away from the door. Max resists and pounds harder. Linus hasn't moved.*) Let him call them, Asel! They're not going to be very happy about our little discovery. They'll toss him on the garbage heap now that he's of no use to them. (*Max stops beating on the door. A pause. Max's heavy breathing can be heard.*) Come over here. You can clear up a few things. (*Desperate, Max starts pounding again.*) Oh! You fear me more than you do them? There must be a reason.

ASEL: Shut up, Linus! (*He struggles with Max.*) Thomas, help me! (*Thomas goes to his assistance.*)

LINUS: Why it's very easy! (*He goes over and seizes Max by the neck with one hand.*)

MAX: (*Choking.*) No! . . . (*Linus leads him to his bedroll and shoves him down on it. Max is gasping for breath.*)

THOMAS: (*Listening near the door.*) They're coming!

LINUS: (*He strikes Max on the neck.*) You damn snake! Don't open your mouth!

(*He crosses and sits on his own bedroll. Asel leans on the edge of the bed. Thomas retreats downstage. After a few seconds, we hear the sound of a key in the door. The door opens. In the background, the closed cells. The Superintendent and his aide appear in uniform, their expressions impenetrable. The aide remains in the doorway. The Superintendent enters. Max jumps up and runs to his side. Linus gets up too but not quickly enough to hold him back.*)

MAX: It was me! I was the one shouting! Take me out of here, please! Take me out!

SUPERINTENDENT: (*Pushing him aside roughly.*) You be quiet! C-73.

ASEL: (*His expression changes; he stiffens.*) I'm C-73.

SUPERINTENDENT: Come with us. (*Asel looks at the others with an expression of dread. Then he addresses the Superintendent.*)

ASEL: With everything?

SUPERINTENDENT: You were told to leave; nothing more.

LINUS: (*To Asel.*) They didn't call you over the loudspeaker . . .

ASEL: It's for questioning. (*With a deep sigh.*) I have nothing to say and I'll say nothing.

SUPERINTENDENT: Get going!

ASEL: Can I say goodbye?

SUPERINTENDENT: For what, if you're coming back?

ASEL: Who knows? (*He takes Linus's hand.*) Good luck, Linus.

LINUS: (*His voice husky.*) Courage. (*Asel looks at Max with profound sadness. Max avoids his eyes. Then he goes to Thomas and clasps his hand.*)

ASEL: Don't forget, Thomas. Your landscape is real. (*He exits to the gallery. The aide directs him to the left. The Superintendent exits in turn. Asel stops an instant.*) Yes . . . Yes . . . (*Suddenly he breaks into a run toward the right and disappears.*)

AIDE: Stop! (*He takes out his pistol and aims it.*)

SUPERINTENDENT: Where's he going? (*To the aide.*) Don't fire. (*He disappears running to the right. We hear his voice.*) Stop! There's no way out! (*Thomas, Linus, and Max go closer to the door.*)

ASEL: (*We hear his victorious exclamation.*) There is a way!

SUPERINTENDENT: (*His voice farther off.*) What's he doing? Don't move! (*Thomas, Linus, and Max crowd into the doorway.*)

AIDE: Get back, all of you! (*He pushes them back. We immediately hear the Superintendent's voice.*)

SUPERINTENDENT'S VOICE: Come here, but don't fire! (*The aide disappears running.*) And you, don't move! (*Urgent blasts from a whistle. The aide is hardly out of sight when Max goes out onto the gallery and looks to the right, holding on to the railing. With more caution, Thomas and Linus look out the door. We hear the Superintendent's voice.*) Get back inside! (*Thomas and Linus step back into the room; Max doesn't move. The commotion increases. More whistle blasts, followed by shouting.*) Stay where you are! Get down from there!

AIDE'S VOICE: (*From a distance.*) Don't do anything stupid! Nothing's going to happen to you! . . .

MAX: He's going to jump!

SUPERINTENDENT'S VOICE: Don't!

AIDE'S VOICE: No!

MAX: Asel! . . . He threw himself over.

THOMAS: To keep from talking.

(A *dull banging far off. We begin to hear the prisoners pounding on the cell doors. Soon the sounds become more frequent and more intense until they are thunderous. Added to the clamor are numerous voices shouting: "Murderers! Murderers!"*)

SUPERINTENDENT'S VOICE: Damn bastard! (*Shouting.*) You two down there! Pick him up, quickly! (*Cries, whistle blasts, running, the thunder of the doors. In a fit of outrage, Linus lurches toward Max.*)

LINUS: You too! (*He seizes him by the legs, and with a quick Herculean push, he throws him over the railing.*)

THOMAS: (*Crying out from the door.*) Linus! (*We hear Max's scream as he falls. Linus enters rapidly.*) What have you done?

LINUS: They didn't see me.

THOMAS: We're going to pay dearly for that!

LINUS: He was guilty!

THOMAS: But you've ruined everything!

LINUS: I couldn't help myself. Those cries went to my head. (*He listens at the door.*)

THOMAS: Linus, I can no longer pass judgment on anything . . . except myself. But that murder was wrong!

LINUS: They're coming! (*The sound of footsteps running toward the cell.*)

THOMAS: I'll try to fix things. Go over there! Quickly! (*He points left. Linus runs to his bedroll. The Superintendent and his aide enter hurriedly. The din outside goes on.*)

SUPERINTENDENT: (*He grabs Thomas roughly.*) What happened here? (*Linus stands up.*)

THOMAS: (*Displaying the greatest indignation.*) That's what I'd like to know! What's going on in the Foundation?

SUPERINTENDENT: Don't talk nonsense!

THOMAS: (*Pulling free violently.*) Let go of me! How dare you lay hands on the holder of a Fellowship in the Foundation? I'm not talking nonsense and I demand that you explain what's going on! For days now, very strange things have been happening, and you are to blame! Yes, you! (*He goes from the Superintendent to the aide reprimanding them.*) Have your jobs gone to your head? You're nothing but arrogant subordinants! (*He shouts at the aide.*) Put away that pistol! How dare you carry arms in the Foundation? I'll have you fired! I said, put away that pistol!

SUPERINTENDENT: Put it away. (*The aide puts it in his holster.*)

THOMAS: That's better. And now, tell me: why have you permitted those noises, those terrible accidents? Why did Asel fall? Did you two push him? (*He takes the Superintendent by the holster belt.*) What horrendous conspiracy is this?

SUPERINTENDENT: (*Looking at him hard.*) Don't touch me. (*He pushes his hand away.*)

THOMAS: (*In an emotional outburst.*) A conspiracy against me?

AIDE: (*Stepping forward with a vicious look on his face.*) And who pushed C-96?

THOMAS: No one!

AIDE: What do you mean no one?

THOMAS: He climbed up on the railing and jumped! I saw him from here. And it's your fault! You'll have to answer for that misfortune too! The good name of the Foundation demands it! Now get out! (*The Superintendent brushes him aside with disdain and faces Linus.*) Don't push me, you swine. (*The banging and shouting have been dying down.*)

AIDE: They seem to be getting tired . . .

SUPERINTENDENT: (*To Linus.*) Who threw C-96 over the railing?

LINUS: Since I was forbidden to watch, I didn't see anything.

AIDE: (*In a low voice.*) Could he have done it?

SUPERINTENDENT: (*To the aide.*) Too afraid, maybe. Start collecting their belongings.

AIDE: Yes, sir.

(*The banging has ceased. The chorus of voices goes on, deliberately and monotonously: "Mur-der-ers! . . . Mur-der-ers!" The aide goes out and signals. Then he comes back in and takes two plates, two tumblers, and two spoons from the shelves.*)

SUPERINTENDENT: Why did C-73 want to be moved to a punishment cell? (*The aide stops and listens.*)

LINUS: (*Pretending surprise.*) That's the first I've heard of it.

SUPERINTENDENT: Don't try to fool me!

LINUS: (*Laughing.*) Why would he want to go down to those rat-infested holes? (*He and the Superintendent are looking at each other fixedly. The two waiters appear in the doorway and wait. They are dressed as when they appeared as janitors. The accusing voices begin to die down.*)

AIDE: (*Harshly.*) Which are their bedrolls?

LINUS: (*Pointing.*) This one and this one. (*Only a few voices are now repeating the accusation. Soon almost all are silent.*)

AIDE: Their duffels!

THOMAS: (*He goes to the rack and takes down two.*) Take them and get out of here now. (*The aide collects them and starts to put one of them on Max's bedroll.*) That belongs to the other one! (*The aide puts down the other bag and carries Asel's to the bed. A single voice says: "Mur-der-ers!"*)

AIDE: (*To the two at the door.*) Take these things. (*The waiters enter; each one picks up a bedroll and bag. They exit with them to the gallery and go off left.*)

SUPERINTENDENT: Let's go. (*The Superintendent and the aide exit. The latter slams the door shut. Pause. Very faintly and for the final time, we hear the accusation of a single voice: "Mur-der-ers!" Silence. Exhausted, Thomas goes to the table and sits on its edge. Linus sits on his bedroll again.*)

LINUS: They fell for it.

THOMAS: It seems so.

LINUS: You were admirable . . . Thank you. (*Thomas responds with a gesture of indifference.*) I'll cede the bed to you. I prefer the floor.

THOMAS: There won't be any need for that.

LINUS: Why not?

THOMAS: If they believe that Max lied to them, they no longer have anything to learn from us. If they think he didn't deceive them, they probably believe that you and I don't know what Asel was up to either. In any case, they have no reason to wait. They'll take us out of here today.

LINUS: To execute us?

THOMAS: Maybe.

LINUS: (*With a motion of rebellion.*) I hope they all get what's coming to them!

THOMAS: They will. These administrators of death will also fall one day. And if the hour has come for us, it doesn't matter much. (*He turns and looks at Linus.*) Linus, we'll face them like Asel. With courage. Asel wasn't a coward. He sacrificed himself for us, to save our comrades, and to give us one last chance.

LINUS: You and me?

THOMAS: Don't you see? (*He gets up and goes over to him.*) Within an hour, or a minute, they'll take us out of here. Yes, to kill us. Almost for certain. (*Brief pause.*) But they might decide just to move us to a punishment cell. Even if they believed that Max threw himself over the railing, they would have to set an example with those in the cell where it started.

LINUS: Are you sure you aren't fantasizing?

THOMAS: Perhaps. It's only the tiniest of possibilities; maybe only an illusion. If it happens, tonight we'll give the signal. And for six days . . . (*ironically*) if they don't send us to the firing squad first . . . we'll live that other curious fantasy of hands blistered from digging, of anxiety in a dark tunnel, of exhaustion from lack of sleep, of the hope of embracing Berta again one day . . . of life and a struggle which goes on.

LINUS: (*Standing up; tense.*) How I wish . . .

THOMAS: I won't be driven insane by that illusion, or by any other. If the time has come to die, I'll face it. For Asel this strange cinema has vanished. And for Tulio. We have no right to survive them. (*A smile transfigures his face.*) But as long as I live, I'll hope! Until the last second! (*He takes a few steps and looks through the invisible window.*) I'll hope in the face of the rifle barrels . . . for all that will have been a hologram! (*Brief pause.*) We owe that strength to Asel. And I thank him . . . I no longer feel fatherless. (*With a glance upstage, he murmurs.*) Yes, the landscape is real. (*He goes toward Linus.*) If he were still here, he would repeat it to you, Linus. Prudence, cunning, since they force us to use it. But not one mistake more. Throwing that poor devil off the gallery was a useless atrocity, and very dangerous.

LINUS: Not so useless . . . if they take us below.

THOMAS: It's not certain. We barely saved the day. Your fit of anger could have ruined everything. We must learn to dominate even the most just indignation. If we don't succeed in separating violence from cruelty, we'll be destroyed. Asel was right, Linus. He knew more than we . . . and I'll never forget his words. (*Pause.*)

LINUS: We have the right to our indignation . . .

THOMAS: And the duty to conquer it. (*Brief silence.*)

LINUS: Yes, I've ruined everything. I still have to learn to think.

THOMAS: And I . . .

LINUS: . . . to understand what all this is. Do you know?

THOMAS: (*Ironically.*) The hologram . . . of the wild beasts.

LINUS: Maybe it is what you call it. But it's so obscene, so cruel . . Aren't we ever going to succeed in changing it?

THOMAS: (*He goes closer and presses his shoulder.*) It's changing already. Even within us. (*He walks away and sits down.*) And now, let's wait. (*Linus sits down.*)

LINUS: For death?

THOMAS: Or the punishment cell. The frightening tunnel toward freedom. (*A long pause.*)

LINUS: (*Lowering his voice.*) Don't you hear footsteps?

THOMAS: (*He lifts his smiling face.*) Yes. (*They look toward the door.*)

LINUS: They've stopped. (*They both stand up. Softly.*) They won't tell us where they're taking us.

THOMAS: We'll know soon. (*Sound of a key. The door opens. The aide enters.*)

AIDE: C-46 and C-72. Leave with all your possessions. (*Thomas and Linus look at each other.*)

LINUS: Yes, sir. (*He goes to the wall rack, takes down the two duffel bags that are left, hangs his over his arm and leaves the other one on Thomas's bedroll. Thomas goes to the metal shelves and takes down plates, tumblers, and spoons.*)

THOMAS: Here. (*He hands Linus his. Linus puts them in his bag. Thomas does the same with his, hangs the bag over his shoulder, and casts a circular glance around the cell.*)

AIDE: (*Sarcastically.*) You seem very happy.
THOMAS: (*With a faint smile.*) Naturally. Shall we go, Linus?
LINUS: Yes.

(*They hoist their bedrolls to their shoulders and exit. The aide goes out behind them and closes the door. A brief pause. We begin to hear, very softly and far away, Rossini's "Pastorale." The light grows iridescent. The alcove curtain descends and hides the corner with the toilet. The left wall rises to reveal again the bookshelves, the television set . . . The telephone reappears on the table. At the head of the bed, the little lamp comes out. The lower panel at right slips back and the refrigerator door gleams again. The large, multicolored shade descends slowly until it reaches its former position. Finally, the large window is revealed, and behind it the marvelous landscape is glowing. The music grows louder. The door opens. The Superintendent appears and immediately stations himself in the doorway. In the background, behind the railing, is the distant countryside. The Superintendent is wearing his formal attire, and with his most obsequious smile he invites new occupants, who are approaching, to enter the room.*)

END

# The Inmates of the Convent of Saint Mary Egyptian

## José Martín Recuerda

## THE INMATES OF THE CONVENT OF SAINT MARY EGYPTIAN
### [The Pavilion Theatre, Penn State University, 1980]
### Directed by Manuel Duque

CHARACTERS:

Townspeople of Granada:
  Baker, Lolilla, Guitarist, Dancer #1, Dancer #2, Dancer #3, Singer, Four Men's
  Voices, Woman's Voice

The Inmates of the Convent of Saint Mary Egyptian:
  Carmela, Chirrina, Concepción, Paula, Rita, Eva, Aniceta, Francisca, Rosa,
  Mariana Pineda, Rosita the gypsy

The Sisters of the Convent of Saint Mary Egyptian:
  Mother Superior, Sister Encarnación, Sister #1, Sister #2, Sister #3, Sister #4,
  Sister #5

The Prosecutor: Ramón Pedrosa

The Military:
  Guard #1, Guard #2, Guard #3, Guard #4, Guard #5, Captain Casimiro Brodett

# PRELUDE

*Granada. The year is 1831. Street in front of the Convent of Saint Mary
Egyptian. Over the solid oak doors of the convent, a weathered sign proclaims: "House of God and Saint Mary Egyptian—Asylum for Wayward
Women." The word "Whores" has been painted under "Wayward
Women." The walls on either side of the doors have remnants of old
posters; a new poster announces the week's bullfight. Other spaces on the
walls are covered with anti-royalist graffiti. A revolving delivery door is
built into the wall. The Baker enters, pushing his cart, opens the delivery
door and places bread inside; closing the door, he rings the bell next to it
and continues on his way. As he exits, faint sounds of music can be heard.
The music grows louder and finally a troupe of flamenco dancers and
guitarist appear on the scene, forming a "Tablao Flamenco." Lolilla leads
the clapping and dancing; she is wearing a green shawl around her waist
over the traditional flamenco dress of Andalusia. Shortly, the spirited
clapping and dancing to the guitar accompaniment is joined by the voice
of the Singer, who enters and joins the Tablao. He sings the traditional
repertory of Andalusian folk songs. As his song ends, the voices of several
men are heard offstage.*

MEN'S VOICES: (*Off.*) Let's head for the Tavern!
    A hearty red wine!
    Some singing and dancing!
    Their wenches are fine!
WOMEN'S VOICES: (*Off.*) They say that all of Granada
    is out for the fiesta today,
    but if you should look in some houses
    you'd see something other than play.

    People are praying in secret
    that freedom and justice may come.
    And bands of guerillas are fighting
    to topple the King from his throne!

The King has become such a tyrant
that rebels abound in our lands.
Granada, which leads in the battle,
has suffered the most at his hands.
MEN'S VOICES: (*Off.*) The cockfight is on in the plaza!
The fiesta is starting off right.
We'll go to the bullfight tomorrow.
But I'll wrestle a woman tonight!
WOMAN'S VOICE: (*Off.*) Some people are singing and dancing,
they carry their joy to the street,
but many are hiding in houses
for fear that their throats may be slit.

And there, behind walls, is the convent
a house not of love but of hate
where nuns are the jailers of women
imprisoned for reasons of State

(*Lolilla unties the shawl which is around her waist and dances before the convent doors; she opens the shawl to reveal sewn on the reverse the words "YOU ARE NOT ALONE."*)

WOMAN'S VOICE: (*Off.*) Have faith in the people, you Inmates!
We're with you! You are not alone!
Today we are with you suffering.
Tomorrow our triumph will come!

(*The Baker returns to the scene and joins the others as they add their voices in the final stanza.*)

ALL: Tomorrow! Tomorrow! Tomorrow!
The jails will be full when we try
the King and his henchmen tomorrow.
Tomorrow we'll see them all die!

(*Blackout. In the darkness, shouts intermingle with the lively music of the fair. Voices of a mob scream out "Down with the tyrant!" "Traitor!" "The Constitution!" "Restore our rights!" "The Constitution!" "Death to the King!" "Freedom! Freedom! Freedom!" "Release the prisoners!" "Free the Inmates!"*)

# PART ONE

*The singing of the "Salve" is heard; the voices of the Sisters in the Convent of Saint Mary Egyptian fill the theatre as the lights come up. The stage basks in the bright late afternoon sunshine of Granada. The setting is a patio, the inner courtyard of a former Renaissance palace which now houses the Sisters and the Inmates. The walls and other structures are in disrepair; the feeling throughout is one of seediness. A functional water trough and a hay storage shed reflect the origins of the space as a horse corral. The massive oak doors to the street, seen in the "Prelude," are flanked by two stairways. One leads to a tower which has a locked iron gate; the other is to an upper level with several caged areas visible, obviously a later addition to the original building. The delivery door and bell are next to the doors. Off the patio are entrances to the chapel and to the cells of the Sisters, the refectory and other rooms of the convent. When the singing of the "Salve" ends, the Sisters begin filing out of the chapel into the patio and towards the convent proper; they are led by Mother Superior, who steps aside to let them pass. As she does so loud pounding is heard from the caged area.*

MOTHER SUPERIOR: (*To one of the Sisters.*) Sister Encarnación, unlock the cages. (*Gives a set of keys to the nun.*)

SISTER ENCARNACION: (*Taking the keys.*) Yes, Mother. (*As she proceeds up the stairs to the caged area, Mother Superior exits. The sounds of cell doors being opened and closed is heard; the Inmates appear on the steps by twos or singly. Aniceta is combing lice out of her hair. Francisca, an aristocrat fallen on hard times, strolls distractedly. Paula and Rosa, who have been in the visible cell, come down together; Rosa's hands are chained. Chirrina, once a dancer, dances down the steps; Sister Encarnación follows, crosses to the convent entrance and exits; Carmela, a stocky, manly woman, descends after her.*)

CARMELA: I thought they'd never finish that damn hymn. Thank the Lord for small favors. (*Muffled fiesta sounds underlie the dialogue.*)

FRANCISCA: Can't you be a little more respectful? After all, this is a convent!

CARMELA: (*Sarcastically.*) Yes! A very holy convent. And the bars? And the locked gate? Are they to keep the holiness in? (*Francisca walks away in disgust.*) Keep that in mind, your Ladyship. (*Carmela motins to Chirrina to help her bring in the table from the shed; as she goes to help, Rita, Eva and Concepción come down the stairs with jugs of water, dishes and drinking mugs.*)

CHIRRINA: (*To Concepción.*) You look like you need a good scrubbing. Who's going to eat from those things after you touched them?

CONCEPCION: I washed my hands . . . What do you want, blood?

PAULA: (*To Concepción.*) Why don't you try some lye?

RITA: Listen to the viper! She's all ears!

PAULA: That's the last straw! What do you expect me to do, cover up my ears? I couldn't hear the sounds of the fair if I did.

EVA: It's wonderful to hear the singing and laughing in the streets.

ANICETA: When I would go to the fair I'd wear a big comb in my hair and my fanciest dress. But that was in Madrid. It seems so long ago! (*Pause.*) Now I look at myself in the mirror and wonder what my general would say if he could see what has become of his beautiful Aniceta.

CARMELA: Shut up, you old bag.

ANICETA: Like hell I will! All of you are always talking about "the good old days." Well, I'm going to say what I like. (*Strolling.*) My general asked me to hundreds of bullfights. His carriage would come under my balcony and he'd bow to me. Handsome as a gypsy! We'd be greeted by jeers when we took our front-row seats because I sold flowers and he was a general, but we were so good together that class differences didn't matter. Afterwards, we'd stroll shamelessly through the streets of Madrid. (*She drinks from the jug and spits out the water.*) The water's bad; it's full of grit. And the nuns tell us it comes from the well . . . (*She spits again.*)

CARMELA: (*To Chirrina.*) Put the table closer to the lemon tree.

CHIRRINA: What the hell do you think I'm doing?

CARMELA: I'm not sure you know what you're doing since you heard about those guards.

CHIRRINA: (*Feigning ignorance.*) What guards?

CARMELA: The new soldiers. The reinforcements.

FRANCISCA: (*Excitedly.*) Reinforcements! (*Regaining her composure.*) Have new troops arrived?

CARMELA: (*Ignoring Francisca.*) A lot of men! That's what Rita told me. (*Turning to Rita.*) And you certainly know about men, don't you? (*Rita ignores the taunt.*) But they're probably only "infants" in the infantry.

FRANCISCA: Such an uninspired pun . . .

PAULA: (*Dreamily.*) Infantrymen! (*To Rosa, who has been apart.*) Rosa, did you hear? More soldiers!

ROSA: I heard . . .

CARMELA: The great and glorious infantry. There's a whole regiment out there, I'll bet.

CHIRRINA: If that's true, these buttons are in the way. (*Unbuttons her blouse, showing her decolletage.*) After all, why hide what one's got when there are men around?

FRANCISCA: Whore! (*Chirrina flaunts her breasts at her.*)

PAULA: (*Peeking through a crack in the outside door.*) Why are there so many soldiers?

ROSA: The King is afraid of the rebels but he has the army with him and until the officers come to their senses, until they see how the people suffer under our great Constitutional Monarch, our case doesn't have a chance. Of course there are more soldiers out there; the King can afford a whole regiment to guard a miserable bunch of women!

(*A bell rings at the delivery box on the wall next to the outside door; the Inmates become silent, their eyes on the delivery box. Sister Encarnación crosses from the convent; she hastens to the delivery box, unlocks it with a key and turns the inner dolly; she takes out the package inside, puts it on the ground, closes the delivery door and locks it. She smiles at the Inmates and starts to exit.*)

ANICETA: Aren't we ever going to eat?

SISTER ENCARNACION: The sisters in the kitchen are preparing something special. (*She exits.*)

ANICETA: It's the eve of Corpus Christi; they *should* do something special for us on such an important Holy Day.

CHIRRINA: Special, but only if you go to confession and receive communion.

ANICETA: (*To Chirrina.*) And you, have you gone to confession? If you haven't, you should! Look at you! Why don't you cover your teats?

CARMELA: Leave her alone.

ANICETA: (*To Chirrina.*) Are the teats for the soldiers or (*turning to Carmela*) for you? (*Aniceta avoids Carmela, who has started for her.*)

ROSA: Can someone get some vinegar for my bruises? (*No one replies.*) Paula?

PAULA: (*At the outside door.*) Get it yourself. I'm looking for *my* soldier.

ROSA: Can't you see I'm sick? I'm burning up with fever!

ANICETA: I'll be happy to help you.

ROSA: Get away from me, you filthy whore. You disgust me.

PAULA: (*To Rita.*) Where's the new regiment from?

RITA: (*Whispering.*) From Burgos? The revolution has been getting stronger there. Some high ranking officers have defected.

PAULA: From Burgos! I wonder . . . Fermín could be with them!

CARMELA: What if he is?

PAULA: (*With deep resentment.*) I'd show him what I think of him for serving the King while I rot in one of his jails! (*Pause.*) Waiting, waiting for a trial! When will I get out of here?

ANICETA: (*With bitter laughter.*) When you're as old as I am you'll understand. You're not going to be tried in a civil court. Do you think they'd give you the chance to buy your freedom? No. You'll be tried in a military court. And that goes for everyone here. Don't you know how the law works in Spain? If the King betrays the Constitution so openly, how can you expect to get justice in his courts? You should know better. But then what can you expect from people who can't read or write. All you know to do is get in bed with a man. How are the rebels ever going to win with the likes of you. You don't even know what's happening out there!

CARMELA: Who the hell does? Lay off the sermon!

ANICETA: (*Killing a louse.*) Someone has to put some sense into your heads.

CARMELA: Take care of your own lousy head.

ROSA: (*In pain.*) My hands! Paula, my hands . . .

PAULA: All right, I'm coming. You act as if no one else had ever worn chains! What you need is a maid. (*In an aside meant for Francisca.*) The good old days of servants are over.

FRANCISCA: (*Strutting proudly.*) I know you all have it in for me. But I'm not about to stoop to your filth. It's hard being a lady in this stable and maintaining one's manner when there's no one of breeding to converse with . . . I'll talk to the walls if I have to rather than be like you. (*Pause.*) To think that it's the feast of Corpus Christi and I'm here! I used to have soirees in my palatial home, with its gardens . . .

CARMELA: Soirees! I've heard about those aristocratic orgies!

FRANCISCA: It's incredible that I who have fought so hard to break down class barriers should end up here having to fight for acceptance . . .

CARMELA: You lost your money! That's what happened to you. You only became a Liberal because you had no money.

FRANCISCA: Fortunately, I understand you and can resign myself to your attitude. It should be enough to convince you that I'm a prisoner like the rest of you. I swore allegiance to the Constitution, as did the King, but I didn't break my oath as he did. And I'm proud to have served the Liberal cause, even if it put me here.

CARMELA: (*With irony.*) How wonderful! (*To the Inmates.*) Our lady of the Liberal cause!

CHIRRINA: (*Coquettishly, to Francisca.*) Milady, could I have some of your cologne? It has such a lovely fragrance, and with new soldiers in town . . . Who knows what could happen tonight if I entice one of them through the crack in the door . . . Give me some!

FRANCISCA: Such insolence! You should have some respect for a lady!

CHIRRINA: Lady? The women who end up here ran around too much and found themselves with big bellies; they were brought here for "correction." If you were a political prisoner and nothing more, they would have taken you somewhere else. The hell with all your airs of the great lady! The hell with her (*points to Aniceta*) general. And the hell with all the kings and aristocrats! And that goes for our Liberal cause too; this is where ideas of equality and justice have brought me. And who's going to save me now? Not a damn one of those rebels . . . and those

good people out there going to the fiesta as if we didn't exist . . . as if
we were already . . . dead. No one rises up . . . no one fires a shot! No
one cares about us! (*Pause.*) That's why I need your cologne . . . to entice the guards!

ROSA: (*Crying out.*) My wrists!

ANICETA: Will you shut up. What a delicate rose she is. You can tell her
husband kept her in style. How did he do it, Rosa? With the bribes he
picked up on the side as a policeman? He performed some fine services
for the King, didn't he?

ROSA: Get out of my sight, you old bitch!

ANICETA: You'll look like me before long. You'll see. Days become years in
this convent. You may have been beautiful in the past but in this prison
. . .

ROSA: Leave my past alone. If you don't (*threateningly raising her chained hands*), I'll bash your head in . . .

ANICETA: (*Moving away.*) I know why the nuns keep you in chains.

ROSA: What I did, I did for the cause of freedom.

ANICETA: Freedom. Yes, it was for freedom, alright. (*To the others.*) Did
you know that she killed her husband? (*The other Inmates react.*)

ROSA: What of it? He was corrupt; he took advantage of others. I'd do it
again.

ANICETA: Didn't I tell you? No one can free herself from her past. She
wouldn't do it again. She lies. She'd give anything not to be here. The
cause of freedom indeed! Ideas about liberty don't liberate; they condemn . . . She's an example and so are we. And Mariana Pineda . . .
she's trapped like the rest of us. Where did all her liberal ideas and her
friends in high places get her? Into the same rotten prison as the rest of
us.

ROSA: (*Rushing towards Aniceta.*) I'll shut you up forever!

PAULA: (*Holding Rosa.*) No, Rosa! Stop it!

ROSA: Let go of me! (*Paula overcomes her and Rosa falls to the ground,
moaning.*)

CARMELA: Be quiet or the nuns will hear us.

CHIRRINA: (*Looking towards the convent.*) I'll bet we won't get a hot meal
today. (*The marching of soldiers is heard beyond the outside door.*)

CARMELA: What's going on?

CHIRRINA: It sounds like the changing of the guard.

CARMELA: Let's take a look. (*She looks through a crack in the outside
door.*) There are soldiers everywhere—more than ever!

PAULA: If I could, I'd flirt with them. I'd take off everything, a little at a
time, then they'd do anything I told them.

CHIRRINA: That's why I wanted the cologne.

CONCEPCION: We ought to try to escape before more soldiers arrive!

EVA: Be careful who hears you. (*Pointing to Francisca.*) Carmela thinks she's spying for the nuns.

RITA: Francisca's a little odd, that's all. She's just living in the past.

CONCEPCION: What I can't understand is why they've placed so many soldiers around the convent. Something must have happened.

*(Mariana Pineda appears. The first impression is that of an attractive, well-dressed woman, but her dress is torn and her face is gaunt from suffering, lack of sleep and poor nutrition. Her hair is unkempt. Yet, when she appears in the brilliant sunlight, there is visible a lingering zest for life. She stands motionless, unseen by the other Inmates.)*

EVA: When I was helping Sister Encarnación get the bread from the delivery box, I overheard the baker tell her that a rebel colonel and his troops were killed in the mountains . . .

CONCEPCION: What's so unusual about that? They're always killing some politician or officer, on either side.

EVA: But they were coming to Granada . . . to join forces with Captain Brodett.

RITA: Casimiro Brodett! *(Mariana, who has been listening, is moved by the name.)*

CARMELA: *(Stepping away from her post at the outside door.)* Who is he? What about this Captain Brodett?

RITA: He's an officer from Burgos . . . he rebelled against the King.

CHIRRINA: He's one of Mariana Pineda's lovers.

EVA: You should show some respect for Mariana; she's a lady.

CHIRRINA: A lady? Mariana Pineda? Listen, I'm from Granada and I know how many men she took to bed. She's no better than we are. And she'll hang like the rest of us too.

EVA: You're cruel, Chirrina. *(Walks away.)*

CHIRRINA: You're an innocent, Eva.

CARMELA: *(To Chirrina.)* What else do you know about this captain?

CHIRRINA: Brodett has a very shady history. But he's with the Liberals now; he'll be in the new government if the King is deposed.

CARMELA: He'll have to survive first; the King's troops are everywhere.

CHIRRINA: *(Seeing Mariana, she speaks secretively.)* Anyway, he is one of Mariana's lovers; she embroidered the revolutionary flag for him. I wouldn't be surprised if those reinforcements are his former troops; they might still be loyal to him, not the King. Maybe they're waiting for the right moment to change sides; then they'll rescue Mariana . . .

CARMELA: *(Interrupting.)* And leave the rest of us, the riff-raff, to rot here.

ANICETA: *(At the outside door.)* Be still! I want to hear what they're saying.

PAULA: *(Nervously.)* Ask them where they're from. I know they're from the north. They have to be from Burgos!

ANICETA: As long as you talk, I won't be able to hear what they say.

PAULA: Please ask them about my sergeant . . .

ANICETA: (*Moving away from the door, grabs Paula.*) Will you be quiet?

PAULA: (*Becoming very agitated.*) He's got to be with them! (*Struggles with Aniceta.*)

RITA: (*To Chirrina.*) That woman frightens me.

CONCEPCION: The nuns will hear you.

EVA: (*Fearful.*) Please stop. Let's finish setting the table.

ANICETA: (*Who is trying to hold Paula.*) Someone help me. I can't hold her myself.

(*Paula screams and fights with Aniceta. Rosa tries to help Paula. Mother Superior and Sister Incarnación rush into the patio on hearing the screams. Other nuns follow them. When Mother Superior grabs Paula, Aniceta lets go of the inmate and retreats.*)

MOTHER SUPERIOR: (*To Sister Encarnación, who has been uninvolved in the action.*) Sister Encarnación! Can't you see that I need your help! (*Sister Encarnación approaches Paula.*)

PAULA: (*Picking up a jug and holding it threateningly.*) Don't come any closer! Don't touch me! (*Both Mother Superior and Sister Encarnación stand firm.*) Why are you keeping me here? I haven't done anything. Why won't you listen to me?

MOTHER SUPERIOR: (*With restrained cynicism.*) We will. Very soon. (*Looking at Sister Encarnación and nodding an order to her, then again to Paula.*) You'll have your day in court, I promise you. (*As she speaks, Sister Encarnación manages to grab Paula's arm and wrests the jug from her. Mother Superior is now holding Paula from behind, hand over the inmate's mouth; Sister Encarnación is visibly upset at her own role.*)

MARIANA: (*Pleading with Mother Superior.*) Let her go! (*Mother Superior tightens her hold on Paula.*) For the love of God . . . you call yourselves nuns! Is this Christian charity? (*Sister Encarnación immediately releases Paula and stands aside, head bent. Mariana then confronts Mother Superior, their eyes meeting in a fierce stare.*) Let her go or . . . (*Picks up the jug.*)

MOTHER SUPERIOR: Your threat will be added to the list of your other crimes! (*She releases Paula.*) Pedrosa will hear of this! You can be certain that the prosecutor will not let this insult pass.

MARIANA: Justice has been denied us and we must help each other. (*Puts down the jug.*) God knows I didn't want to threaten you, Reverend Mother.

MOTHER SUPERIOR: (*Still smarting.*) Only those going to the gallows dare to do what you have just done.

MARIANA: (*Stunned.*) Gallows . . . (*Recovering her self-assurance.*) I will not be taken to the gallows. You had better look to what you're saying, Reverend Mother. One day we'll be out of here and then the Pope himself will hear about your *holy* convent.

MOTHER SUPERIOR: That remains to be seen, doesn't it? We are here to carry out the King's orders; it is the mission of the convent of Saint Mary Egyptian to assist His Majesty in protecting the Faith in moments of national crisis.

MARIANA: Nothing can justify your abuses, your mistreatment of these women, your lack of charity. You should give comfort, not pain; you should bring the word of God to these women . . .

MOTHER SUPERIOR: (*Interrupting.*) How dare *you*, a woman without morals, presume to lecture me! You, who's given herself to so many men . . .

MARIANA: I'm a political prisoner, not a prostitute. I've addressed you with respect, Reverend Mother. You might have the same consideration for me.

MOTHER SUPERIOR: Respect! Indeed! You'd like all of us to think of you as a grand lady, a victim of political oppression. (*Pause.*) Well, there are no political prisoners within the walls of this convent. Move aside, whore!

MARIANA: Reverend Mother!

MOTHER SUPERIOR: Oh, but I do you an injustice. I haven't given you your other title: Traitor.

MARIANA: Not even the King can prove that I've committed treason! There is no proof because there is no treason. But there is a God who will judge your malice and your disservice to His cause.

MOTHER SUPERIOR: You'll fall from your high pulpit soon enough, Señora Pineda. (*To Paula.*) Once again you have lost the privilege of being in the patio. (*To Sister Encarnación.*) Sister, lock her in her cell.

SISTER ENCARNACION: Yes, Mother. (*She exits with Paula.*)

MOTHER SUPERIOR: (*To the other nuns.*) Come, Sisters. To the chapel. (*They exit. The Inmates stand silently in place. Sister Encarnacion returns alone and hastily goes towards the chapel door; she stops, looks at the Inmates with sympathy and then exits.*)

ROSA: (*To Mariana.*) Sister Encarnación is the daughter of a weaver who joined the rebels . . . You could tell she did not want to hurt Paula. She feels as we do, Mariana. I'm sure she's one of us!

MARIANA: I must find a way to speak to her alone . . .

ROSA: (*Interrupting.*) Be careful! Mother Superior knows her background. I think she's testing Sister Encarnación. Be patient. There will be an opportunity to talk to her when she's not being watched.

MARIANA: (*Now unsure and despondent.*) I wonder, Rosa. We've been here so long, without word from the outside, not knowing what is happening . . . Sister Encarnacion could be our ally, bring us news . . . Something has to end this uncertainty. We can't go on like this. (*She hides her face in her hands, leaning against the bars of the cell. The strains of a sad song are heard off.*)

WOMAN'S VOICE: (*Off.*)

"Women enclosed in a convent,
a palace whose walls are a prison,
wear beautiful dresses now tattered
like remnants of hope in their hearts.

Women whose love has been stifled,
while lovers and friends cannot see them;
they sigh in the bright sun of day,
they cry in the darkness of night.

In prison, they're learning to see
the dawn they had never beheld
and now in their last days of life,
are finding what living can mean."

PAULA: (*In her cell, shouting.*) I want Fermín! I want to get my hands on Fermin!

MARIANA: Tell me about him. Who is he?

PAULA: (*Bitterly.*) The man who denounced me. The one responsible for my being here.

MARIANA: Was he your lover?

PAULA: Lover? Yes, he was my lover. But he was much more than that. He was everything to me! He was my husband. (*Sobs.*)

MARIANA: And he denounced you? How could he?

PAULA: Because I left him. I was tired of his devotion to the King. The King always came first! One day I forced him to choose between us and the King won. So I left him. But not before I ripped off his stripes with my teeth!

MARIANA: All of us despise what the King stands for . . . but there's more to your hatred that that. What is it?

PAULA: (*With difficulty.*) He had my father imprisoned . . . then they stood him against the wall of our parish church and shot him. (*Pause.*) I saw it all from the balcony of our house. (*Sobs.*) I had to leave the city after that. That's when I confronted Fermín and left him. (*Regaining her composure.*) I went to work on the docks. Later, I was told that Fermín had avenged himself by denouncing me to the authorities. I fled to the mountains and joined a band of guerillas. (*Pause.*) I fell in love with their leader. I stayed with him until he was captured. I saw him being led through the streets in a cage. They had beaten him. I ran to wipe his face with this handkerchief. (*Removing the handkerchief from her bosom.*) Before I was arrested I was able to kiss him one last time. (*Pause.*) Then I was brought here by Fermín.

MARIANA: What are the charges against you?

PAULA: (*Very hesitantly.*) I'm accused of being a heretic.

MARIANA: (*Turning her back to Paula, horrified.*) My God!

PAULA: No, it's not what you're thinking! They called me a Freemason because I wanted to think for myself.

MARIANA: (*Getting as close as she can to the cell.*) Try to forget what he's done to you, Paula. Put him out of your mind.

PAULA: Never! I won't rest until I see him die at my hands! I keep thinking I hear his voice outside. Maybe the moment is here. Maybe he is among the reinforcements . . . I know you helped many prisoners to escape; they must be plotting your rescue now. You're a great lady, Mariana. Important men have trusted you. They've shared their secret plans with you. No one trusts me. I won't even be brought to trial. I'll die without the chance to defend myself. I've seen the same thing happen to others. They were taken from the convent to be executed. There's a rumor that troops are coming from Burgos to rescue you. Take me with you when they come. If you don't, I'll be executed. Please, I don't want to die! (*Cries.*)

ROSA: (*Who's been eavesdropping on the last part of the conversation.*) You must take me too. I'll be silent as a tomb.

PAULA: The troops are under the command of Captain Brodett!

MARIANA: (*Very defensive now that Rosa has joined the conversation.*) Who is this Captain Brodett?

PAULA: Your lover . . . The man for whom you embroidered the revolutionary flag.

MARIANA: I haven't embroidered any flag . . .

PAULA: (*Imploringly.*) Don't lie to us. It's time we told each other the truth. We might be dead by tomorrow. (*Mariana moves away nervously; some Inmates approach them.*)

ROSA: I know all about you. We lived near you. We could see your house from ours. We'd hear the music of your parties and see you in the midst of the orgies. The worst politicians and assassins in Granada were your guests. I can rattle off their names if you like. And when the festivities were over, you'd close the shutters of your bedroom because one of your important guests always spent the night with you. (*Mariana turns away.*)

PAULA: (*Appeasingly.*) The reinforcements must be here because of you. They're waiting for Brodett to make his move; they know he's on his way here. Is it fair that only you be saved?

ROSA: If they come for you, they'll have to take the rest of us.

PAULA: But if they don't rescue you, I'll be with you to the end, Mariana.

ROSA: What choice do any of us have?

CONCEPCION: We can fight. I led a march from my village to the sea. But the troops were waiting for us when we reached the coast. I was the only one who survived. I didn't survive for nothing; I was spared so I could fight again. (*Pause.*) The schoolteacher brought the village children on the march. All of them were slaughtered, even my little boy!

MARIANA: I'm sorry, Concepción. I have a son too and I don't know what has become of him.

(*Mariana becomes pensive. The bell at the delivery box rings. The Inmates become expectant. Sister Encarnación crosses to the wall, unlocks the delivery box, turns the dolly, and extracts the green shawl Lolilla had worn in the "Prelude." She opens the shawl, reads the message on its reverse, looks at the Inmates, and locks the delivery box. Sister Encarnación exits, obviously leaving the shawl for the Inmates to see. When she has left, Concepción runs over to the shawl and picks it up, looking at it intently.*)

CARMELA: What are you doing?

CONCEPCION: (*Holding it up.*) There's something written on it!

CHIRRINA: (*Taking the shawl from her.*) "YOU ARE NOT ALONE." That's what it says.

CONCEPCION: It could be from Casimiro Brodett! (*She takes the shawl back, climbs the table, and starts waving the shawl.*) This is our flag. The beautiful flag of hope! (*The other Inmates become jubilant.*)

CARMELA: (*To Concepción.*) Get off the table! Quickly! (*Concepción does so and Carmela takes the shawl from her and hides it. There is tension in the air because Carmela has seen Francisca watching. To Francisca.*) And you, milady? Now that you've seen our "flag," what are you going to do?

FRANCISCA: I'd carry it through the streets if I could!

CARMELA: If you could ever stop fanning yourself.

CHIRRINA: Listen! (*The sound of marching is barely audible.*)

EVA: What's wrong?

CHIRRINA: (*Looking through the crack on the outside door.*) Soldiers . . . I can see them. (*The Inmates become exctied.*) They're in formation now . . . They're presenting arms.

EVA: Someone important must be coming here.

CARMELA: It must be Aniceta's general coming to take her to the bullring.

ANICETA: Shut up, you witch!

FRANCISCA: Could it be an officer? (*Mariana, Paula and Rosa react.*)

CARMELA: (*Seeing that the Inmates are becoming afraid again, she needles Francisca.*) No doubt for you! You with the fancy fan. Finish setting the table. (*Francisca ignores her.*) Look at this table. There are footprints all over it. (*Starts cleaning the table with the hem of her dress.*) Someone's got to care what we eat on.

EVA: With all this going on they won't feed us today.

CHIRRINA: Listen, I hear a carriage. They must be bringing more prisoners.

EVA: Not on the eve of a Holy Day!

CARMELA: They never stop making arrests.

PAULA: (*To Mariana.*) They're coming to rescue us, Mariana. (*Mariana embraces her.*) All those soldiers . . .

CARMELA: Don't build up your hope. (*Pause.*) It's hell not knowing what's really going on.

ANICETA: I'll tell you what's going on. Newspapers are forbidden. The universities are closed. The jails are bursting with prisoners. The streets are full of soldiers. What more do you want to know? When we're going to the gallows?

MARIANA: Don't talk like that. (*Pointing to where the shawl is hidden.*) "You are not alone," remember? Someone out there has sent us this message. There *is* hope.

CARMELA: And that's all it is. Hope! And what happens when the prosecutor, Ramón Pedrosa, arrives? All our hope disappears. That could be his carriage Chirrina heard.

PAULA: Pedrosa! Oh, God, no!

MARIANA: Our day will come, Paula. It will come. But if it is Pedrosa, I don't want to give him the satisfaction of seeing me look like this. (*Exits.*)

CHIRRINA: Someone's coming . . .

(*Silence. The women wait tensely. They face the convent. Two nuns appear escorting a frail gypsy girl into the patio. The nuns exit immediately. The girl walks slowly, head bent, hands tied.*)

CONCEPCION: She's just a child!

EVA: (*Lifting the girl's head.*) A gypsy girl. (*The Inmates gather around the newcomer.*)

CONCEPCION: Who are you, child? (*No reply.*)

FRANCISCA: Why are your clothes so tattered? (*No reply.*)

CARMELA: Who brought you here? (*Still no reply.*) Were you with the rebels?

CHIRRINA: (*Lifting the gypsy's head up.*) I thought so. I know her. Her name is Rosita. I've seen her selling castanets in the plaza. (*To Rosita.*) Aren't you working as a seamstress now?

ROSITA: (*Crying.*) I don't know how to sew. I can't embroider . . .

CARMELA: What are you talking about? (*Unexpectedly tender.*) That can't be why you're crying. (*To Eva.*) Fetch some water for her. Her mouth is as dry as an old bone.

EVA: (*Bringing a cup of water.*) Here. (*But Rosita can't take the cup.*) Untie her hands, Chirrina.

CHIRRINA: (*Doing so.*) Her hands! My God! They've broken all the bones! (*The Inmates are overcome by the revelation.*)

CONCEPCION: (*Embracing Rosita.*) How could they do this to a child? (*Rosita faints in her arms and Concepción carries her to the table. The Inmates gather around the table.*)

EVA: Will she . . . die?

ROSA: (*Banging her chains.*) Murderers! Cowards!

INMATES: Bastards! Cowards! Murderers!

PEDROSA: (*Who appears as the Inmates cry out "Murderers!" accompanied by Mother Superior, nuns and guards.*) Good afternoon, ladies! My, what a delightful fragrance! Ah, lemon blossoms. A cool breeze, the music of the fiesta, the sounds of the bullring . . . It is quite pleasant out here.

MOTHER SUPERIOR: I can assure you that the accommodations are not appreciated by our guests, Señor Pedrosa. They show nothing but contempt for the convent and the good sisters.

PEDROSA: Oh? Yet they have clean cells, good food and a pleasant enough routine. How very odd. (*Recognizing Francisca, he approaches her.*) Well, Dôna Francisca. You are well, I take it. (*He bows and kisses her hand.*)

FRANCISCA: (*Proud of his attentions.*) It's good of you to remember me, Señor Pedrosa.

PEDROSA: How could I forget? Your hospitality, those lovely evenings at your palace . . . Unforgettable! The people of Granada are so kind to strangers.

MARIANA: (*Who entered as Pedrosa greeted Francisca, composes herself after an initial revulsion at seeing him.*) Generosity is so hard to forget. Isn't it so, your excellency?

PEDROSA: (*Turning quickly to Mariana.*) Ah, my lovely friend, Mariana Pineda! (*Taking her offered hand and kissing it.*) Needless to say, I cannot forget that you were the first in Granada to open her doors to me.

MARIANA: Yes, on an evening such as this we had our first dinner together . . . Have you come now to attend my last supper?

PEDROSA: You're as witty as ever, Mariana. Such stimulating conversation at your house . . .

MARIANA: But the setting has changed.

PEDROSA: Your days in this holy convent have been well spent, I trust. Undoubtedly you're read the writings of Saint Paul and other devout authors; there's certainly been time enough for meditation on the holy lessons they teach.

MARIANA: Time enough. But I'm afraid my mind has been on other things.

PEDROSA: Ah, yes! The "progressive" ideas which the French Enlightenment has lobbed over the Pyrenees!

MARIANA: I'm sorry to disappoint you. Rousseau and Voltaire have never been my favorite reading; I can't understand the current passion for them. Their ideas can lead only to a grave spiritual crisis . . . I lack the words to express how I really feel . . .

PEDROSA: (*Unctiously.*) Does the lady wish to talk in the privacy of the chapel?

MARIANA: The chapel is for praying to God, not for confiding in men.

PEDROSA: Just so. But it is most suitable for an examination of conscience; I can help you with that, Mariana. (*Approaches her too closely and she backs away.*) But if my role as father confessor is not to your liking, you can confess your sins to the priest who came with me; he's in the reception room.

MARIANA: And why not right here, before this audience? (*Indicating the Inmates.*)

PEDROSA: They are not worthy of such intimacies.

MARIANA: And *you* are.

PEDROSA: (*Seriously, taking her arm.*) Mariana, let me help you. We could be on the same side.

MARIANA: But we are not. These are my people. These fellow prisoners and people like them on every corner.

PEDROSA: (*Himself again.*) Very well. Your attitude saddens me. Are these the only conclusions you've come to here?

MARIANA: I have had other thoughts . . . (*Fear and anxiety show on her face.*) What has become of my son? Is anyone caring for him? Is he safe?

PEDROSA: He is well. Your servants are caring for him at home. Your friends visit him often.

MARIANA: Thank God!

PEDROSA: You should thank me. I too am concerned with his well-being. As with yours, Mariana. (*She does not back away now as he touches her arm.*) You could be back with your son very soon . . .

MARIANA: If only I could believe that.

PEDROSA: Your case has been discussed in Parliament. It will undoubtedly claim the attention of the King . . . But then, after things have settled down somewhat, a compassionate word in His Majesty's ear . . .

MARIANA: And the King would . . .

PEDROSA: The national situation is better than people here suppose. Granada is distant from Madrid and the mails are slow; you're the last to know what is happening elsewhere. And, of course, the people of Granada are fond of making much out of nothing.

MARIANA: They've had to live with so little for so long . . .

PEDROSA: (*Ignoring her remark.*) Things have become more tranquil.

Don't you hear the excitement of the bullring? The people of the city have flocked to see the new matador.

MARIANA: I remember your fondness for the killing of bulls. I'm surprised that you've missed this opportunity to see a few more slaughtered.

PEDROSA: I am very fond of the *art* of bullfighting. But one isn't always free to do as one wishes. Duty has kept me from the corrida today.

MARIANA: Was it on my account?

PEDROSA: A lesser man would flatter you now. No, I had to attend to that little gypsy.

MARIANA: How could one so young require the personal attention of the great Pedrosa? She's only a child! And you have tortured her!

PEDROSA: Scarcely a child. Gypsies, with all their singing and dancing, may not keep track of their age, but they learn very quickly how to get what they want out of life. Some even have grandiose dreams!

MARIANA: It must be wonderful to have dreams in times like these.

PEDROSA: You could dream too, Mariana. And yours could come true.

MARIANA: Like that little gypsy's? What has she done to be brought here? To be tortured like this? Who is she?

PEDROSA: (*Approaching Rosita and holding up her head.*) I thought you knew her, Mariana.

MARIANA: I've never seen her before.

PEDROSA: (*To Rosita.*) And you, little gypsy, have you ever seen this lady? (*Rosita nods no.*) This innocent-looking girl has committed a very serious crime: she was caught embroidering a certain flag. (*Nods to Mother Superior, who unfurls the revolutionary banner; Inmates react.*)

MARIANA: What a lovely piece of embroidery! The letters are so well done.

PEDROSA: You are surprised. Have you never seen it before?

MARIANA: Should I have? I've seen flags in Granada but none so fine.

PEDROSA: The embroidery has impressed you.

MARIANA: (*Sensing a trap.*) I don't know much about embroidering but I can recognize good work.

PEDROSA: Yes, it is fine. A pity to have wasted it on such a flag.

MARIANA: A revolution doesn't need a flag, only men and weapons. When you have those things, any rag will do. It was a waste to embroider that flag.

PEDROSA: Unless, of course, it was done out of love . . . out of love for a man.

MARIANA: No man could inspire such artistry. Only an ideal could do that.

PEDROSA: And you'd have me believe that this gypsy had such lofty inspiration?

MARIANA: (*Turning to Mother Superior.*) Reverend Mother, this child has suffered enough. Can't she be taken inside? (*Mother Superior looks at Pedrosa.*)

PEDROSA: All in good time. (*Becoming the prosecutor.*) Mariana Pineda, isn't this the flag found in your home? The one you helped embroider?

MARIANA: It could be the one you *claim* was found in my house.

PEDROSA: (*To Rosita.*) Listen to me, Rosita Heredia. If you admit that this woman (*pointing to Mariana*) gave you this cloth and asked you to embroider the letters, you can go free right now.

ROSITA: (*With difficulty.*) But . . . I . . . don't know . . . this lady (*murmuring among the Inmates who agonize over Rosita's condition*) I never . . . learned . . . to embroider. I swear it! (*Trying to cross herself.*) The nuns at school tried to teach me but I could not learn. You can ask them. I only know how to dance . . . I sell castanets in the Plaza but I can't embroider. I swear it by the sweet nails that pierced the hands of Jesus.

ROSA: (*Banging her chains.*) Leave her alone! (*Paula quiets her immediately.*)

MARIANA: (*Taking Rosita in her arms, to Pedrosa*) Enough! I beg you. Let her rest.

PEDROSA: The lady is very concerned with a mere gypsy . . . Let me tell you what else this "innocent" gypsy has done: she became the mistress of a young man who was destined for the priesthood; she seduced him away from the seminary, away from God. He will burn in Hell. But the law will rectify her mistakes here; these holy sisters of Saint Mary Egyptian will instruct her in the way of humility and decorum. (*He pushes her brusquely to Mother Superior.*)

MARIANA: Pedrosa! She's only a child!

INMATES: (*Approaching Pedrosa threateningly.*) Coward! Coward!

PEDROSA: Guards! (*The guards stand between Pedrosa and the Inmates.*)

MARIANA: (*To the Inmates.*) No! Not like this. Not like a mob. Violence will only make us like they are. Our revolution will triumph some day. And when it does, we will deal with the likes of Pedrosa. But justly. Our Constitution is humane and just. (*The Inmates heed her words.*)

PEDROSA: You've just admitted before witnesses that you are a revolutionary. Your own words condemn you. I need no further proof of your treason to the crown. The flag is only additional evidence now. You will be tried very soon. I will plead for clemency only if you give me the names of your fellow conspirators. (*Pause.*) Who are they?

MARIANA: Those who will assassinate you and the King.

PEDROSA: There are men you consider your friends who are willing to betray you to save themselves. I would rather execute them than you. Denounce them before they denounce you. Save yourself. I am trying to help you.

MARIANA: Like you helped so many others! You have no evidence against me that would stand up in a proper court . . . words alone cannot condemn anyone. The flag was "discovered" in my house by the policeman who put it there at your orders. (*Turning to Rosa.*) Do you know why? Because he came to my bedroom after one of my parties and tried to make love to me; but I kept him at a distance. His hands were never on my body. I swear to that. (*Kissing her crossed fingers.*)

PEDROSA: You've been known as a fallen woman for a long time, Mariana. You will pay for the sins of your body as well as for those of your soul.

MARIANA: And you for yours, Pedrosa. You have enemies everywhere. One of your own soldiers, someone in the street . . . anyone might assassinate you at any moment. It is you who must live in fear. (*Removing the lemon blossoms from her hair.*) I wore these thinking of my own death, but now I throw them at your feet because I see you as a dead man. These are the only flowers you'll receive.

PEDROSA: We will see each other again, Mariana.

(*He takes the flowers with him as he exits. Mother Superior and the soldiers follow Pedrosa out; Sister Encarnación remains on the scene, apart. Mariana goes to Rosita and comforts her. She helps Rosita to sit on the table.*)

CARMELA: (*With disdain.*) Look at those nuns bowing to Pedrosa.

CHIRRINA: What do you expect? They live on the crumbs from the King's table.

ANICETA: I remember Pedrosa when he was a kid with torn clothes begging on the streets of Madrid. Now he rides in a carriage and has power over life and death. But one of these days he'll end up dead in the same gutter where he started.

CARMELA: We should have killed him ourselves.

CHIRRINA: The guards would have stopped us.

ANICETA: I'm not so sure . . . Didn't you see how they hesitated to confront us? I could swear they're on our side.

CARMELA: Not so loud. Francisca might hear and report it to her great friend Pedrosa. (*To Francisca.*) Listen to me, you are going to be watched night and day.

MARIANA: The child's hands . . . We must do something for them.

CARMELA: (*Turning on Mariana.*) You should be concerned. She's one of your victims.

CHIRRINA: You had her making that flag and now look at her.

CARMELA: (*To Mariana, threateningly.*) Don't touch her again. Get away from her. (*Mariana moves away from Rosita.*) Child, did you embroider that flag?

ROSITA: No . . . but I held it in my arms and kissed it.

MARIANA: Bless you! (*To the Inmates.*) We must help this child. *The Inmates remain impassive.*) If we don't help each other all that awaits us is death.

CARMELA: That'll never happen to you; you have a chance to save yourself. You're well connected.

CHIRRINA: Yes! Under the sheets!

CARMELA: Pedrosa will come through for you.

MARIANA: I feel sorry for all of you. Your distrust and hatred of one another will drag us all down. We are all prisoners here. If we have to
die, we could die with dignity. We could help each other like human
beings instead of fighting among ourselves like animals. (*Tearing off a
piece of her petticoat.*) This will have to do. (*She starts to bandage
Rosita's hands.*)

SISTER ENCARNACION: (*Coming to Mariana's side and ripping a piece of
her own petticoat.*) I'm with you, Mariana.

(*Inspired by her action, the Inmates begin ripping their petticoats and
giving Mariana the pieces. She and Sister Encarnación bandage Rosita's
hands. As they console the gypsy girl, castanets are heard off; their
rhythm brings Rosita to her feet. When guitar music joins in, Rosita starts
to dance, her arms in the air. The Inmates begin to clap in accompaniment. The music increases in loudness. As Rosita dances, the spirit of optimism wells up in the Inmates, the last two verses of the "Prelude" are
now heard, but with greater vehemence.*)

WOMAN'S VOICE: (*Off.*)
    Have faith in the people, you inmates!
    We're with you! You are not alone!
    Today we are with you in suffering.
    Tomorrow our triumph will come!

(*Carmela retrieves the green shawl from its hiding place and starts to
march with it; the other Inmates follow her, joining in the chant.*)

ALL:
    Tomorrow! Tomorrow! Tomorrow!
    The jail will be full when we try
    The King and his henchmen tomorrow.
    Tomorrow we'll see them all die!

END OF PART ONE

# PART TWO

## Scene 1

*The house lights dim to total darkness. The sound of hammering is heard. The slamming of doors and muffled cries, mixed with shouts, pierce the night.*

VOICE: (*Off, over music.*)
"Oh, what darkness there is in Granada,
even the stars have departed;
while people in houses lay sleeping
the night has been stripped of its gladness.

Sounds in the night were of hammers
joining the planks into scaffolds.
Their dirges resound through the blackness
while women in prison are dying."

## Scene 2

*The next morning, the Feast of Corpus Christi. Festival music is heard, some of it discordant. The day is bright and in the courtyard of the convent some of the Inmates are in small groups while others are alone. Carmela, Chirrina, Eva and Concepción wash their faces and arms in the water trough while Rita works the pump. Francisca is primping. Rosa, whose hands are still chained, has her hair combed by Paula. Aniceta is washing her feet in a wooden tub. When the washing is through, each inmate sits in the sun to dry.*

ANICETA: What a concert! Not exactly the sound of cherubs, is it? You can tell the musicians aren't from Madrid. And on Corpus Christi! You'd think they'd have only the best musicians for the Holy Day.
CHIRRINA: How I wish I could throw some rose petals in the procession.
CARMELA: You?
CHIRRINA: Yes, me! I love feastdays. I have a great devotion to Saint Rita; I used to carry a candle and sing in her processions. She's already performed two miracles for me.
CARMELA: Let's see her get you out of here!
ANICETA: That would be some miracle.
CARMELA: (*To Rita.*) Did you overhear the baker say anything else? (*Rita shakes her head no.*)
RITA: Only that more strangers have arrived in Granada. I already told you the important news.
CARMELA: That a priest was dragged off to prison.

EVA: (*Blessing herself.*) A priest! Why?

CARMELA: Because he was preaching against the abuses of the King . . .

ANICETA: (*To Rita.*) Is that all the news? What about the hammering last night?

RITA: How should I know? I'm not a newspaper. I only helped the nun collect the loaves of bread.

CARMELA: You ought to talk to the baker. Don't just stand there getting the bread. Ask him questions! Find out what's going on!

RITA: It'll be your turn next; you ask him. You try to get more information with one of the nuns standing next to you. (*Going to the water pump.*) Besides, my mind's been on our little gypsy. They took her away during the night. Poor Rosita must be in the hospital by now.

ANICETA: (*Feet still in the tub.*) I wonder if the hospital is where they took her . . .

PAULA: (*To Aniceta.*) When are you going to finish with that tub? The rest of us need to wash our feet.

ANICETA: Why don't you use the trough? There's no one using it now.

PAULA: What a pig. That's for faces and hands, not for feet!

CONCEPCION: (*Going to Chirrina, who is at the trough, splashing water.*) Stop it! You're getting me wet!

CHIRRINA: (*Splashing her.*) You need a good bath, anyway.

CONCEPCION: If you get my petticoat wet, I'll have nothing that's dry!

CHIRRINA: (*Mockingly.*) So? You can't go to the chapel in your petticoat. (*Splashes her again.*)

CONCEPCION: (*Pushing Chirrina's head into the trough.*) Let's see how you like it. (*Runs off.*)

RITA: Stop arguing. This is the most beautiful day of the year; it's Corpus Christi!

CARMELA: (*Mockingly.*) St. Rita, I presume. All that church crap. It's really stuck to you, hasn't it?

ANICETA: (*Seemingly sincere.*) Stop abusing her. Can't you see she's heading for the cloister after she's been laundered here? (*Pinching her cheek.*) She's such a good girl . . . (*Rita pushes her away.*) Why did they put you here with all these bad women? Did some dirty old man lift your skirt? (*Laughs. Others lift their skirts or stick out their bellies.*)

CONCEPCION: (*To Aniceta.*) Will you stop it? You're even making me blush.

ANICETA: I only want to find out why she's here. No one knows anything about her.

EVA: (*Indignant.*) Why don't you mind your own business? No one gave you the right to meddle.

ANICETA: (*To Eva.*) Your own situation's a little shady too.

EVA: I was a weaver . . . I had my own shop and I worked very hard to get it. You know all that.

ANICETA: And what else did you do?

EVA: It's none of your business . . . but I'll tell you anyway because I've nothing to be ashamed of, like some people . . . It's very simple: I fell in love with a man and we lived together until he joined the guerrillas in the mountains; afterwards, he went to Gibraltar. I haven't seen him since. I've never even received a letter . . . I don't know if he's alive . . . and our children . . . I've had no word about them . . . I can't sleep; I wake up hearing them call me and I come to the patio thinking they're out here. But I never hear their voices in the patio . . . My only crime is that I loved a rebel!

CHIRRINA: That's all most of us are guilty of.

CARMELA: Not you, darling. They threw you in here for posing as a dancer (*the others laugh*) among other things.

CHIRRINA: (*Ignoring the taunt.*) I could have bought my way out of here with all the money I earned as a dancer. When Napoleon's soldiers were in the country they loved to see me dance! (*Lifting her skirt.*) They were mad about my dancing . . . and other things. I could have danced for Napoleon's brother when he sat on the Spanish throne. But I didn't want to because he was a foreigner; the bastard didn't deserve to see *me* dance!

CARMELA: Ole! And what happened to all your money?

CHIRRINA: I spent it all on myself. There was always more whenever I needed it. (*Serious.*) I should have kept some of it after all. These days justice can be bought and sold. (*Mariana appears and stops to listen.*)

ANICETA: A friend, even your best friend, will cheat you or turn you in. A coin in your pocket is all you can count on.

MARIANA: Justice has always been bought and sold. That's how it is and you have to make the best of it. Even if it doesn't always turn out as you thought. In spite of everything, I still have hope.

CARMELA: (*Tired of Mariana's optimism.*) Hope, again! Bah!

CHIRRINA: My hope is in my body. (*Tossing her long hair.*) I used to dance in the best cafes! (*Strikes a pose.*) My blood boiled in me when I danced. And in the customers!

CARMELA: (*Sarcastically.*) Ole!

CHIRRINA: Look at these arms . . . (*pulls up her skirt*) and these legs. And what about these thighs? (*Sexily in front of Carmela.*) Hard as rocks.

CARMELA: (*Turning away.*) I pity the poor bastard who gets caught between them!

CHIRRINA: (*Menacingly, to Carmela.*) These legs can trample anyone to death! And these arms are strong enough to choke a man! (*Lunges at Carmela; a fight ensues.*)

RITA: Stop it! (*She attempts to separate Carmela and Chirrina.*) It's a Holy Day! (*Other Inmates help Rita.*)

CARMELA: God damned Holy Day! As if that mattered . . . after last night. (*Taking Rita's arm.*) Didn't you hear what went on last night?

RITA: (*Pointing to Eva.*) Ask that one about last night; she never sleeps.

EVA: (*Lying.*) I didn't hear anything. (*Walks to Mariana's side seeking her protection.*)

CHIRRINA: (*Accusingly.*) Well, I heard strange sounds in the night . . . something . . .

EVA: (*Trying to change the conversation.*) Mariana, would you let me comb your hair some morning.

MARIANA: (*Embracing her.*) I would really like that! Thank you, Eva.

EVA: (*Hesitantly.*) Could I do it . . . now?

MARIANA: Of course, Eva. (*Mariana sits and Eva proceeds to comb her hair.*)

PAULA: (*Who has been washing herself.*) What am I going to dry myself with? There aren't any sheets or blankets in our cells.

ANICETA: They're afraid we're going to hang ourselves.

PAULA: Or them! (*She lets loose her hair, drying her hands on it, then combing it out.*)

ANICETA: Such a fine head of hair! Too bad it's full of lice.

PAULA: They're probably yours. (*Picks one and throws it at Aniceta.*)

ANICETA: Keep your filth to yourself. That's not the kind of visitor I want.

EVA: Why can't we have visitors?

MARIANA: They're afraid to let us talk to anyone who could tell us the truth.

CHIRRINA: Even the nuns are afraid of the truth; none of them face up to it.

RITA: Sister Encarnación was acting as if she wanted to tell us something yesterday.

CARMELA: She left the shawl for us to see; she helped with Rosita's hands, but she hasn't *said* anything, has she?

CHIRRINA: She's afraid of something.

RITA: I think she'll find a way to talk to us.

ANICETA: (*Who has rejoined Paula.*) Hand me the comb. You'll never finish doing it like that.

PAULA: What can I do with this toothless comb? (*Continues combing Rosa's hair. To Rosa, who has been crying.*) You should see how beautiful I'm making you look. (*To Aniceta.*) Isn't she striking with her hair parted like that? (*To Rosa.*) Rosa, if you stop crying, I'll comb your hair and make you look pretty. Let me see. (*Touching her face. To Inmates.*) She's burning with fever!

ANICETA: (*Rushing to the cage.*) My God. Her wrists! You can see her bones.

PAULA: She's too ill to go to Mass. She looks as if she's in a trance.

ROSA: (*Dreamily.*) No one heard what I heard last night. It must have been four in the morning. (*The Inmates start gathering near the cage.*) There was a roundup last night . . . from my cell I could hear the police pounding on the doors of all the houses . . . I heard shouting and crying! I couldn't sleep. All night long I heard doors opening and slamming shut. Over and over! They were taking people away . . . They're coming for us next!

MARIANA: (*Putting her arms around Rosa and trying to calm her.*) I heard it too, Rosa. But we have to be calm so we can help ourselves when the time comes. (*Two nuns appear and cross. The Inmates feign indifference to Rosa.*)

ANICETA: (*As the nuns open the chapel door and exit, a chant can be heard; Aniceta sarcastically.*) What a joyous sound!

MARIANA: We still have time. They can't hold trials on Holy Days. They may still be loyal to the King but it's Corpus Christi; they're still religious.

CARMELA: (*Makes an obscene gesture.*) That's what I think of them and their "religion."

ROSA: (*Frightened.*) They've all been arrested . . . our friends . . . the soldiers who were going to rescue us. I know it!

MARIANA: (*To Paula.*) We can't let her stay here alone while we go to Mass. She has to come with us so we can take care of her.

PAULA: (*Reacting to a bell.*) There's the first call to Mass. I'll help you with Rosa. (*They help her to stand.*)

CARMELA: (*Mocking Francisca, who has entered wearing a once-splendid French wig.*) Is milady joining us for Mass?

FRANCISCA: I should say so. And on this special day with my finest veil. (*Putting it on top of the wig.*) Isn't it beautiful? It's from Morocco, you know.

CHIRRINA: It is a shame to hide such lovely curls.

FRANCISCA: One can do so while one is still young and attractive.

CHIRRINA: Milady is sixty if she's a day.

FRANCISCA: I can still make love as if I were twenty.

CARMELA: Make love! Who'd have you?

FRANCISCA: (*Touching Carmela.*) You, if you could.

CARMELA: (*Angrily.*) You're nothing but a painted has-been. (*To the others.*) And she says she's one of us! Look at her and her foreign airs. Just a rotten aristocrat.

FRANCISCA: (*Superior.*) Being a lady comes naturally to some. I know how to dress and how to wear a fashionable wig. (*With disdain.*) You on the other hand . . . You poor have always envied us. What you really want is to be rich. You want to take our place but you haven't the talent for it.

CARMELA: The poor, as you call us, won't be kicked around forever. My hair may be a mess, my dress torn, my shoes falling apart, (*menacing-*

*ly*) but one day . . .

FRANCISCA: (*Serene.*) Think what you like. I have my own way of dealing with fear. (*Walks away.*)

CARMELA: By hiding from it. I don't make believe that we're going to a fiesta, milady. I'll tell you what there is to fear. (*Looks at all the Inmates.*) We all know what that pounding was last night. (*Pause. The Inmates are apprehensive.*) They were building a scaffold! (*The Inmates are dismayed. The chapel bell rings another call to Mass but it sounds in the ears of the Inmates like the knell of death; some cover their ears. Carmela approaches Francisca.*) We are going to die!

CHIRRINA: (*Taking Carmela away.*) That's enough!

CARMELA: (*To Chirrina, obsessed.*) I feel it in my bones.

ROSA: (*Desperate.*) That scaffold is for me! Mariana, I've been sentenced to death! (*Mariana consoles her.*) Don't leave me, please. They'll take me away while you're in the chapel. (*Cries.*)

MARIANA: (*To Rosa.*) You're coming with us. No one will take you away, Rosa.

MOTHER SUPERIOR: (*Who appears, followed by the nuns and Sister Encarnación.*) Mariana Pineda!

(*There is silence. The Inmates freeze in place; Mariana presents herself and Mother Superior unlocks the outside door, admitting two guards. They are followed by Pedrosa. The Inmates are confused and frightened. The door is locked.*)

PEDROSA: (*Standing before Mariana.*) Mariana Pineda, I put the question to you. For whom did you embroider the revolutionary flag? (*No reply.*) You can save yourself from the dire consequences of these acts of treason . . . Give me the names of your co-conspirators. (*No reply.*) Mother Superior, you may proceed.

MOTHER SUPERIOR: Sister Encarnación. (*Hands her a document.*)

SISTER ENCARNACION: (*Looking nervously at Mother Superior, who nods to her.*) Mother Superior, I . . . (*Seeing Mother Superior's glare, she turns to the Inmates.*) Mother Superior has ordered me to read this official document for all to hear. (*Hesitating.*) I cannot. Please.

MOTHER SUPERIOR: Sister Encarnación! You have taken a vow of obedience.

SISTER ENCARNACION: (*Her voice trembling.*) "In compliance with Article Seven of the Decree of October 1, 1830, the criminal charge of plotting against the Crown is leveled against Mariana Pineda, a native of Granada. (*The Inmates react to the unexpected name; Rosa sinks to her knees, both relieved at her momentary reprieve and saddened by Mariana's plight.*) It has been demonstrated to the satisfaction of all that said Mariana Pineda has incited the populace of the city to rebellion against the lawful authority of their sovereign through a nefarious act of the greatest magnitude, there having been found in her possession, within the confines of her domicile, the flag of the rebellious subjects lately risen against the Crown. It has been further ascertained that said Mariana Pineda herself embroidered the emblem of the uprising and that she openly associated with traitors. The penalty for acts of treason is death." (*Sister Encarnación drops the document.*)

CARMELA: (*Picking up the document angrily.*) I'll show the bastards what they can do with their document! (*Approaches the soldiers, who form in front of Pedrosa; other Inmates follow Carmela. The soldiers affix bayonets.*) Bayonets? Bastards! (*She lunges at one of the soliders, but Aniceta stops her. Mother Superior wrests the document from Carmela. Silence ensues. Under Pedrosa's fixed stare, Mariana falls to her knees, face in her hands. The last call to Mass rings out. Pedrosa exits with his guards.*)

MOTHER SUPERIOR: (*Pointing to the chapel, she indicates that the Inmates file in one by one. They enter as if defeated. Rosa enters with Paula's help.*) Sister Encarnación, you may bring Mariana Pineda into the chapel when she has composed herself. (*Exits.*)

SISTER ENCARNACION: (*Kneeling next to Mariana.*) I'm sorry, Mariana.

MARIANA: I'm resigned to my fate now that I've heard the pronouncement. But, strangely, I haven't lost hope. I don't think I ever will. (*Recovering, she brings Sister Encarnación to her feet.*) Come, let us go into the chapel.

SISTER ENCARNACION: Is there any way that I can help you? (*Mariana shakes her head negatively.*) Forgive me for having hurt you, Mariana. I should have refused to read that document.

MARIANA: It's not your fault. You were only doing what they told you. It was your duty. If not you, someone else would have read it to me. I'm grateful that it was you. (*Pause.*) Come to Mass.

SISTER ENCARNACION: (*As Mariana starts to leave.*) Wait . . . I have to talk to you . . . I've had no news of my father. I'm as ignorant of what has happened to him as you are about your child . . . They won't tell me anything. And I can't sleep . . . Instead of praying, I curse them. (*Nuns sing in the chapel.*) I'm going to lock myself in the cathedral and refuse to eat. I want to cause a scandal. My rebellion would scandalize everyone and then, perhaps, the Pope would hear of it . . . The Holy Father would wonder about the cause of my actions and he'd send someone to investigate . . .

MARIANA: (*Maternally.*) You'd only succeed in making enemies; even your friends would be afraid to help you . . .

SISTER ENCARNACION: Friends! Do you know that one of your friends is the person responsible for the document I just read to you? (*Mariana is shaken.*) Pedrosa is only a means to an end; it was Andrés Oller who demanded your death. That way he saves his own skin. I heard Mother Superior say it.

MARIANA: A friend . . . a good friend.

SISTER ENCARNACION: They make us hurt one another. They make us lie to one another, distrust one another, sacrifice those we have loved . . .

MARIANA: There are many in Granada who will demand my death if the revolution fails. Many have been friends . . .

SISTER ENCARNACION: How can people be like that? How can they say they're for freedom and justice?

MARIANA: Perhaps they really believe that the cause will only survive if they live. And perhaps one day they'll accomplish what I haven't been able to do.

SISTER ENCARNACION: (With sudden hope.) Your sentence must still be approved by the King! Perhaps the courier will be caught by the guerrillas . . . Or someone might assassinate the King before he can sign it . . .

MARIANA: (*Tenderly.*) How can a sweet nun like you think such thoughts? . . . It's ironic that I find myself here, in these circumstances, when what I wanted long ago was to enter a convent and live in peace like you.

SISTER ENCARNACION: Peace! I am not at peace. You haven't seen the real struggle inside me! I looked for the purity of the Church in this convent but I've found only hypocrisy.

MARIANA: Encarnación, what you're saying is blasphemy!

SISTER ENCARNACION: The Church supports the very King who oppresses the people! How can the Church be so blind? I've knelt before the altar seeking an answer and the only answer I hear is to leave the convent.

MARIANA: If the search for God in this convent is so disillusioning, what can you expect out there? (*Pointing beyond the walls of the convent.*)

SISTER ENCARNACION: What good are my vows in here?

MARIANA: God may be testing you.

SISTER ENCARNACION: Then He can have my answer now. (*She removes her veil, revealing her beautiful hair, and then tears off her habit, remaining in her petticoat.*)

MARIANA: Sister Encarnación!

SISTER ENCARNACION: No, Mariana, only Encarnacion. Let them judge me as I really am . . . without the habit of Saint Mary Egyptian.

MARIANA: Oh, my God . . .

SISTER ENCARNACION: One more inmate! Let them sentence me! I'd rather die as an inmate than live a life of hypocrisy.

MARIANA: (*Embracing her.*) You must not do this. Please save yourself!

SISTER ENCARNACION: I am saving myself. (*She embraces Mariana and runs into the convent. The chanting of "Salve Regina" becomes louder;*

*Mariana enters the chapel as darkness fills the stage.*)

### Scene 3

*Later that same day, the Feast of Corpus Christi. Full sunlight. The chapel door is wide open. Some of the Inmates are in the cells, others on the patio. Chirrina is dancing to the distant music of the fair, disguising the fact that she's trying to listen at the doorway that leads to the tower. All the Inmates are nervous as they go about their tasks. Rita and Mariana are the only Inmates not on.*

CARMELA: Damn this sweat! It's even running between my teats.

ANICETA: Stop bitching. Look at me. (*Wiping her forehead.*) I wash every day, whether it's a Holy Day like today or not. You don't hear me bitching, do you? You work, you sweat; that's life. (*Continues washing her clothes in a wooden tub.*)

CARMELA: What's the good of all that washing if you don't have a place to dry it?

ANICETA: Those bars (*pointing to the cells*) will do, as always. I like to be clean even if I have to live in this filthy hole.

CARMELA: You're beginning to sound like our fine lady. (*Gesturing to Francisca who, as always, is primping.*) I wonder who washes her rags and combs her French wig?

CHIRRINA: She has a private laundress, of course. (*Continues dancing while Francisca reacts silently.*) I wonder when Rita will come down. How long can it take to spread out the linens?

CARMELA: (*To Aniceta, who is wringing out her wash; and moving towards Francisca.*) I'd like to wring her neck like that.

CHIRRINA: (*Exhausted from dancing.*) It's too hot to dance. And it's only May!

ANICETA: (*Splashing her playfully.*) This will cool you off!

FRANCISCA: (*Approaching Carmela, who gestures menacingly, and then veering towards Chirrina.*) You are attacking me because I didn't join your protest. You did a terrible thing leaving the chapel like you did. Not going to confession! Not receiving Holy Communion! (*Blesses herself.*) And how could you heap such abuse on the saintly nuns of this convent? (*The Inmates look at Francisca angrily.*) You'll regret it some-day. The Constitution guarantees that Catholicism will always be the religion of Spain. Even if the Liberals win. They're fighting for that Constitution. You'd be better off in the chapel praying for your souls!

PAULA: I'd rather die in mortal sin than pray in that unholy chapel. How can anyone have faith with the likes of those nuns around? I don't understand their brand of religion: they condemn us to death in order to save our souls!

CARMELA: Like the old days of the Inquisition. But there will be a day of reckoning.

CHIRRINA: (*To Francisca.*) You expect us to go to confession. To tell everything to a priest who is on the side of the enemy . . . He would report it all to Pedrosa!

ANICETA: That priest who comes with Pedrosa is the one who should pray for his soul. He's the one who has broken God's law by breaking the seal of confession.

PAULA: God's been betrayed by some of the very people who are supposed to serve Him. They've made a pact with the Devil.

FRANCISCA: All of you have a talent for twisting things to suit you. (*Chirrina "twists" into a dance position and stomps her feet in front of Francisca, who jumps back.*) Have any of you heard of the Ten Commandments? You're here because you have no respect for God's law.

CARMELA: . . . I'll give you some human law! (*Francisca moves quickly to the other side of the water trough.*) I'm going to commend your body to a living hell, you old whore. It's time you examined your own conscience!

FRANCISCA: I won't be intimidated by you. My conscience is clear. I'm ready to face God at this very instant. But what about your own conscience? Didn't you curse God when your lover was executed? (*Carmela reacts painfully.*) Listen to me, all of you. You must not forget God. Pray for His help.

CARMELA: I remembered God. I prayed to Him for Juan Martín's life because I was a good Christian. I prayed for "El Empecinado," my fury of a man. He was a hero! The people loved his valor, his heroism . . . everyone loved him, except the King. When Juan Martín died, I cried for him. But I no longer even dream of him. I was his woman; there will never be another man in my life. (*Distant gunshots are heard. Commotion in the patio.*)

CHIRRINA: Did you hear that?

CONCEPCION: It's our soldiers! They're here!

PAULA: (*Moves towards the chapel.*) Mariana! Mariana!

CARMELA: (*To Paula.*) Do you know something we don't? Those weren't shots. They were fireworks. From the fair.

CONCEPCION: Those were shots! I have ears . . .

EVA: They *were* shots. I heard them plainly. I swear they came from the river.

CARMELA: Don't get your hopes up. That's worse than having none. (*Mariana and several nuns enter; the nuns cross the stage hurriedly.*) I wonder what they're up to?

PAULA: (*Excitedly, to Mariana.*) Mariana, did you hear? Those were shots! Our soldiers . . . (*Mariana embraces Paula.*)

ROSA: Where's Rita? She'll know what's going on!

CARMELA: Shut up! Do you want the nuns to hear you? (*The marching of soldiers is heard outside.*)

CHIRRINA: (*Runs to peer through the outside door.*) Some soldiers are leaving! They must be expecting an attack somewhere else . . . (*Male voices are heard beyond the outside doors.*)

EVA: (*Who has been looking through the crack of the outside door.*) It's the Bishop and several priests from the cathedral . . . (*Afraid, turns to Mariana.*) Mariana!

CARMELA: If the bishop's here there must be an important reason. I don't like it. I've never trembled before, not even when I was fighting in the hills.

EVA: What's going to become of us?

MARIANA: Don't be afraid, Eva. Everything will turn out as God wills it. Have faith . . .

CARMELA: (*Interrupting.*) Faith? In what? I've had enough preaching from that "whitened sepulcher." (*Nodding towards Francisca.*) Don't you begin! And I've had my fill of these "holy" nuns!

MARIANA: They're as afraid as we are.

CARMELA: Not that Mother Superior! She knows what's going to happen to us. She enjoys her role as warden of this prison.

ROSA: (*Who is pacing her cell like a caged beast.*) Where is Rita? Why doesn't she come down and tell us what's happening out there? Rita!

MARIANA: Rosa, you musn't scream. If the nuns suspect that Rita's spying from the tower, they'll never let her go up again. (*Rosa nods in agreement but continues to pace her cell.*)

EVA: (*Still at the door.*) One thing is certain: there are fewer sentries.

CONCEPCION: (*Picking up something.*) Look! (*She holds up a nun's veil.*) Whose veil is this?

MARIANA: (*Unintentionally.*) Sister Encarnación . . .

EVA: (*Surprised, leaves the door.*) What? Sister Encarnación's veil?

CONCEPCION: Come to think of it, I haven't seen her pass by lately. (*To Mariana.*) What happened?

MARIANA: (*Defensive.*) I don't know . . . I can't . . . I don't know anything about it. (*Turns away.*)

CARMELA: (*Turning her around.*) You *do* know. You were with her when the rest of us went into the chapel. And you went in without her! Where is she?

MARIANA: Leave me alone. I have to think.

CONCEPCION: Did she leave the convent?

EVA: Are you trying to spare us some bad news?

PAULA: Did she join the rebels in the hills? What?

CARMELA: For God's sake, tell us! (*Mariana remains withdrawn, pensive.*)

EVA: Maybe they took her away because of her father . . . (*The Inmates react with shock.*)

CHIRRINA: (*Hearing keys jangling.*) Listen . . . Rita is coming! (*Everyone crowds around the tower door.*)

(*The tower door opens and Rita appears with a laundry basket full of altar linens. She places the basket on the table and walks back to lock the tower door, then returns to the basket.*)

RITA: (*To Mariana.*) Will you help me fold the altar linens?

MARIANA: (*Assisting her.*) What is it? (*The others have grouped around them.*)

RITA: They've removed guards from the convent and sent them to the cathedral.

EVA: But why?

RITA: A woman on the street said "Sister Encarnación" loud enough for me to hear. Then a man across the street wrote on a piece of paper, wrapped it around a stone and threw it to me on the tower.

CONCEPCION: What does it say?

RITA: (*Hesitantly*) I . . . can't read. (*Ashamed, she hands the paper to Mariana.*)

MARIANA: (*Looking to see if any nuns are near, begins to read in a low voice.*) "Twenty women followed Sister Encarnacion into the cathedral and locked themselves in. (*Pauses as the Inmates are surprised.*) They're willing to starve to death if necessary." (*Holds the paper to her breast.*)

FRANCISCA: There's more. (*Continues reading.*) "Some men with rifles have barricaded themselves in front of the cathedral to protect the women. They've piled up chairs, mattresses, tables . . . Some troops are there already and some shots were fired a while ago."

EVA: (*Excited by the news, embraces Mariana.*) Mariana!

MARIANA: (*Returning her embrace.*) I'm going to pray for them . . . and for us.

CONCEPCION: Our men *are* out there. They haven't forgotten us. No one has to die!

CARMELA: (*Stopping Mariana.*) How can you go in there to pray? Why do you need God? There's no doubt about the outcome now. The troops are on the defensive.

MARIANA: There's always a chance . . . I can't help doubting. Even when faced with death one doubts that it will happen. I must pray.

CARMELA: First it's faith and now it's doubts. What's going on inside you? Are you waiting for something to happen? Or is it that you're waiting for a special someone to come?

MARIANA: (*Relieved.*) Yes! There is one hope. Casimiro Brodett. He's leading the revolutionary troops to Granada . . . He's our hope. (*She becomes excited.*) Now I must pray.

CARMELA: You'd better get out of the sun. Maybe you *should* go to the chapel; it's cool there.

MARIANA: Yes! Yes! (*She walks into the chapel while Carmela looks on.*)

EVA: Sister Encarnación! I can't believe she left the convent! She looked so timid.

CARMELA: Timid . . . We're the ones who are timid. She *did* something.

ROSA: I always felt she was one of us at heart.

PAULA: I wish I could be with her in the cathedral.

FRANCISCA: (*Unexpectedly.*) If I were in that church . . . If I had a gun, I'd face an army!

CARMELA: You?

FRANCISCA: I know how to handle a rifle better than anyone here. I never miss. I had the best hunting instructors money could buy. Wealth prepared me for more than fans and wigs. You'll see me yet on the streets of Granada. I'll show all of you how to shoot . . . to kill!

PAULA: Why are you here, Francisca? Don't you think it's time you told us?

FRANCISCA: I suppose I should tell you . . . the time has come! It can't harm him now if I tell why he brought me here.

EVA: Who is "he?"

FRANCISCA: A Count. He's Captain General of the King's Army. Like the King, he had sworn to uphold the Constitution of 1812; but when the King became a tyrant, my general turned secretly against him.

PAULA: Were you in love with him?

FRANCISCA: I still am . . . and he with me.

EVA: How could he put you in prison then?

FRANCISCA: Everyone knew my political sympathies. He became suspect in the eyes of those who advised the King. They resented him; they feared him. He had to show the King that he was loyal. He brought me here and promised to come for me as soon as the Liberals took the offensive . . . After what Mariana told us about Captain Brodett, I know the time has come! Soon the nobility will rebel too!

CARMELA: (*Still suspicious of Francisca.*) Only when it has no money.

(*The sound of troops marching. Scuffling and crying is heard in the street. The Inmates rush to the outside door to peer through the slit or listen.*)

EVA: (*Reaching the door first.*) I see many soldiers. They're carrying bodies! My God, some of them are women!

CONCEPCION: Sister Encarnación, could she be one of them?

EVA: Wait. There are others . . . in chains.

CARMELA: Can you see who they are?

EVA: No. The soldiers are in the way. They're almost out of sight now.

PAULA: Where are they taking the women?

CARMELA: To be tortured like the little gypsy.

ANICETA: They wouldn't dare . . . the scandal.

CHIRRINA: It would only add fuel to the revolution.

PAULA: Everyone would hear of Sister Encarnación's rebellion. It would reach other cities.

CONCEPCION: Even other countries.

ROSA: And the Pope! He'd have to look into the causes! They'll even question us.

CHIRRINA: We've got to find out what the soldiers are up to. (*To Rita.*) Give me the key to the tower.

RITA: I can't. The nuns . . . If they found out, I couldn't go up anymore; none of us would be allowed. Then I couldn't bring back news . . .

CHIRRINA: Now is when we need to know! Give me the key! (*Pulls Rita towards the tower door.*)

ANICETA: Rita's right. We've got to be careful. What if . . .

PAULA: (*Interrupting.*) It won't matter soon. The sun is brighter than ever. The day is ours!

CHIRRINA: Listen! (*The Inmates become attentive.*) I hear footsteps outside . . . (*Listening at the door.*)

RITA: (*Looking through the slit.*) I hear them. They're coming closer.

CHIRRINA: Can you see anyone?

RITA: Now I can. An officer. He's stumbling . . . He's covered with blood.

ANICETA: Is he alone?

EVA: Yes . . . No, he keeps looking back. Two guards are following him.

CARMELA: Get away from the door! I hear the nuns coming. (*The Inmates move away quickly as Mother Superior appears with several nuns following.*)

MOTHER SUPERIOR: Where is Mariana Pineda? (*A nun whispers to her, indicating the chapel. To the Inmates.*) All of you, into the convent!

INMATES: (*Surprised by the order.*) What? The convent? What's going on? (*They fail to move.*)

MOTHER SUPERIOR: Quickly. (*Signals to the nuns to herd the Inmates, which they do. When they're inside, Mother Superior walks briskly, key in hand, to the outside door, places the key in the lock and opens it. Two guards bring in Captain Casimiro Brodett and exit. Mother Superior locks the door and signals to a nun to bring Mariana from the chapel, then exits. Brodett is bloody and weak. His hands are tied behind his back. His uniform is tattered; there are no insignia. He leans against the wall; the door is shut from outside. As he stands catching his breath, Mariana enters from the chapel, followed by the nun, who exits immediately. The silence surprises Mariana and she looks around for the other Inmates; suddenly, she sees the soldier, who is on the ground.*)

MARIANA: (*Recognizing Brodett, she starts towards him impulsively. Sen-*

*sing the trap, she goes to the trough instead and gets a jug of water. She tears a peice of her petticoat, soaks it in the trough and offers Brodett the water.)* Here, drink. *(Seeing that his hands are tied.)* I'll hold it for you. *(He drinks.)* Slowly. *(When he's through, she tries to free his hands.)* I can't do it. *(No reply.)* Where did you come from? *(No reply.)* Can't you speak . . . Let me see your tongue. My God! Casimiro! They've burned it! *(Embraces him, then wipes away the blood on his face.)*

BRODETT: *(Mustering strength, tries rising to warn Mariana, but can only make guttural sounds.)* Ma . . . Ma . . . *(He gestures weakly towards Mother Superior, who retreats into the shadows.)*

MARIANA: *(Catching Mother Superior's movement.)* It doesn't matter that she's spying on us . . . I have you again, my love. *(Embraces him again.)* What have they done to you? *(Cries and embraces him. Slowly recovering from the shock.)* My love, you're safe now. I'll take care of you.

BRODETT: *(Trying again to speak.)* Ma . . . Ma . . .

MARIANA: *(Placing her fingers gently on his lips.)* No, don't . . . I know there are many things you want to ask me . . . Pedrosa *(Brodett reacts violently to the name and Mariana holds him)* . . . told me our son was safe but I don't trust him. Now that I see what he's done to you, I'm afraid for him. *(Pause.)* I'm afraid for us. We don't have much time left. I can see how much you've suffered. I have too. *(Brodett tries to comfort her. Mariana slowly regains her composure. He looks at her expectantly. She kneels to caress him but then, knowing that the hardest part of her story is yet to be told, rises with concern on her face.)* Casimiro, I must tell you what I did after I left Burgos. I know it will hurt you, my love, but I must. I came back to Granada to do what I could for the revolution. *(Painfully.)* I invited military officers and influential men to my house; we drank and laughed together. *(Gathering courage for what she has to say.)* And when the festivities were over . . . I always invited one of my high-ranking guests to stay overnight. *(Brodett reacts painfully.)* I opened my bedroom doors to them . . . All the important men in Granada graced my bed. *(Brodett, hurt and angered, turns away from her.)* Those men controlled the political and military life of the city. They used my body, but I used them against the King. Those powerful men gave me a way to help our cause: they gave me access to the prison; they provided false identity papers, even passports; they helped me get political prisoners out of Granada . . . Many of those who are fighting at this moment are free because of what I did. *(Pause.)* Forgive me. *(Brodett struggles to stand; he faces Mariana with a defeated look and moves towards the outside door. Mariana runs to him.)* Casimiro, please! Please understand . . . *(He stops but doesn't look at her.)* I've always loved you . . . None of the others mattered . . . I only used them to help our cause . . . to save lives! (*Brodett avoids her. She places herself in front of him when he fails to turn.*) I have lived waiting for you! Casimiro, don't shatter the only hope I have left. Please understand. (*Pedrosa and Mother Superior enter from the convent, silently watching the scene.*) Isn't a man capable of forgiving the woman he loves? (*Despondent.*) You have not understood me. You can never understand me now. (*Pause. Pedrosa is visibly irritated. Brodett gestures disdainfully towards Pedrosa. Mariana turns and sees Pedrosa, then turns back to Brodett, who has stumbled closer to the door. Looking at Pedrosa and then back to Brodett.*) Casimiro, they want to kill me! I'm afraid. Please . . . show me that you still love me. (*Brodett pushes her away.*) Don't abandon me now! I love you! Only you. (*Pause.*) I was wrong. (*She turns away from him. Then, nervously, she faces the convent.*) Pedrosa brought you here, didn't he? (*Defiantly.*) Reverend Mother opened the gate so you would enter. Not out of pity. No! Only so they could overhear what I had to tell you. My confession. Well, now they've heard it.

PEDROSA: (*Pedrosa enters, followed by Mother Superior.*) And very touching it was, my lady. (*Suddenly, pounding can be heard from within the convent; at first it is haphazard but it becomes a pounding in unison. Pedrosa is furious but controls his anger. Mother Superior enters the convent.*) I find it hard to believe that this is the same serene Mariana Pineda that I so admired. (*Walking around her and gesturing to Brodett.*) This is what has become of the greatness of your cause. (*The pounding stops as suddenly as it began. Mother Superior reappears.*)

MARIANA: (*Pulling herself together.*) How smug you are. You seem so sure of victory. But it's only a pose, Pedrosa. I've seen you defeated in my bedroom! Remember?

PEDROSA: (*Angered.*) It is the final victory that counts, Mariana. (*Pointing to Brodett.*) Take a last look at your "lover." Both of you have been defeated. Mother Superior. (*She opens the outside door.*) Guards! (*Two guards enter.*) Take this traitor outside.

MARIANA: Casimiro! (*He ignores her.*) We'll be together! In the earth, if we must. (*The two guards exit with Brodett. Mariana holds back her tears.*)

PEDROSA: It takes such a long time to see the truth about ourselves, Mariana. Such a long time before we accept things as they are . . .

MARIANA: You see things only through your selfishness and prejudice.

PEDROSA: That may well be, but my selfishness and prejudice, as you call them, are derived from rightful authority. My reasons are as valid to me as yours are to you. Remember the divine right of kings.

MARIANA: God must be preparing a terrible reward for your holy monarch!

PEDROSA: But in point of fact it is your cause which has suffered His wrath. The rebellious Sister Encarnación and some of the women she led astray have paid for their transgression.

MARIANA: What do you mean? (*Frightened.*) What have you done . . . Encarnación! (*Mariana sinks to her knees under the weight of this realization; she is crushed.*)

PEDROSA: It is too late to concern yourself with her. But as for your lover . . . forgive me, one of your many lovers . . . his fate is in my hands. And in yours, Mariana.

MARIANA: (*Looking up.*) In my hands . . . (*Loathing him.*) What do you want of me?

PEDROSA: (*Formal.*) I have been empowered to offer you the choice of life or death: life if you disclose the identities of your co-conspirators, death if you refuse to denounce the traitors. (*No reply.*) Mariana Pineda, as the Crown's prosecutor of this case, I again put the question to you: Who were your fellow-conspirators? (*Mariana remains silent.*) Very well, I'll refer to a list of names of highly-placed officials with whom it is know you had liaisons: Do you know Diego de Salas, warden of the city prison? (*No reply.*) Do you know . . . Andrés Oller . . . (*Mariana starts at his name*) the public prosecutor? Do you know . . .

MARIANA: Yes! Yes! Yes! I slept with all of them!

PEDROSA: And now they have betrayed you. (*She lowers her head.*) Do you know what this document is?

MARIANA: I can guess. My death sentence.

PEDROSA: (*Nods in agreement.*) But this other document is very different; it is your pardon. You will select your own fate. (*Holds a document in each hand before her.*) The men on this list have betrayed the Crown by helping you free political prisoners; by their deeds they have aligned themselves with the so-called Liberals. They are guilty of treason! But these very men now seek to save themselves by giving evidence against you; your death warrant has been signed by one of them, Andres Oller. They have all betrayed you. (*Pauses.*) Mariana, you can save yourself and Brodett if you sign this other document; it contains the evidence against these men in great detail. Please read it. (*Offers it to her but Mariana does not take it.*) The statements are all true. Sign it!

MARIANA: (*Sobbing.*) They were only my lovers.

PEDROSA: They betrayed you. Sign it.

MARIANA: I cannot . . .

PEDROSA: Now is the time to avenge yourself on your *real* enemies. And you can. Choose to live, Mariana!

MARIANA: Death no longer frightens me.

PEDROSA: Live for your son then.

MARIANA: Someday my son will grow up and know that his mother be-trayed her friends just to live. Those you say have betrayed me are good men. They are human. They've had a moment of weakness. Someday they'll be brave again and fight for our cause. Enough. (*Pause.*) I have made my peace with God.

PEDROSA: But not with me, Mariana. Not with me . . . I listened to your confession before that defeated officer. (*To Mother Superior.*) Leave us. (*She exits.*) Let me save you! Perhaps my pity is greater than you give me credit for. It surprises even me. It stems from depths you will never understand. (*His words reflect sincerity.*) Even a follower of the King can have pity and feelings. (*Pause.*) I already knew all the details of your treason, Mariana, but I needed to hear the confession from your lips in front of witnesses—that is my duty. But I wanted something else—to be your friend . . . I fell in love with you. (*Mariana looks surprised.*) Yes, love. I realized that you did not return that love. But I could not help loving you. I even became jealous of your lovers. And even though I knew that you were using them against the King's authority, my love for you kept me from putting you under arrest.

MARIANA: Don't make a mockery of the word "love." You've only wanted possessions: power, glory, me . . . No, what you felt for me was not love . . .

PEDROSA: (*Ironic again.*) And you? For your captain? (*Pause.*) Is there enough love in you to save his life?

MARIANA: By giving myself to you? No! Once you could have been my lover, helped me to save prisoners, been the good man that is locked inside you . . .

PEDROSA: I would have given anything to be that man. (*Impulsively, he kisses her.*)

MARIANA: (*Momentarily giving in, she then pushes him away and wipes off his kiss with disgust.*) You will never possess me!

PEDROSA: I've shown you my feelings openly. I may have lost you, Mariana, but you will lose your life. (*Facing the convent.*) Mother Superior! (*Mother Superior appears at the convent entrance.*) I want everyone out here. (*Mother Superior exits. To Mariana.*) When you're on the scaffold and the rope is placed around your neck, the people of Granada will be helping the hangman! Everyone will breathe easier with your death.

MARIANA: You especially, Pedrosa.

PEDROSA: No, Mariana. I will grieve more than any other man. (*The Inmates begin to enter the patio, followed by Mother Superior, the other nuns and several guards. Pedrosa addresses the Inmates.*) I have tried to reason with the prisoner Mariana Pineda in order to find a way to save her from the terrible fate which has been decreed for her. (*Pacing.*) The law demands that Casimiro Brodett be executed as a traitor. But his life and hers will be spared if she agrees to denounce her other conspirators. All she has to do is sign this document. (*Inmates murmur.*)

MARIANA: Terms of betrayal! Never!

PEDROSA: The betrayal is theirs. Even Brodett has deserted you. Having been separated from you, he desired you. He returned to you as a hero bloodied in combat. But his reaction to your confession proves that he desired only your body. (*Inmates react.*) Not you, not your spirit. Your liberal ideas are as expendable to him now as when he had to save his skin by giving you up for his career.

MARIANA: When I was hounded by the military, accused of being a whore because I was living with Casimiro Brodett, he wanted to give up his commission and take me away from Burgos. But I would have despised him if he had done it; I wanted him to stay at his post. We needed him to protect the interests of the Liberal cause. It was I who refused to marry Casimiro; I preferred to be his mistress, to bear his child out of wedlock. I made him remain in the King's service. He never gave me up to save his skin. He made a sacrifice and I made a sacrifice. (*Stronger.*) All of us here have! We're all inmates in this convent because we fought for the cause of justice, truth and freedom. Each in her own way. Even that poor little gypsy girl you tortured . . . and Sister Encarnación whom you have killed! (*She becomes distraught. The Inmates react to the news of Sister Encarnación's death.*)

PEDROSA: (*To Inmates.*) Her hero did not rescue her; the people of the city who put up barricades are no longer a threat to law and order; Granada is subdued. Many will rest better when she's been executed. Her death means peace of mind for those who fear that she will talk.

MARIANA: The cause for which I struggled with will continue, even if I die, even if others betray it.

PEDROSA: I have tried to save you. I have given you every opportunity. (*To Inmates.*) I am an instrument of the court, only that. I did not decree her death. Her execution has been demanded by her so-called *friends.* The King has granted their request. I tried to save her in spite of the political turmoil in Granada, but I have been forced to sign her death warrant and without a public trial. I was obliged to send it to the King, not because I wanted to do it but because she refused to denounce those who sacrifice her to save themselves. (*To Mariana.*) Your execution has been decreed by other hands. Now you must stand alone. (*He walks away from her. Mother Superior joins him.*)

CARMELA: She's not alone! (*The Inmates follow Carmela's lead and gather around Mariana. Pedrosa remains apart, silent. Mother Superior is upset.*)

ANICETA: We won't let them take you! (*Eva runs to Pedrosa and starts beating him; one of the guards pushes her down with the butt of his rifle. The other Inmates start towards Pedrosa and the guards fix bayonets.*)

FRANCISCA: (*Helping Eva up; to Pedrosa.*) I see that you will never escape what you are. Filth! (*She spits at his feet. Inspired by Francisca's action, the other Inmates surge towards the guards.*)

MARIANA: (*Placing herself between the Inmates and the soldiers.*) No! No more bloodshed! There's been too much already. (*Pedrosa gestures to the guards and they hold Mariana firmly.*) All they can do is kill us! But they can never kill our cause! (*Pedrosa gestures for the guards to remove Mariana. Mother Superior unlocks the gate.*)

MARIANA: (*Being led away.*) Our cause will live on! You are not alone!

(*The nuns lower their heads as Mariana is led away; Mother Superior stands with head erect next to Pedrosa; the guards protect them from the Inmates, who are still facing them defiantly.*)

CARMELA: Mariana! We're with you! (*She runs to where the green shawl bearing the words "You Are Not Alone" had been hidden earlier; she waves it triumphantly.*) You are not alone, Mariana! (*Facing Pedrosa defiantly.*)

EVA: Mariana! No! (*Pounds the table.*)

INMATES: (*In chorus.*) Mariana! Mariana! Mariana! (*Protected by the guards, Pedrosa exits hurriedly. Mother Superior locks the outside door hastily and crosses to the convent entrance, gesturing to the nuns to follow her. The Inmates continue shouting Mariana's name; some begin pounding in unison. The rhythm of their pounding is picked up by Lolilla and her group outside the convent and converted into flamenco clapping, accompanied by the guitar. The sounds inside and outside the convent fuse, in an ironic note of triumph.*)

WOMAN'S VOICE: (*Off.*)
Have faith in the people, you Inmates!
We're with you! You are not alone!
Today we are with you in suffering!
Tomorrow our triumph will come!

INMATES:
Tomorrow! Tomorrow! Tomorrow!
The jails will be full when we try.
The King and his henchmen tomorrow.
Tomorrow we'll see them all die!

(*The lights dim. As they do, the sound of hammering outside the convent increases till it becomes all pervasive. Blackout.*)

END

# The Cock's Short Flight

## A Play in Two Acts

## Jaime Salom

THE COCK'S SHORT FLIGHT [Teatro Espronceda 34, Madrid, 1980]
Directed by Manuel Manzaneque

CHARACTERS:

Pilar [Mother]
Agustina
Pilar [Daughter] ———┐
Agustina [Daughter] —┘  — Played by one actress
Servant ——————┐
Neighbor's Wife
Madame Alfonse   — Played by one actress
Another Servant ——┘
Nicolás [Father]
Ramón
Nicolás [Son]
Army Messenger ———┐
Ambrosio
Neighbor
Conductor   — Played by one actor
Notary
Sergeant
Official ——————┘

# ACT ONE

*A modest apartment on Fuencarral Street in Madrid. The set imprecise, open, and symbolic, avoiding naturalism—though always realistic and functional. For a good while we hear the sound of a doorbell. Onstage, motionless, as if waiting for a signal to begin to speak, Agustina and an Army Messenger with a letter in his hand. 1939. Although no longer young, Agustina is still attractive and sexually desirable. She dresses carelessly. Farther upstage, Nicolás-Father will appear, looking mature but still strong and virile. By no means the old man of eighty that he is, but as he sees himself and would like to be at this moment. His clothes are shabby.*

AGUSTINA: He's an insufferable, dirty, drunk, foul-mouthed old man, and I don't know how I put up with him another minute. But I do. For our daughter's sake. For some stupid memory of other times . . . At heart I've always been a God-awful romantic.

*(The bell stops ringing.)*

MESSENGER: The envelope.
AGUSTINA: Has it been another month?
MESSENGER: Another month, señora. May.
AGUSTINA: Well, tell whoever sent you that the Commandant receives a pension appropriate to his rank and doesn't accept charity from anyone.
MESSENGER: It comes from Lisbon. The order is to bring it here, to this address, and return the signed receipt to the Ministry.
AGUSTINA: Well, he won't sign it.
MESSENGER: I'll sign the receipt the way I do every month. I'll be in hot water if I don't bring it.
NICOLAS-FATHER: Agustina!
AGUSTINA: Leave it there and go, so he won't see you.

NICOLAS-FATHER: Agustina! Who was at the door?

AGUSTINA: Nobody, Nicolás. Go about your business.

NICOLAS-FATHER: (*Coming closer.*) Could it have been the slave my grimy, tightfisted son sends to humiliate his father?

MESSENGER: I'm only carrying out orders, sir.

NICOLAS-FATHER: I'm a man of honor, I'll have you know. And I don't want anything from that pack of mediocre swellheads. I'm not a useless old man. I can still do justice to a woman and a bottle of Valdepeñas.

MESSENGER: I have other messages to deliver.

NICOLAS-FATHER: Don't be afraid of them, boy, don't let yourself be dazzled by appearances, no matter how much they cover themselves with medals and decorations. They're rotten to the core, empty . . . and they know it. That's why they don't want anyone to remind them of it. Will you do it?

MESSENGER: I'm sorry, but I'm on duty.

NICOLAS-FATHER: Well, you tell my son Nicolás that I'm on to his deals. That his cars, his parties, and his whores . . . we're all paying for them. You too, son, and her. (*Referring to Agustina.*)

MESSENGER: I don't know anyone. Only the sergeant at the motor park who hands me the messages to deliver.

NICOLAS-FATHER: Then tell your sergeant, so that he can repeat it to whom it may concern, that as a Spaniard and a Navy man I am outraged.

MESSENGER: I wish you wouldn't shout.

NICOLAS-FATHER: I'm not afraid of anybody.

MESSENGER: But you can get me into trouble.

NICOLAS-FATHER: You won the war! . . . And now you crap in your pants when you hear a piece of truth the whole world knows! You can leave.

MESSENGER: Yes, sir.

NICOLAS-FATHER: Stand at attention before a superior as you're supposed to.

MESSENGER: At your orders.

NICOLAS-FATHER: You have a button undone on your jacket.

AGUSTINA: Leave the boy alone.

NICOLAS-FATHER: A uniform is the pride and dignity of a soldier. Even if he's only a slave who drives a motorcycle.

MESSENGER: Until next month, señora. (*He exits.*)

NICOLAS-FATHER: Look what's happened to our youth.

AGUSTINA: You silly fool. So much swearing and shouting just because they didn't bring you the envelope on time.

NICOLAS-FATHER: It was more than a week late.

AGUSTINA: Well now you have it. Here.

NICOLAS-FATHER: I'll never accept anything from him. You know that . . . But I want to know if he still remembers his father. Only one envelope?

AGUSTINA: Of course. What did you expect?

NICOLAS-FATHER: And from his brother . . . nothing. Not a word.

AGUSTINA: Has he ever had a word to say to you?

NICOLAS-FATHER: Always surrounded by bishops, posing in every cathedral . . . without ever mentioning he has a family, and in all this time not even a how do you do for the father who sired him. But what the fuck does it matter to me! (*He opens the envelope.*) A thousand pesetas. It's not much.

AGUSTINA: The same as every other month. Are you going to tear it up again?

NICOLAS-FATHER: Naturally.

AGUSTINA: It would come in handy. We could pay . . .

NICOLAS-FATHER: Shut up and don't tempt me. I don't sell myself like a whore to the ones who have the upper hand. I am an officer in the Spanish Navy!

AGUSTINA: Who doesn't know one ship from the other except the ones in the books about the Spanish Armada.

NICOLAS-FATHER: That's an insult. I was in the Phillipines and Cuba too.

AGUSTINA: Years ago. Now you're an armchair sailor who prefers wine to salt water.

NICOLAS-FATHER: Just shut up, witch. A thousand pesetas. You see, that clever opportunist is the best of my children, the only one who still has a little bit of heart under his billfold. Do you know why? Because he's a Navy man too. Not like his brother, who couldn't get into the Naval Academy and now wears an admiral's uniform when he feels like it. What a joke! Nicolás is the best, even if he does have a weakness for schoolgirls and collects government jobs like stamps. At least he knows how to live. You can't blame him too much for living the way he pleases . . . since his own brother gives him the means to do it. Don't you agree?

AGUSTINA: One is as big a scoundrel as the other.

NICOLAS-FATHER: I forbid you to talk that way about my sons! It's true he could be a bit more generous with me. What would it cost him! Fifty, a hundred thousand, what's that to him?

AGUSTINA: A hundred thousand pesetas used to be enough to last us a lifetime.

NICOLAS-FATHER: And why not a million?

AGUSTINA: Why not? I'd buy myself some new clothes. What I have were already old when the war started . . . And I'd stock the pantry up to the rafters, and I'd send our daughter to a good school instead of being an apprentice in a workshop . . .

NICOLAS-FATHER: And a German car. A black Mercedes with a uniformed chauffeur so that he could drive you around Madrid like royalty.

AGUSTINA: What would I want a car for? They'd have a good one if I drove up in a black car to buy coal.

NICOLAS-FATHER: Shall I take you to the best jeweler on the Gran Vía?

AGUSTINA: First we'll have lunch in some elegant restaurant.

NICOLAS-FATHER: With a good wine and Galician brandy.

AGUSTINA: And afterwards, to see a show at the Martín.

NICOLAS-FATHER: In a stage box . . . so that everyone will say: "Who is that pretty, elegant woman? The stepmother of the most powerful man in Spain!"

AGUSTINA: And that well-dressed gentleman is his father. You'd have to put on your dress uniform every day, the one you were wearing at the dance the night we met . . .

NICOLAS-FATHER: With saber and silk sash . . . (*They are silent for a moment and then both break into laughter.*) You're hopeless, you crazy witch . . .

AGUSTINA: So are you, you old drunkard . . .

(*Their laughter freezes.*)

NICOLAS-FATHER: Do you realize? It's better that he sends us only a thousand. It would be harder for me to tear it up. (*He rips up the thousand pesetas.*) Go on, throw the pieces in the toilet. And pull the chain, so that I can hear it and be sure that they're going straight into the sewer.

(*Agustina exits. We hear the cistern emptying. The Servant Girl enters.*)

SERVANT: He's a dirty old man . . . The moment I drop my guard he's got his hand up my skirt. I let him feel around . . . poor guy, at his age he has few pleasures left.

NICOLAS-FATHER: Run along, sweetheart, and bring me a glass of wine.

SERVANT: Señora Agustina won't let you have it.

NICOLAS-FATHER: Señora Agustina isn't at home.

SERVANT: It's not good for you to drink. Wine's going to be the death of you yet.

NICOLAS-FATHER: I'm eighty years old . . . Do you want me to live to be older than Methuselah? You'd all be thrilled if I kicked off now.

SERVANT: Don't say that. (*She goes for a glass of wine.*) Only one glass.

NICOLAS-FATHER: Are you wearing your pink panties today?

SERVANT: What does it matter to you?

NICOLAS-FATHER: They're your nicest ones. If I had money, I'd buy you a set of silk underwear and one night I'd make you the happiest woman in the world.

SERVANT: You're a little old for that now.

NICOLAS-FATHER: You pretty thing. Your lips are like cherries. (*He kisses and embraces her.*)

SERVANT: You devil! At your age and still able to get a girl all excited. (*Getting away from him.*) You're a shameless man.

NICOLAS-FATHER: And you're a charming child.

SERVANT: You must have been quite a ladykiller when you were young.

NICOLAS-FATHER: Women haven't exactly disagreed with me. I think I left a few memories along the way. (*He laughs.*) I managed to get two chocolate bars. You can have them. Here. A gift. (*He gives them to her.*)

SERVANT: Umm, how good!

NICOLAS-FATHER: Even my sons, when they were children, they caught me sometimes with my hands in the dough.

SERVANT: They way you and I are now? That's funny.

NICOLAS-FATHER: In El Ferrol! You can't imagine what El Ferrol was in those days. Like a convent!

SERVANT: Jesus, not that bad I should hope.

NICOLAS-FATHER: You have the firmest little breasts in the world . . . a good place for a sailor to run aground for a while.

(*Nicolás-Father kisses her again. Nicolás-Son, Ramon, and Pilar enter. They're young, between 20 and 25.*)

PILAR: What is Papa doing to the servant girl?

RAMON: Can't you see? He's touching her. Papa's touching Florita, Papa's touching Florita's ass!

NICOLAS-SON: That's a lie. Florita would never allow it.

NICOLAS-FATHER: How many times have I told you not to enter the parlor without knocking. I was helping her tie the knot in her apron. How's that? You can leave now, Florita.

FLORITA: Thank you, sir. (*She withdraws.*)

NICOLAS-FATHER: You're quite welcome. And you . . . why aren't you in school this time of day?

NICOLAS-SON: Today's the day of the Virgin.

NICOLAS-FATHER: Which one? Anything will serve as an excuse for those deadbeats to stop work and rob decent parents of their money. Spain is hopeless. The more Catholics there are the more holidays. And what about Pacita?

RAMON: She died two years ago, Papa. Don't you remember?

NICOLAS-FATHER: Of course I remember that angel! It's just that sometimes my memory gets dates and ages a bit confused. She was the sweetest, most loving of my children, the only one who would never have abandoned me, who would have consoled me in my old age. (*The Servant has entered again.*)

FLORITA: Shall I serve you a glass of wine, sir? (*She does.*)

NICOLAS-FATHER: I wouldn't complain . . . And what about your brother?

PILAR: Francisco went with Mama to the Sanctuary at Chamorro.

NICOLAS-FATHER: Always hanging on to her skirts! She'll end up turning him into a plaster saint like his grandfather, or something worse. (*He takes the wine glass and caresses Florita's cheek.*) Thanks, sweetheart.

NICOLAS-SON: That's enough, Papa!

NICOLAS-FATHER: What's eating him?

NICOLAS-SON: Just because Florita works in this house doesn't give you any right . . .

NICOLAS-FATHER: Well, well, this tops everything.

NICOLAS-SON: I've seen you often in the hallway with your arms around her and even leaving her room.

NICOLAS-FATHER: I won't tolerate this lack of respect. If I had talked that way to my father . . . It's my fault for indulging you all so much. But this time you're going to get your punishment, unless you apologize right now, to Florita and to me.

NICOLAS-SON: She knows that I didn't mean to offend her . . . but I won't ask your pardon because I saw you with my own eyes.

NICOLAS-FATHER: You and I are going to have a long talk right now, you young whippersnapper . . . Bring me your grade reports. And the two of you go play. Out! You too, Florita.

PILAR: Yes, Papa.

RAMON: (*To Florita.*) Will you let me go with you to the laundry?

FLORITA: No sirree. And don't get it into your head to hide in the washroom again when I'm going to take a shower so that you can see me naked. The mischief that gets into that boy's head.

(*Ramón, Pilar, and Florita withdraw upstage. Nicolás-Son gives the report card to his father.*)

NICOLAS-FATHER: So you like Florita . . . Apparently what your father does doesn't matter to you, but you're jealous. You'd like to be the one who squeezes her around the house and gets into her bedroom at night. I suppose you're also the one who puts the flowers on her bedside table.

NICOLAS-SON: Did she tell you that? But, how could. . . ?

NICOLAS-FATHER: I saw them, dummy. Some wild daisies, wilted and dirty, beneath the picture of Saint James . . . A failing grade in Geometry. Barely passing in Geography . . . Don't you know that the sea is the most amazing and fascinating study of all? That's a lover worthy of a future Navy man, the most accommodating and the most passionate lover who'll never deceive you . . . Do you go to bed with Florita?

NICOLAS-SON: Papa! How could you think that?

NICOLAS-FATHER: At your age women can only give you diseases. Anemia, consumption, and the French disease . . . So now you should put more effort into your studies. There'll be plenty of time for all the rest. Ah, and don't get any ideas about masturbating in the toilet because that's even more harmful.

NICOLAS-SON: Papa, I didn't know . . .

NICOLAS-FATHER: Well now you do. If I find out you've touched your dingaling for anything except pissing, I'll cut it off for you with a knife. Understood? So you got your highest mark for good conduct. That's really funny. At the head of the class! I'd give you . . . (*He returns the grade reports to him.*) Until you bring me better grades, you're going to do without supper. And while the rest of us are eating, you'll stay under the sofa as punishment, where we can't see you. Oh, and with your face to the wall so that you don't start drooling over the servant's legs, you little degenerate. And if you dare go back to Florita's room, don't forget that I'm on the lookout. Now go study. (*Nicolás-Son goes upstage in silence. Florita has approached Nicolás-Father.*) Let it be absolutely clear, Florita, that I'm the master and the only man in this house, and don't get any ideas about enticing the boy with your airs and your flirting . . . I know you!

FLORITA: How can you think that of me, sir!

NICOLAS-FATHER: And lock your door every night.

FLORITA: I always do, as soon as the master leaves.

NICOLAS-FATHER: But, if you forget sometime . . . be careful with him. He's only a child. Slowly, delicately, everything natural, with no strange positions. You understand me. With that sly way of yours you can be downright bestial at times. Pour me another glass of wine.

FLORITA: Yes, sir.

NICOLAS-FATHER: Good girl!

(*Florita withdraws. Pilar-Mother appears.*)

PILAR-MOTHER: The day we married was the twenty-fourth of May. My father and his father were both Naval Commanders. I was twenty-four. He was already thirty-six. With a reputation for loose living and gambling, like almost all the men in El Ferrol, until they got married and settled down. Only Nicolás never settled down.

NICOLAS-FATHER: It's raining . . . It's always raining in this sad, sleepy town. (*We hear the sound of a bugle. Far-off.*) A bugle sounding taps from a barracks or church bells are all you ever hear on this damned street. God, if I could only go somewhere else!

PILAR-MOTHER: Come along, children. We're going to say the Rosary for the blessed souls in Purgatory and our departed loved ones. (*Nicolás-Son, Ramón, and Pilar-Daughter cross themselves and pray with their*

*Mother.*) By the sign of the Holy Cross . . .

(*Ambrosio has entered dressed in a Navy uniform.*)

AMBROSIO: (*To Nicolás-Father.*) Tuesday there's a touring company opening in town, and the chorus girls are staying at the Hotel Varela.

NICOLAS-FATHER: Last time they turned out to be a bunch of leeches.

AMBROSIO: No comparison. These are real young ladies. They come from Madrid.

PILAR-MOTHER: Ave Maria gracia plena dominus tecum . . .

THE OTHERS: (*Including Nicolas-Father and Ambrosio.*) Benedicta tu in mulieribus et benedictus fructus ventris Jesus.

AMBROSIO: By the way, you owe me thirty duros. [150 pesetas]

NICOLAS-FATHER: Where do you think I can find thirty duros now?

AMBROSIO: If you hadn't lost them at cards . . . When your money runs out, you get up from the table, and that's that.

NICOLAS-FATHER: Listen, I'm a man of honor and I've never failed to pay a gambling debt.

AMBROSIO: I know, but I need the money.

NICOLAS-FATHER: I'll see what I can do when I get paid.

AMBROSIO: What's your wife going to say?

NICOLAS-FATHER: I have the say-so in my own house, don't I? Oh, but you're lucky to be a bachelor!

PILAR-MOTHER: In the name of the Father, the Son, and the Holy Ghost.

THE OTHERS: Amen.

NICOLAS-FATHER: (*Putting on his raincoat.*) I'm going with Ambrosio to take a walk down by the harbor. If any of you children want to come along . . .

PILAR-MOTHER: We've finished the Rosary, but I intended to read to them a while from the lives of the saints.

NICOLAS-FATHER: A little fresh air would do them more good.

AMBROSIO: You used to like to stroll around the city and explain to your children the names and structure of the ships you could see from the shore . . .

(*Pilar-Daughter, Nicolás-Son, and Ramón have put on their raincoats and follow their father and Ambrosio downstage. The sound of the ocean and seagulls. Pilar-Mother reads without moving from her chair.*)

NICOLAS-FATHER: Over there is north, do you see? Toward the Cape . . . and that way is south.

PILAR-DAUGHTER: How big the ocean is, Papa? Who owns it?

RAMON: Silly, the ocean doesn't belong to anybody, it can't have an owner.

NICOLAS-FATHER: You're wrong, Ramón. It does. The ocean belongs to us all.

PILAR-DAUGHTER: To me too?

NICOLAS-FATHER: To you too, daughter. To anyone, man, woman, or child who dares to cross it. That's why it's better than the land. Out there there are no greedy owners who put fences around their property so that nobody can walk over it. Only on the ocean are we truly free . . .

RAMON: And in the sky . . . Seated in one of those flying machines they've invented in America.

NICOLAS-FATHER: The only bad part of it is that no matter how big the ocean is, or the sky, we always end up returning to port.

AMBROSIO: Did you know that once upon a time this was the leading port of Spain, when half the world was ours? Go on, tell them what the English thought of El Ferrol?

NICOLAS-FATHER: Prime Minister Pitt said that if it were his, he would have covered it with silver armor.

AMBROSIO: What do you think of that?

NICOLAS-FATHER: But I don't see the silver anywhere . . . only those dirty sheds and that packing plant. A garbage heap, like all of Spain.

NICOLAS-SON: Spain is the greatest country of all, Papa.

NICOLAS-FATHER: It could be if we'd forget about lost colonies, and Pitt, and so much nonsense, and finally look ahead. But we're too proud, too lazy . . .

AMBROSIO: Look, a sailboat.

NICOLAS-FATHER: Give me the telescope. (*He looks.*) It's an old clipper, with full sails to the wind . . . What a beautiful sight! Do you know what I'd like more than anything else? To be free and cross the ocean proudly, with full sails like that clipper. What about you? What would you like?

NICOLAS-SON: I . . . to be happy.

RAMON: I, to fly.

PILAR-DAUGHTER: Well, I want to have a husband, a lot of children, and a lot of money.

NICOLAS-FATHER: What about you, Ambrosio?

AMBROSIO: Me? Just for you to return the thirty duros you owe me.

NICOLAS-FATHER: You're a fool. Let's go home, it's raining harder.

AMBROSIO: He was an intelligent man, but eccentric, with a great personality that led him to do what he felt like, without worrying about what people would say.

(*He exits with the children. Nicolás-Father goes over to Pilar-Mother, who continues reading. He takes off his raincoat slowly.*)

NICOLAS-FATHER: Hello, Pilar.

PILAR-MOTHER: Hello, Nicolás. (*They kiss routinely.*) Isn't it early to be coming home from the office?

NICOLAS-FATHER: I left a little early so that I could talk to you. It's something important.

PILAR-MOTHER: Go ahead.

NICOLAS-FATHER: My promotion has finally come through. I'm now a Naval Commandant, like your father and mine . . .

PILAR-MOTHER: Congratulations.

NICOLAS-FATHER: Thank you . . .(*He shows her the notification.*) They're going to transfer me.

PILAR-MOTHER: Where?

NICOLAS-FATHER: I don't know yet.

PILAR-MOTHER: You always wanted to leave El Ferrol . . .

NICOLAS-FATHER: (*Emphatically.*) A Navy man is a bird of passage . . . bound for any part of the world.

PILAR-MOTHER: Save your fancy speeches for the Men's Club. They don't impress me . . . I suppose you were the one who requested the transfer.

NICOLAS-FATHER: There's no opening here. I owe it to my career.

PILAR-MOTHER: You just want to get out of sight. Your conduct and your drinking sprees are not exactly a good recommendation for a brilliant career.

NICOLAS-FATHER: I do my job like the best. They've never had a complaint.

PILAR-MOTHER: But when we go to Mass on Sundays people look at you as if you were some kind of freak. And in many places they avoid me because I'm your wife, or worse yet, they feel sorry for me.

NICOLAS-FATHER: This is a mediocre provincial city inhabited by dull people devoid of imagination.

PILAR-MOTHER: The superior man!

NICOLAS-FATHER: Envy is at the root of it all.

PILAR-MOTHER: Like it or not, this is and has been your home and your family's.

NICOLAS-FATHER: Well take a good look around; from now on it's going to cease to be.

PILAR-MOTHER: The demons of pride are tempting you, Nicolás, as they tempted our Lord. One has to learn to conform.

NICOLAS-FATHER: Conformity is an invention of priests to keep us silent and in line.

PILAR-MOTHER: Nicolás! (*Transition.*) Have you asked them to send you to the capital?

NICOLAS-FATHER: Why not?

PILAR-MOTHER: It's a big place, with a lot of people, and everything can be concealed, even your escapades.

NICOLAS-FATHER: The palace of your beloved royalty is there. You could applaud them when they pass by in their carriage, decked out in jewels and furs, while you are shivering from the cold in your cheap, flimsy coat.

PILAR-MOTHER: Don't tell me you've turned republican. Or joined the Masons.

NICOLAS-FATHER: I'm not a Mason, Pilar. Actually I don't know very well what I am . . . But I don't like this world that's been my lot to live in. I don't like kings, I don't like vassals, I don't even like myself.

PILAR-MOTHER: Keep on talking that way and they'll throw you out of the service. If your father could hear you.

NICOLAS-FATHER: It's possible we'll have to move before summer.

PILAR-MOTHER: We?

NICOLAS-FATHER: Well, I mean the whole family.

PILAR-MOTHER: Why would you want to take us with you? To keep on offending me and setting a bad example to the children? God knows what I've suffered and the tears I've shed all these years because of you. And how much I've prayed for you to change.

NICOLAS-FATHER: Then it's one or the other. Either it doesn't matter to God what I do or He doesn't pay you any damn attention.

PILAR-MOTHER: Don't be blasphemous . . . (*Transition.*) It would upset the children's lives too much.

NICOLAS-FATHER: Why? Nicolás is already fifteen and he's studying at the Naval Academy. Francisco is going to enroll too as soon as he finishes the school year.

PILAR-MOTHER: Admissions are already closed for the next term.

NICOLAS-FATHER: That can change in twenty-four hours. If not, he can enroll at a military academy. But by no means should he stay on with us. With your pampering and your priggishness you've made him a strange, timid boy.

PILAR-MOTHER: You hate him, Nicolás. The poor child realizes it, that's why he avoids you . . .

NICOLAS-FATHER: What are you talking about? How could I hate him? But I have to admit that he scares me sometimes. When he fixes those black eyes on me with that faraway look of his. I don't know whether he's showing me contempt or indifference. He'll be better off away from us, believe me.

PILAR-MOTHER: You don't love him and you don't understand him.

NICOLAS-FATHER: He doesn't love me either . . . and maybe not even you, though he always runs to your skirts for protection. It could be that he only loves himself.

PILAR-MOTHER: Why don't you hang your head in shame for saying such awful things about your own son?

NICOLAS-FATHER: Time will tell. But God will that I'm wrong.

(*Pause.*)

PILAR-MOTHER: Pacita is buried here.

NICOLAS-FATHER: We'll come back every time I have a leave and cover her grave with white flowers.

PILAR-MOTHER: Don't waste your breath, Nicolás. Neither I nor my children are moving from this house.

NICOLAS-FATHER: We'll see about that. The law obliges you to follow me wherever I go.

PILAR-MOTHER: If necessary, I'll speak to the admiral who was Papa's friend at school, and I'll tell him the sad truth about our marriage. The whole truth.

NICOLAS-FATHER: Well, don't forget to tell your father's friend what's been happening in our bed ever since we got married.

PILAR-MOTHER: That's enough.

NICOLAS-FATHER: With the light out and your nightgown laced up to your neck, it was a major engineering feat to find the mineshaft.

PILAR-MOTHER: Don't be vulgar.

NICOLAS-FATHER: Still as a marble statue, without the slightest collaboration, an authentic Christian martyr prepared for the great sacrifice. Do you think that hasn't been humiliating for me? Any other man would have lost his hard-on every time he tried.

PILAR-MOTHER: I won't tolerate your barracks language. I'll stay in El Ferrol because I, and my children, were born here, and the stones and streets of this town are familiar to us. Maybe it does rain too much, as you say, and it's sad and boring . . . but the people here are decent, proud of their land and God-fearing. Just as our ancestors were and as I'd hoped our children would be too, and our grandchildren, and our great grandchildren. Leave whenever you like for that rowdy city, but don't try to get us to go with you, because you'll have to drag us away by force to do it.

NICOLAS-FATHER: What are you after? For me to give up my career?

PILAR-MOTHER: I only ask you to leave us in peace once and for all.

NICOLAS-FATHER: Let it go on record that you're the one who is causing the separation.

PILAR-MOTHER: Don't be a hypocrite. You are the only one responsible for our coming to this lamentable situation. I've restrained myself to bear your continuous affronts with decorum.

NICOLAS-FATHER: Keep your voice down. The children might hear us.

PILAR-MOTHER: Don't worry, they're not at home. Though I don't think it would surprise them too much. They know it better than anyone.

NICOLAS-FATHER: This is a veritable conspiracy to get rid of me . . . Well, congratulations! I don't say that I've been a man without faults, and of course I'm not the paterfamilias they've implanted in your mind from the pulpits . . . but I've done my best for you and for my children . . . and I don't deserve this.

PILAR-MOTHER: Please, enough playacting. I can't take any more.

NICOLAS-FAHTER: And now the tears.

PILAR-MOTHER: I'm not crying, Nicolás. I've had enough experience over the years to face my troubles without tears. (*Pause.*) Are you going to take the girl with you?

NICOLAS-FATHER: I don't know what you're talking about.

PILAR-MOTHER: About the dressmaker's daughter. Agustina or whatever her name is . . . Don't try to deny it. Everybody in El Ferrol knows.

NICOLAS-FATHER: Ah, so that's it! This damn town is full of gossips. You can rest at ease, it means nothing. It's not worth your jealousy, I assure you.

PILAR-MOTHER: I'm not jealous of anyone. Not any more. You've managed that too.

AGUSTINA: (*Appearing between the couple.*) He was the vainest and most charming man I'd ever met. My mother always used to warn me: "Be careful, Agustina, he's married and he has a terrible reputation . . ." But he had me under his spell and he only had to do this with his fingers . . . (*she snaps her fingers*) and I'd follow him like a fool wherever he wished.

PILAR-MOTHER: Servants, actresses, dressmakers . . . you aren't very choosey.

NICOLAS-FATHER: What do you know about it! (*Transition.*) Your pride gets the better of you too, Pilar. Your display of virtue and your modesty are only a way of feeling superior to other people. Because you went to a school taught by dignified nuns, because you're the daughter of a naval officer . . . Do you know why you really want to stay here? Because in any other place in the world you'd be only a poor, ignorant provincial who goes around showing off her piety.

AGUSTINA: I'm going to Madrid, mother, I'm going to Madrid. I'm going to Madrid! Of course with him. Who else?

PILAR-MOTHER: When do you intend to leave?

NICOLAS-FATHER: As soon as the transfer order arrives. I think it will be soon.

PILAR-MOTHER: I'll have the big trunk brought down from the attic.

(*Pilar-Mother exits. Nicolás-Father remains motionless for a few moments during which we hear the sound of a doorbell.*)

AGUSTINA: Nicolás. Nicolás.

NICOLAS-FATHER: Damn it, can't you stay off my back for one blessed moment!

AGUSTINA: Those neighbors have come again.

NICOLAS-FATHER: I don't want to see anybody.

(*A moment before, the Neighbor and his Wife have entered.*)

NEIGHBOR: Forgive us for bothering you, don Nicolás, on a day like today, when they're celebrating the end of the war with a great parade .·. . But it's a very serious matter, a question of life or death.

NICOLAS-FATHER: And what the hell do I have to do with your damn problems?

NEIGHBOR'S WIFE: You see? I told you so. Excuse us, we'll come back another day.

NICOLAS-FATHER: You, offer them a glass of wine.

NEIGHBOR'S WIFE: Don't go to any trouble, please.

NICOLAS-FATHER: Madam . . . I am yours to command.

NEIGHBOR'S WIFE: Oh, thank you very much, you're too kind . . . we live in this building, on the second floor . . . that's why we dared to come by. Since it's so urgent and we don't know where to turn. (*She is crying.*)

NICOLAS-FATHER: Drink, drink . . . (*He offers her the glass of wine that Agustina has brought.*)

NEIGHBOR'S WIFE: Yes, thank you. (*She drinks.*)

NEIGHBOR: Around the neighborhood they've been saying, I don't know if it can be true, that you belong to the family of . . . well, of . . . you know what I mean. The family name, at least, is the same. It may be only a coincidence, but people do talk . . . you know how the people of Madrid are . . . So my wife said to me: "You can't lose anything by asking . . ."

NICOLAS-FATHER: I'm the only one in my family.

NEIGHBOR: That's what I told my wife. If there were any connection, would you be living in this house, suffering the same hardships that we endure. Come now, that's absurd. (*He drinks.*) To your health.

NEIGHBOR'S WIFE: But if you knew, just by chance, some bigwig who had influence . . .

NICOLAS-FATHER: I don't know anybody.

NEIGHBOR: In our home we've always been strictly conservative and very devout. All our lives. And patriotic . . . too patriotic maybe. If one can be too patriotic, of course.

NEIGHBOR'S WIFE: When you go outside, take a look at the flag we've hung on the balcony. It's the largest in the building . . .

NEIGHBOR: And I'm returning to work with all my papers in order. They cleared me in less than a month. And you know how hard that is . . .

NEIGHBOR'S WIFE: And the same for the whole family . . . that is, all except a cousin of mine. And bear in mind he grew up around us and only had the best examples . . . Honest and hardworking as they come, that's for sure, but he had this thing against priests, he couldn't stomach them, not even from a distance.

NICOLAS-FATHER: I swear, neither can I! They're to blame for all that's happening in this country.

NEIGHBOR: Please, don Nicolás, you shouldn't say those things . . .

NEIGHBOR'S WIFE: They led him astray, you know. They filled his head with all that business about democracy, equality, and other nonsense . . . And since he's really such a simple soul, they sent him to the front.

NEIGHBOR: They say he volunteered, but who can say. The upshot is, smart and likeable as he was, they soon made him the leader of something or other . . .

NEIGHBOR'S WIFE: He even had a car, and without fail when he came to visit us the kids in the street all made it their plaything.

NEIGHBOR: So at the time of the retreat they caught him just before he got to France and put him in a concentration camp . . . Yesterday we found out that he'd been tried and sentenced to death.

NEIGHBOR'S WIFE: No matter what ideas he had, I swear to God he doesn't deserve that . . . Take pity on him and us. Please, I beg you, please . . .

NICOLAS-FATHER: I?

NEIGHBOR'S WIFE: (*Kissing his hand.*) You're a good man, don Nicolás, I can see that in your eyes . . . please . . .

NICOLAS-FATHER: (*Taking his hand away.*) Señora, don't. You musn't. (*He takes a swallow of wine. He doesn't know what to say.*) Why are you all looking at me? What do I have to do with this? Do you think I signed his sentence? Do you think me capable of ordering anyone's death because he wants equality and can't stand priests? Agustina, tell them not to look at me that way! (*Martial music begins to be heard very faintly.*) What do they expect me to do? Plant myself in the middle of the parade, face the reviewing stand and shout to my son what I think of him? . . . It's been so long since he's seen me that he wouldn't even recognize me . . . Throw that old drunk out! (*He drinks.*) Today is your day. The great day you've been looking forward to since you were a child, the one your dark, empty eyes always saw in the future . . . They're all obeying you and applauding you . . . They're shouting our name. Thousands of soldiers turn their eyes toward you, marching in step . . . They're all afraid of you, all except me. Not I. What can you take away from me? Yes, you're right, I *am* only an old drunk that you're ashamed of . . . But listen carefully, boy, listen to me. It would all go better if you had a few drinks and let yourself go, like your father. I'm sure of that. (*He drinks again.*)

AGUSTINA: Leave me his name, the place where they're holding him, and all the information. I don't know what success he'll have, but he'll try something . . .

NEIGHBOR: Then he really is . . .

AGUSTINA: Yes . . .

NEIGHBOR: I can't believe it . . .

NEIGHBOR'S WIFE: My heart tells me he'll succeed. How could he refuse his own father anything? Bless you, señora. (*The Neighbors exit.*)

NICOLAS-FATHER: Agustina, close the windows and close the curtains. I don't want to hear that music.

AGUSTINA: Don't drink anymore.

NICOLAS-FATHER: What else can I do, Agustina? (*Pause.*) Where is our daughter?

AGUSTINA: In the street, watching the parade, like everyone else.

NICOLAS-FATHER: I forbade her! Doesn't anyone pay attention to me?

AGUSTINA: All her friends from the workshop got together to go. If she hadn't they would have called her unpatriotic.

NICOLAS-FATHER: So only one man and one color represent patriotism now.

AGUSTINA: Besides, she had a certain curiosity to see her brother, even from a distance.

NICOLAS-FATHER: You don't say. Why don't you go too and cheer your stepson with a little flag in your hand?

AGUSTINA: Nicolás . . . are you going to write to him?

NICOLAS-FATHER: Me? Write to that one? I'd hang myself by the neck first.

AGUSTINA: Not even to ask a pardon for that poor boy?

NICOLAS-FATHER: He wouldn't pay the slightest attention . . .

AGUSTINA: Then send the letter to your oldest son. He sends you news from Lisbon every month.

NICOLAS-FATHER: He sends me a measly thousand pesetas. That shows you how much I matter to him.

AGUSTINA: Would you want that man's death on your conscience, because of your silly pride.

NICOLAS-FATHER: That's the limit. Why would it be on my conscience? You're confusing the issue, as always. Leave me alone. And close the curtains!

AGUSTINA: They already are.

NICOLAS-FATHER: That music, my God, it's going to drive me mad. And now all that noise! . . .

AGUSTINA: Hundreds of airplanes are flying over Madrid . . .

NICOLAS-FATHER: My son Ramón was the most famous aviator in the world.

AGUSTINA: Yes, Nicolás . . .

NICOLAS-FATHER: Will you just get out. (*Agustina withdraws.*) Ramón . . . Ramón! (*Ramón appears.*)

RAMON: Papa! It doesn't seem true to find one's father on Echegaray Street. And with a glass in his hand.

NICOLAS-FATHER: You shouldn't drink so much. It's bad for your health, it softens your brain.

RAMON: Hey, I'm no longer the little boy you left in El Ferrol seven years ago! Your certainly look fine, very handsome. I suppose you're still the lady-killer you always were.

NICOLAS-FATHER: Not any more.

RAMON: I like women a lot too. I inherited it from you. Thank you, Papa, for such a nice inheritance.

NICOLAS-FATHER: You're a rascal.

RAMON: You're someone to be talking. Well, isn't there something else you should say to me? I'm a second lieutenant!

NICOLAS-FATHER: I heard about it . . .

RAMON: Promotion 1914, still wet behind the ears. You would have preferred a Navy man and Mama a priest . . . but like it or not you have two sons in the Army. It looks like they're going to send me to the 8th Zamora Regiment in El Ferrol, where Francisco was. Though I'll never be like him. Tough as nails. With that little boy's face of his and that squeaky voice, I swear he had the whole base shaking in their boots.

NICOLAS-FATHER: And where is he now?

RAMON: In Africa. Doesn't he ever write you? I'm going there too as soon as I can. It's the only way to get promoted. Better a bullet than dying from boredom in the orderly room. As they used to say at the Academy: promotion or death.

NICOLAS-FATHER: Have you ever stopped to think about the lives that promotion costs?

RAMON: Don't be a defeatist.

NICOLAS-FATHER: I live in a modest neighborhood, among modest people don't give a hoot about rank . . . They have a different view of things there. By the way, you don't happen to have twenty duros [100 pesetas], do you? I left the house without any money . . .

RAMON: Still addicted to cards? Careful, Papa, it's an ugly vice that's the ruin of families. (*He laughs.*) Five duros. [25 pesetas] That's all I can give you.

NICOLAS-FATHER: You're tightfisted and a bad son to boot. Aren't you ashamed? You see your father in difficult straits and you offer him this pittance that won't even help in the slightest.

RAMON: In that case . . .

NICOLAS-FATHER: (*Snatching the money.*) Let me have it. At least I can gain some time. Your brother Nicolás is a bit more generous.

RAMON: He makes more than I do. Ask him for it.

NICOLAS-FATHER: Who knows where he is.

RAMON: I'm meeting him at an apartment near here. Madame Alfonse's house. Another round? Oh no, wine is bad for our health. Let's go, old fellow. Let's go see him. (*Nicolás-Son appears.*)

NICOLAS-SON: You're a half hour late.

RAMON: Don't get so upset. Look what I've brought you.

NICOLAS-SON: Hello, Papa.

NICOLAS-FATHER: Do you think this is a proper meeting place for two brothers from one of the most decent families in Galicia?

RAMON: I hope you won't punish me this time by making me lie under the dining-room sofa.

NICOLAS-SON: Do you know, Papa, that I still dream that I have bad grades and you make me stay under that damned sofa all night?

NICOLAS-FATHER: Maybe you're a naval engineer and the pride of your family because of it.

NICOLAS-SON: You wanted to cover up your own shenanigans by being hard on your children. You were a hateful man.

NICOLAS-FATHER: I'm sorry . . . In that atmosphere, I believed that I was fulfilling my duty . . . Now I know I was wrong and I ask your forgiveness.

RAMON: Careful. Don't defile this happy house by talking of serious things. Lend me a hundred pesetas, Nicolás. I'll give them back to you. On my word of honor.

NICOLAS-SON: I warn you that this time I'm going to hold you to the last cent.

RAMON: Our father is so right. You are the pride and joy of the family. (*He takes the money and gives it to Nicolás-Father.*) If you give me five duros [25 pesetas], I'll give you your hundred pesetas. Agreed?

NICOLAS-FATHER: Agreed.

RAMON: It's all arranged.

(*Madame Alfonse appears.*)

MADAME: (*Kissing Ramón.*) Hello, Ramón, dear. This gentleman was waiting for you a long time. Ah, what a distinguished man. Welcome. You'll have to wait a few minutes. Can I offer you a glass of sherry?

RAMON: We don't touch alcohol. It softens the brain.

MADAME: There are some magazines to pass the time. I'll see you shortly, gentlemen.

NICOLAS-FATHER: I'm leaving. It doesn't seem proper for me to be here with you two, the three of us out on the town.

RAMON: Ora pro nobis, my favorite saint.

NICOLAS-FATHER: Neither of you has any principles.

RAMON: Don't be too hard on Nicolás. He has certain problems in his sex life, and I'm sure he can solve them here.

NICOLAS-SON: Keep your mouth shut, stupid.

RAMON: Ever since you threatened to cut off a certain appendage, it hasn't worked too well.

NICOLAS-SON: That's enough.

RAMON: (*Referring to a photograph in the magazine.*) Hey, look at this baby!

NICOLAS-FATHER: You don't have the slightest respect! Showing your father a woman without her clothes!

RAMON: It's the airplane, Papa. On the opposite page. The advocates for the dirigible can talk all they want, but the future is in heavier-than-air machines, not in balloons . . .

NICOLAS-FATHER: Do you still want to fly, like you did when you were a child?

RAMON: Yes, Papa. Someday I'll fly higher than anyone.

*(Madame Alphonse enters again.)*

MADAME: The young ladies are waiting for you in the salon.

RAMON: I invite you and Nicolás to dinner afterwards. I've just won five duros, and dinner with the family will be an occasion to remember.

MADAME: If you please, gentlemen . . .

RAMON: *(To Nicolás-Son.)* After you . . .

*(Nicolás-Son exits. Ramón embraces Madame Alfonse.)*

RAMON: You get better every day, you pretty thing.

MADAME: You little devil.

NICOLAS-FATHER: I'm leaving. This is too much for me at my age.

MADAME: For heaven's sake, you look sprier today than you did a few years back, when you were honoring us with your visits . . .

NICOLAS-FATHER: This is the first time I've ever been here.

MADAME: Forgive me, I must have mistaken you for someone else. So many gentlemen pass through here . . . But the first three rooms in the house have been reserved for you . . . It would be a pity not to use them all . . . This way.

NICOLAS-FATHER: I'll only stay a minute. I'll just go in to satisfy my curiosity about the girls.

MADAME: As always, they're the prettiest in Madrid. This way . . . *(Winking at him.)* Nicolás. *(They all exit. Agustina and Pilar-Mother appear.)*

AGUSTINA: Señora, such . . . such a surprise. To see you **here in Madrid** . . . come in . . . Forgive my appearance . . . but I just **got up** . . .

PILAR-MOTHER: Inform my husband.

AGUSTINA: As you wish, señora. He's still asleep. I'll wake him immediately . . . Don Nicolás! Don Nicolás! *(To Pilar-Mother.)* Can I get you a cup of coffee?

PILAR-MOTHER: No, thank you. You can leave us alone.

AGUSTINA: I prefer to remain here, if it's all the same to you. He has his coffee and biscuits the moment he opens his eyes. *(She pours a cup from a thermos.)*

PILAR-MOTHER: You're Agustina, aren't you? The daughter of the dress-maker who used to come to our house on Tuesdays and whom I had to dismiss because her sewing got poorer and poorer.

AGUSTINA: Arthritis deformed her hands. She died last year.

PILAR-MOTHER: I'm sorry. Are you my husband's servant now?

AGUSTINA: I wouldn't say that I'm his servant.

PILAR-MOTHER: Sleeping with him doesn't make you anything else. He did it with all of them, always.

AGUSTINA: He also slept with you, señora, I suppose.

PILAR-MOTHER: I don't want to see any more of you. Leave.

AGUSTINA: I don't believe the señora has realized it yet, but this is not El Ferrol. I beg your pardon, but this is my house.

PILAR-MOTHER: This is my husband's house. And consequently mine, and I'll throw anyone I please out of it.

AGUSTINA: Nicolás!

NICOLAS-FATHER: (*Appearing.*) That's enough shouting! (*Seeing Pilar.*) Well, well . . .

PILAR-MOTHER: I have to talk with you. You've probably guessed that it's a very serious matter if I've lowered myself to come here.

NICOLAS-FATHER: Very well.

PILAR-MOTHER: Alone.

NICOLAS-FATHER: Don't be concerned about her, she's like family. (*He begins to sip his coffee.*) Would you like some?

PILAR-MOTHER: Get her out.

NICOLAS-FATHER: Would you let us be alone, Agustina?

AGUSTINA: No.

NICOLAS-FATHER: You heard her. I can't. She's the stubbornest woman in the world . . .

PILAR-MOTHER: As you prefer. I've come to bring you this train ticket. The Andalusian Express leaves in an hour and a half.

NICOLAS-FATHER: And why do you think I'd be going off to Andalusia?

PILAR-MOTHER: Francisco has been seriously wounded. By now he may even have died. The War Department sent these tickets. Here is yours. Goodbye.

(*She crosses to the sofa which will become the train compartment and sits down.*)

NICOLAS-FATHER: Did you hear? My son is dying. And Ramón is in Africa too. It could happen to him any day . . . Put a few things in a suitcase for me.

AGUSTINA: I'm sorry, Nicolás. Truly.

NICOLAS-FATHER: Promotion or death. That's what they drum into the heads of the young officers . . . Well, you got what you were looking for, fool. You're already a captain at twenty-two, but a captain with a wound in his body that can finish him off at any moment. What stupidity, Agustina! While they're killing one another in Europe, here we are sending our sons to conquer a few rocks that are worthless and don't really belong to us . . . Bring me my jacket . . . Brrr, what bilge! This coffee is cold.

AGUSTINA: I can warm it for you in a jiffy.

NICOLAS-FATHER: To hell with it. We're really all in shit up to our necks. What a disgusting mess! (*He puts on his jacket, picks up his suitcase, and sits in silence beside Pilar-Mother. Suggestion of a train station. Agustina exits.*) Will it bother you if I smoke?

PILAR-MOTHER: You always smoked whenever you took a notion without worrying about me.

NICOLAS-FATHER: You see, time has taught me a few manners. One thing is certain, the years haven't touched you. You're younger and prettier than ever.

PILAR-MOTHER: You have a gift for remembering things at the wrong time.

(*Pause.*)

NICOLAS-FATHER: Tell me what happened to our son.

PILAR-MOTHER: A bullet in his stomach. It appears that it affects vital organs, and his condition is very grave. They rushed him to the camp at Kudia-Federico. Then they transferred him to the hospital in Seville. That's all I know.

NICOLAS-FATHER: Poor Pilar.

PILAR-MOTHER: They wounded him when he was assaulting a hill where the rebels were firing on our troops. He led the company on until he was hit. Francisco was brave, he's a hero. If you only knew the admiration he inspired in the detachment at El Ferrol. An example for Spain.

NICOLAS-FATHER: Which Spain? Yours . . . or mine?

PILAR-MOTHER: The one that's decent and God-fearing, that loves peace and has respect for the law.

NICOLAS-FATHER: What peace are you talking about? We've been trapped in this stupid, useless war for fifty years, and nobody knows why it started in the first place.

PILAR-MOTHER: To save those poor savages from their ignorance and bring them the truth of our faith.

NICOLAS-FATHER: But how are we expressing that truth, tell me that. With bullets?

PILAR-MOTHER: How can you repeat the slanders that traitors have dreamed up? I don't understand you.

NICOLAS-FATHER: And I don't understand how you can accept with resignation and even pride that they kill your own son.

PILAR-MOTHER: We've been separated for nine years, Nicolás. We no longer have anything in common.

NICOLAS-FATHER: With all that slaughter? So that half a dozen generals can be decorated and four mining companies exploit the mineral deposits?

PILAR-MOTHER: I don't want to argue with you.

NICOLAS-FATHER: Do you really think it's worth the lives of our sons?

PILAR-MOTHER: For the last time, please.

NICOLAS-FATHER: Listen to me, Pilar. You live in a provincial city, surrounded by people who think and feel like you. But you're greatly mistaken if you imagine that El Ferrol is the whole country. You aren't the only woman. There are thousands of mothers who are crying with you at this very moment.

PILAR-MOTHER: I know that.

NICOLAS-FATHER: But not for a son like ours who has made war his career, who pursues honors and promotions and accepts risks and sacrifices by his own choice. Those other mothers are terrified when they see their sons growing up and approaching military age. They can't sleep from anxiety, not knowing when a new drawing will send them off to a dangerous war in Africa. They say their tearful goodbyes in train stations without understanding why the sons they've borne and raised are being carried off to a land they know nothing about. It's not that they're less Spanish than you, Pilar; it's just that they can't conceive of a country that has no respect for their pain and the lives of its own people. And there's that God you've incriminated in the killing, taking for granted it was His will. The God of those weeping mothers is not your God, Pilar. He's the God of all the people . . . even those poor ignorant men who are defending their land, their country.

PILAR-MOTHER: You're crazy. Or drunk.

NICOLAS-FATHER: Crazy perhaps. Drunk, no, not yet. But I feel the need for a drink to keep from thinking any more. With your permission. (He drinks from a bottle that he takes from his suitcase.)

PILAR-MOTHER: You're nothing but a clown.

NICOLAS-FATHER: There was a time when that comment would have wounded me deeply. Now I know that you say it because you don't know what to say. (He takes another drink.)

PILAR-MOTHER: Please . . .

NICOLAS-FATHER: Relax. Francisco isn't going to die. Your son is a winner and he won't let a ridiculous little piece of metal cut short his career. He'll go on being the wonder of the army barracks for years and years. (He drinks again.) I can assure you of that.

PILAR-MOTHER: Don't drink any more. You're already drunk.

NICOLAS-FATHER: You're right. I'm beginning to feel it . . . You're pretty,

Pilar. Your body has stayed young and desirable . . . Actually I've always desired you, because I never managed to possess you completely or plant my flag on the last redoubt.

PILAR-MOTHER: If you continue with your obscenities, I'll have you thrown out of the compartment.

NICOLAS-FATHER: You can't. I have my ticket with a seat reserved to the end of the trip. Down deep you're flattered . . . But don't worry, this would be an adventure sanctified by the Church, with the special blessing of the bishop of the diocese and the station master. (*He laughs.*) Why did you marry me? Were you beginning to think you were an old maid and that it didn't look good in the eyes of the city? Or did you fall in love with my mustache like a common dance-hall girl?

PILAR-MOTHER: Please . . .

NICOLAS-FATHER: Didn't I ever make you happy?

PILAR-MOTHER: It could have been beautiful . . . A decent husband, a respectable family. That was what I wanted and you never gave me. You, obviously, wanted something else, something I couldn't give you either.

NICOLAS-FATHER: Pilar . . .

PILAR-MOTHER: It wasn't easy for me to come looking for you.

NICOLAS-FATHER: Come here, sit closer to me.

PILAR-MOTHER: No. You've already hurt me enough.

NICOLAS-FATHER: Be good to me.

PILAR-MOTHER: If you touch me, I'll go out into the passageway and call for help.

NICOLAS-FATHER: Have no fear, I'm not going to force myself on you. I did it too many times during all the years we lived together . . . and it's disappointing. (*He embraces her.*)

PILAR-MOTHER: (*Getting up and starting toward the passageway.*) You stink of wine. Conductor, there's a drunk man in my compartment who is disturbing me.

CONDUCTOR: (*Entering.*) Hey, you. Let me see your ticket. (*He examines it.*) Please leave the lady alone.

NICOLAS-FATHER: The lady is my wife. I had my arms around her because the law and the Church give me every right, including the basest ones. We're going to Seville to visit our heroic son, a captain in the Foreign Legion, wounded in battle for the greatest glory of God and Country. And now, stand at attention. I'm a naval commandant.

CONDUCTOR: Yes, sir. (*He exits.*)

NICOLAS-FATHER: At least the railroad company will have an excellent opinion of us. I've spoken like an exemplary husband from our exemplary town.

(*Transition. Ramón and Nicolás-Son appear.*)

RAMON: Congratulations, Papa.

NICOLAS-SON: My compliments.

RAMON: We've just entered posterity gloriously through the front door.

NICOLAS-FATHER: Me too?

NICOLAS-SON: You too! At least by association . . . Today at noon your son became the most popular Spaniard of his generation.

NICOLAS-FATHER: Good for you, Nicolás. I'm proud of you and the Navy.

NICOLAS-SON: It's not me, Papa . . . it's him.

RAMON: My seaplane has reached Buenos Aires, after crossing the Atlantic for the first time, in the most fantastic flight in the annals of aviation.

NICOLAS-SON: The 10th of February, 1926.

RAMON: The King has decorated me.

NICOLAS-SON: (*As if putting the decoration on him.*) For the renown that you have achieved and for the daring that you have displayed, which will live in history. (*He embraces him, after simulating the pinning on of the medal.*)

RAMON: I've been honored by the Republic of Argentina, by Uruguay, and by all America.

NICOLAS-SON: He has passed triumphantly, in an open car, along Fifth Avenue in New York.

RAMON: While they threw thousands and thousands of pieces of white paper from the windows of the skyscrapers to welcome me.

NICOLAS-FATHER: You always wanted to fly higher and farther than anyone. (*He embraces Ramón.*)

NICOLAS-SON: And this is nothing, Papa. Within ten years, in 1936, another son of yours will become no less than the supreme commander of our nation.

NICOLAS-FATHER: Really?

NICOLAS-SON: And he'll keep his job, come hell or high water, for forty years!

NICOLAS-FATHER: It's not me I'm talking about, Papa . . . but our brother Francisco . . .

NICOLAS-FATHER: You don't say . . .

RAMON: They'll name him General of Generals, he'll win the war, he'll get rid of his enemies, and he'll manage to accumulate all the honors you've ever heard of and then some.

NICOLAS-FATHER: God help us!

NICOLAS-SON: And all thanks to me, for I'll pave the way. I'll convince the other officers and I'll even change a word or two in the Officers' Billet to eliminate rivals. What's this? Don't I deserve an embrace too?

NICOLAS-FATHER: (*Embracing his son without conviction.*) I wish you did, son, how I wish it!

RAMON: Now you see how you're going to be the most famous father of the century!

*(Suddenly there is the loud roar of a plane that noses over, falls into the sea, and explodes.)*

NICOLAS-FATHER: What was the date of the accident that cost the life of our son Ramón?

PILAR-MOTHER: I don't know. I'd already been dead for four years when it happened. I was the first of our family to pass away . . . *(She gets up and exits.)*

NICOLAS-FATHER: Agustina! Agustina! You have a great memory and you remember everything. Tell me, what day did my son die?

AGUSTINA: *(Who has just appeared.)* The 28th of October, 1938. At 5:28 a.m. his plane went into a spin at ten thousand feet and fell into the sea off the coast of Valencia.

NICOLAS-SON: I took care of the arrangements. It was a big funeral, and all the church dignitaries and the military were there.

NICOLAS-FATHER: Why, Ramón? You must explain it to me . . .

RAMON: I should have cancelled the flight, but in wartime there's no such thing as bad weather.

NICOLAS-FATHER: Was it sabotage? Did the controls freeze on you? Did your own pursuit planes shoot you down because you were going over to the other side, as people said?

RAMON: For God's sake, Papa . . . what does that matter now?

NICOLAS-FATHER: You had more experience than anyone . . . I can't believe that the accident was caused by human error.

RAMON: I was very depressed. I stayed awake all night remembering things. I couldn't sleep or live. Do you know how many attacks we had to carry out against civilian targets? 170! 2,500 dead, 3,500 wounded . . . To think that only a few years before, when we staged a revolt at the Cuatro Vientos, I refused to bomb the Royal Palace because some children were playing in the square in front of it.

NICOLAS-FATHER: It surprised me that you joined your brother . . . You were a revolutionary. You used to call yourself a deputy of the people. You were hotheaded then.

RAMON: All Spaniards were hotheaded at that moment.

NICOLAS-FATHER: I'll never understand it.

RAMON: I wanted to fly, Papa. It was my calling. I offered my services to the Government, and they told me to get it out of my head, because I'd have a bad time of it.

NICOLAS-FATHER: And for that you joined your enemies?

RAMON: I put myself at Francisco's orders, yes. He was my brother, and he wasn't going to reject me.

NICOLAS-FATHER: I'm his father, and now you see how he treats me . . . Stupid. You took a great risk . . . you were a Mason.

RAMON: Nicolás belonged to groups too, and he was his right hand man.

NICOLAS-FATHER: He made an exception with you, he needed you.

RAMON: And he loved me . . .

NICOLAS-FATHER: Maybe. He never made any exception for me.

RAMON: Face it, Papa, you never made things easy . . .

NICOLAS-FATHER: I don't bow and scrape to anyone . . . I'm proud to be the way I am.

RAMON: Papa . . . you're a stupendous fellow.

NICOLAS-FATHER: Bah! I'm just a loudmouth, a little strutting cock who crows his cock-a-doodle-do every morning but can't manage to fly very far. A cafe rebel . . . who loves freedom as much as you . . . even if I'm not capable of fighting for it.

RAMON: I know that.

NICOLAS-FATHER: Ramón . . . what became of the dreamer who put his fame at the service of the oppressed . . . who was hunted down and jailed for taking part in all the uprisings against the dictatorships? (*The sound of the plane is repeated. It crashes and explodes. To Agustina.*) Ramón died in October of '38, didn't he?

AGUSTINA: His plane went into a spin at 10,000 feet and fell into the sea off the coast of Valencia.

NICOLAS-SON: I took charge of the arrangements, it was a great funeral . . .

RAMON: A great guy, my father . . . A spunky little rooster, even though he never learned to fly.

(*The sons exit.*)

NICOLAS-FATHER: Open the window, Agustina.

AGUSTINA: You won't like it. The sky is black with planes flying in formation over the parade.

NICOLAS-FATHER: Open it.

(*Agustina obeys. We hear the sound of planes and military music.*)

NICOLAS-FATHER: Look everywhere, Agustina, look close. You won't see Ramón's plane up there or me shouting in the streets . . . It's not a great feat . . . but something is something.

(*Blackout.*)

# ACT TWO

*1939. A summer night. Agustina, Nicolás-Father, Neighbor, and Neighbor's Wife are playing dominoes.*

NEIGHBOR: I pass.

NICOLAS-FATHER: Well, you've lost, my friend! Six-double, six-two and I finish . . . Ah, what a night I'm having! I've won more than two pesetas.

AGUSTINA: (*To the Neighbor.*) But you could have closed before with four-three.

NICOLAS-FATHER: And left us all with our asses bare. Tell me, is this some kind of trick?

NEIGHBOR: On my word of honor . . .

NICOLAS-FATHER: You couldn't be letting me win to make me feel good? I'd rather give you back your two pesetas.

NEIGHBOR: Such ideas you get, Don Nicolás!

NICOLAS-FATHER: I'm not playing anymore.

NEIGHBOR: Don't say that. With the luck you've having?

NICOLAS-FATHER: That's exactly why I'm stopping. Bring us something to drink, Agustina.

NEIGHBOR'S WIFE: Don't bother for us . . .

NICOLAS-FATHER: Any news about your relative?

NEIGHBOR: To be honest, that matter doesn't interest us very much any longer. I believe that if they have condemned him, the rascal must have done something we don't know about. Don't you think?

NEIGHBOR'S WIFE: That's not true! My cousin was a very decent person, and they've killed him, like so many others, because he didn't think like them . . .

NEIGHBOR: Will you keep your mouth shut!

NEIGHBOR'S WIFE: He was very good, I swear it. You only had to see him playing with the children in the street when he came to see us in his car.

NEIGHBOR: Stolen, God knows from whom . . .

NICOLAS-FATHER: When did it happen?

NEIGHBOR'S WIFE: Last week. They shot him on Friday.

NICOLAS-FATHER: And why the hell didn't you tell me?

NEIGHBOR: We didn't want to upset you . . . They buried him with a lot of others, in a common grave.

NEIGHBOR'S WIFE: We weren't even able to give him a grave of his own. Nobody will ever know which body is his.

NICOLAS-FATHER: A letter would have been enough, a quick telephone call, a word . . . but no! They have to eliminate all obstacles, no matter how tiny, like that poor devil who was nobody . . . Oh, but they're going to pay for it, I promise you they will.

AGUSTINA: Drink your wine.

NICOLAS-FATHER: (*Pushing it away*) I let my pants down for them. I sent a letter to each of my sons, throwing myself at their feet like a lackey . . . And you see how much attention they paid! Well, young fellows, we'll see who has the last laugh.

AGUSTINA: Who do you want to have the last laugh? Get your head out of the sand.

NICOLAS-FATHER: When the messenger returns, I'll kill him. Wait and see if I don't kill him.

AGUSTINA: But how can that boy be to blame?

(*Agustina and the Neighbor's Wife withdraw.*)

NEIGHBOR: Would you like to roll yourself a smoke from my pouch?

NICOLAS-FATHER: I've given up smoking.

NEIGHBOR: Well, now that they've left us alone, my friend, I'd like to make you a little proposition . . . This isn't made from butts like what they sell around here. Look at that pure white smoke . . .

NICOLAS-FATHER: What are you suggesting?

NEIGHBOR: As anybody can see, life is hard and I'm afraid it's going to get worse. This postwar, or whatever they call it, is going to be harder than the war itself, I promise you that. Not to mention the mess we'll be in any day now when the French and the English start a shooting match with the Germans . . .

NICOLAS-FATHER: Hitler is a dangerous lunatic.

NEIGHBOR: On the contrary, he's the hope of Europe. Don't you read the papers?

NICOLAS-FATHER: My doctor has forbidden it.

NEIGHBOR: What have you done with your tobacco ration card?

NICOLAS-FATHER: I haven't even gotten one.

NEIGHBOR: That's a pity, because a friend of mine would rent it from you at a good price. Shall we play another little game of dominoes, you and I?

NICOLAS-FATHER: To give me two more pesetas? Come, now! Out with it!

NEIGHBOR: Well since the food situation has gotten impossible . . . I was thinking that we could take a little trip South and bring back a few liters of cooking oil, some beans . . . A few things to stock our wives' pantries.

NICOLAS-FATHER: You'd need a trading permit for that.

NEIGHBOR: Of course. And it's not easy to get without a sponsor. But if you and I applied for one . . . nobody would dare refuse us.

NICOLAS-FATHER: Agustina! Our neighbors are ready to leave.

NEIGHBOR: But, man, I'm not suggesting anything illegal. Isn't your name what it is?

NICOLAS-FATHER: Look, sir . . . or whatever you are. It's clear that this is starting to smell, like all dictatorships . . . and only clever fellows like you are going to stay afloat in this immense sea of filth. Look how the tables have turned, I was always the whoring member of the family, and now I'm the only one who has enough sense of shame not to screw everybody in sight. I may not be exactly a saint but I have enough decency left to see the difference between right and wrong.

NEIGHBOR: I think you've misunderstood me, Don Nicolás.

NICOLAS-FATHER: I'm sleepy.

NEIGHBOR: You're right, it's very late. We'll talk about it another time. Good night.

NEIGHBOR'S WIFE: Good night.

AGUSTINA: Pay us another visit soon. (*The neighbors exit.*) You have no manners.

NICOLAS-FATHER: If you knew what that rascal was proposing . . .

AGUSTINA: How could I help knowing. You could hear the shouting all over the house.

NICOLAS-FATHER: And doesn't it make you indignant?

AGUSTINA: But what are you thinking? That if you don't apply for a permit to buy a few miserable things to eat they won't give permits to anyone?

NICOLAS-FATHER: Do you think our neighbor would limit himself to necessities? He'd make one trip after another and turn his apartment into a black market emporium.

AGUSTINA: All of Spain is going to be one great black market before long. And who's going to benefit from it? Others who are less idealistic and a whole lot less deserving.

NICOLAS-FATHER: I am not deserving anything.

AGUSTINA: Why do you think they kept the cousin's death from you? Because they're afraid of you.

NICOLAS-FATHER: Of me?

AGUSTINA: Why can't we take advantage of a bad situation? Do you know what we have left in the pantry?

NICOLAS-FATHER: What does that matter to me?

AGUSTINA: It'll matter a lot when dinner time comes. You have as much right as anyone. If there's any injustice, it won't be your doing but some higher-up's.

NICOLAS-FATHER: I don't want to hear any more. Go to bed.

AGUSTINA: He could get us some tins of sardines . . . and who knows, even some of those cookies you like.

NICOLAS-FATHER: I'm going to let you have it!

AGUSTINA: And you boast that you've never used anyone. Well, you've been using me, I'll have you know.

NICOLAS-FATHER: (*Pulling off his shoe and throwing it at Agustina.*) Just get out!

AGUSTINA: Animal. (*Agustina withdraws.*)

(*Ramón appears. He picks up the shoe and takes it to his father.*)

RAMON: I see that your temper hasn't improved with age.

NICOLAS-FATHER: Leave me in peace.

RAMON: Your shoe, Papa.

NICOLAS-FATHER: Thanks, Ramón . . . (*He sits down.*) Help me put it on, will you? (*Ramón assists.*) What day did you return to Madrid?

RAMON: The 15th. The 15th of April on the Paris Express. But don't you remember?

NICOLAS-FATHER: How could I not remember if we got up at six-thirty to be the first at the station? . . . That was in . . . what year was it?

RAMON: 1931. Papa, for pity's sake . . . Three days after the famous election that changed the government. I could finally return to Spain with my head up.

NICOLAS-FATHER: Yes, of course.

RAMON: I came with others being repatriated, and a lot of newspaper reporters. It was a truly popular reception. It's all over now, Papa. Exile, hunger, persecution, wandering . . .

NICOLAS-FATHER: There's no one who can hold you back!

RAMON: Do you know the first thing I caught sight of from the train when we'd just arrived? The waxed ends of your mustache.

NICOLAS-FATHER: Really?

RAMON: Really! I said to myself, behind that well-trimmed hedge, only a proud man can be hiding. A man of the times, a free thinker. In short, my father.

NICOLAS-FATHER: You're a scamp. I don't believe a word you say . . . But I was at the barber's the evening before, to have the ends trimmed.

RAMON: You see?

(*They laugh.*)

NICOLAS-FATHER: How excited the people on the platform were! And what enthusiasm over you! . . . The whole family came to meet you.

(*The Neighbor and his Wife appear. They approach with Agustina.*)

AGUSTINA: The train will arrive in ten minutes on track 3. I know I'm going to make a fool of myself . . . look how I'm crying.

NEIGHBOR: We'll carry him in triumph on our shoulders. We've prepared a great reception for him.

NEIGHBOR'S WIFE: They say he's very handsome.

(*Now Nicolás-Son and Pilar-Daughter appear.*)

NICOLAS-SON: I don't share your ideas. But I'm your big brother, and I believe that it's my duty to welcome you.

PILAR-DAUGHTER: Well, this is going to be more than I can stand. In my condition and with this crowd . . .

NICOLAS-FATHER: Why didn't Pilar's husband come with her?

PILAR-DAUGHTER: To this kind of revolutionary demonstration? And the smell! Why do you suppose the proletariat smell so much of sweat?

NICOLAS-FATHER: (*To Ramón.*) Maybe because they work more than other people, don't you think?

NEIGHBOR: They've just named him director of aviation!

NEIGHBOR'S WIFE: Well, he deserved to be made president of the Republic!

NICOLAS-SON: One has to change with the times. In the shipyards that I direct I've already given order to re-christen the boats that were named for the daughters of the King.

NICOLAS-FATHER: We'll have to change a lot of other things besides names if we want to get the country moving.

NICOLAS-SON: Don't worry. All the money, the land, and industry will remain in the same hands as always. Everything will stay the same.

PILAR-DAUGHTER: May God listen to you, Nicolás.

AGUSTINA: Here he comes, here he comes.

NICOLAS-FATHER: They're waiting for you. What are you going to say to the crowd?

RAMON: (*Addressing the audience.*) We have the Republic! Now we have to make the revolution! (*Applause.*)

NEIGHBOR'S WIFE: To the Puerta del Sol!

NEIGHBOR: Our hero is home!

(*They all carry Ramón off triumphantly.*)

NICOLAS-FATHER: He seemed thinner to me . . . I said to Agustina: This boy has had some rough times abroad.

RAMON: (*Appearing again.*) Thanks for the money you sent me.

NICOLAS-FATHER: Agustina insisted on selling a ring I'd given her for her birthday.

RAMON: I received help from every part of the world. Even Francisco helped me a bit.

NICOLAS-FATHER: It's not possible. I can't believe my ears.

RAMON: You heard right. With a letter full of advice and warnings. A person from another century might have written it. It sounded like Mama.

NICOLAS-FATHER: Sometimes I think that your brother is nothing more than a shadow of your mother.

RAMON: But I wrote him the kind of answer it deserved. You know how I am. (*Reading a letter he takes from his pocket.*) "Dear Brother, I don't agree with anything you've said to me, and it pains me to see that your 'liberal' ideas are more conservative than the King's. If you came down from your little general's throne and took a stroll in the real world with captains and lieutenants, you'd see that few of them think as you do; those who oppose the will of the people are going to lose all respect . . ."

NICOLAS-FATHER: Good for you! That was fine.

PILAR-MOTHER: (*Appearing.*) Ramón, son, listen to your brother's sensible advice. Besides the sorrow of seeing you in error and blind to reason, I must fear the possibility that you'll end up shot and abandoned by everyone.

RAMON: "Getting shot doesn't frighten me, and if I left Spain it was to stay on the front line . . ."

PILAR-MOTHER: I hope that necessary exile calms your spirits, raises you above all passion and self-interest, and remakes your life.

RAMON: "I'll keep on doing what I wish, following the dictates of a conscience that is a great deal more concerned with civic responsibility than yours . . ."

PILAR-MOTHER: Give it serious thought, Ramón . . . for your own sake and for the worry it causes me and a lot of others.

RAMON: "I hope that this letter will show you the way to go. I still follow a straight path. Your brother, Ramon." (*He exits.*)

NICOLAS-FATHER: And you, Pilar, didn't you want to witness your son's great triumph?

PILAR-MOTHER: That train passed by the one that was taking the Queen and her children into exile.

NICOLAS-FATHER: Didn't you feel proud of him?

PILAR-MOTHER: Do you know what that minister friend of his said when when he saw him? The one who had conspired with him so much? "Now that lunatic is here to upset our future."

NICOLAS-FATHER: Why didn't you go with the rest of us to welcome him?

PILAR-MOTHER: I spent the day at Pilar's house, praying, as always. My life has been a continuous prayer. First for you, for us . . . then for my children, the only thing I had left.

NICOLAS-FATHER: I didn't see you at the station.

PILAR-MOTHER: No, Nicolás, you couldn't see me.

NICOLAS-FATHER: Then how do I remember it so clearly?

PILAR-MOTHER: Perhaps because you wished it so much. It would have been the last time, our last conversation.

NICOLAS-FATHER: I see you now, as young and as pretty as ever.

PILAR-MOTHER: I wasn't young then. I was seventy-five.

NICOLAS-FATHER: You will never be that age for me! I forbid it. (*Pause.*) When you were leaving high mass with your parents . . . you were the most beautiful girl in El Ferrol . . . I saw you with my friends, from the bar in the plaza . . . I would have given my life for a kiss . . . (*He approaches her and kisses her gently.*) If you understood me just once . . .

PILAR-MOTHER: I'm sick of this terribly sad city . . . and this rain!

NICOLAS-FATHER: If you had shared my ideas . . .

PILAR-MOTHER: These prudish people envy your free spirit.

NICOLAS-FATHER: If you had liked to dance . . .

PILAR-MOTHER: You never asked me . . .

NICOLAS-FATHER: I thought you didn't know how! Will you do me the honor of this dance?

PILAR-MOTHER: I'd be delighted . . . (*They dance a few steps.*)

NICOLAS-FATHER: If you had gone with me to Madrid . . .

PILAR-MOTHER: You only have to do this with your fingers (*snapping her fingers*) . . . and I'll follow you wherever you wish.

NICOLAS-FATHER: When I'd come home from the casino at night, I'd go over to your bed full of desire for you . . . But you were always asleep . . . or pretended to be.

PILAR-MOTHER: I'm awake now. What do you want of me?

NICOLAS-FATHER: What you never gave me. To admire your naked body, to feel you warm in my arms . . . to caress your neck, your sweet breasts.

(*Agustina enters. She turns on the light and breaks the spell. She is wearing a plush bathrobe. Pilar-Mother disappears.*)

AGUSTINA: Nicolás, what are you doing? What's going on?

NICOLAS-FATHER: Just leave me in peace.

AGUSTINA: You're acting very strange. Your eyes are shining . . . (*She goes closer to him.*) Well, well. If I didn't see it with my own eyes, I wouldn't believe it. Aren't you ashamed, you old lecher? Eighty years old and as excited as a raunchy dog.

NICOLAS-FATHER: Please, Pilar, please . . . I want to feel your body. I want you . . .

AGUSTINA: Yes, yes, come here, come . . . (*She opens her robe and they kiss at length.*) That was the last time we made love, and I swear that it was as beautiful as the first. (*Nicolás-Father remains motionless, exhausted, on the sofa.*) Are you still alive?

NICOLAS-FATHER: Go to hell.

AGUSTINA: I feel proud of you.

NICOLAS-FATHER: Well my back hurts.

AGUSTINA: Lift up your shirt . . . I'll give you a rub. (*She massages him.*)

NICOLAS-FATHER: What if I told you that tonight . . . I really didn't make love to you?

AGUSTINA: I would answer that you're mistaken.

NICOLAS-FATHER: And if I had been thinking about another woman?

AGUSTINA: You said her name, I realized that . . . But the woman you desired only existed in your imagination, and naturally has nothing to do with your poor wife, may she rest in peace . . . That woman, capable of leaving everything to follow you, unquestioningly, and who can still enjoy being with you when you're eighty, if she existed, would bear a very different name from the one you spoke.

NICOLAS-FATHER: Yours maybe?

AGUSTINA: Maybe. (*She helps him get up.*) Up!

NICOLAS-FATHER: Why wasn't she like you?

AGUSTINA: Are you going to start making comparisons? I'm just a poor country woman. She, on the other hand, was such a lady, so proper . . . one of those who cross themselves three times before they take off their bloomers.

(*The Notary enters with a folder of papers. He sits down facing the audience.*)

AGUSTINA: To bed now.

NICOLAS-FATHER: Yes, let's go.

(*Nicolás-Father, assisted by Agustina, exits. Nicolás-Son, Pilar-Daughter, and Ramón enter. They sit in front of the Notary with their backs to the audience. There is an empty chair.*)

NOTARY: Let us proceed to the reading of the last will and testament of Doña Pilar, may she rest in peace, who passed away in Madrid the 28th of February, 1934. Here present for the act are all the children of the deceased, to wit: Nicolás, Francisco, Ramón, and Pilar . . .

NICOLAS-SON: I beg your pardon, sir, but our father hasn't arrived yet.

PILAR-DAUGHTER: Is his presence essential? In my condition, waiting around is a bother.

NOTARY: Shameful of him! Keeping us waiting an hour and a half—his daughter, me, and his three very important sons: a deputy, although of the left, a future director general of the Merchant Marine and, God bless him, one of the most prestigious generals of our Army. A father like that should be erased from the map. Zas, zas, zas, and zas! And I'm not a fascist.

NICOLAS-FATHER: (*Arriving.*) I'm sorry I'm late, but I had to stop in every bar on the way to get my courage up. I'm appearing in my oldest suit and my house slippers to put you to shame. I don't intend to see things happen the way they did when poor Pilar died, and you forgot to mention me in the obituary.

PILAR-DAUGHTER: Hello, Papa, dear. How happy it makes me to see you looking so handsome and so young.

NICOLAS-FATHER: Hello, Pilar, daughter. I'm not handsome, nor are you happy to see me. And don't take me for a fool. Pregnant again? Don't you and your husband ever stop?

NICOLAS-SON: For heaven's sake, Papa, take off your hat.

NICOLAS-FATHER: How's your son?

NICOLAS-SON: I was going to write you one of these days to tell you about his birth.

NICOLAS-FATHER: According to the reports I've had he's already two years old.

NICOLAS-SON: He has your name. And he's going to be your only descendant to carry the family name in a direct line.

NICOLAS-FATHER: (*To Ramón.*) And how are things going with my dear representative of the people?

RAMON: As you can see, Papa, words don't fix anything. I'm not an orator, or a politician, I'm a man of action.

NICOLAS-FATHER: You can't disappoint Agustina, and all of us who believe in you. Do what you can, whatever it is, in congress, in the air, at the barricades . . . Keep it up, Ramón!

NOTARY: And for your son, the general, not a word, not a glance, as if he didn't exist. I can attest to that.

NICOLAS-FATHER: As far as I'm concerned . . . the chair could be empty.

NOTARY: That's an insult! A soldier sent by providence to put down the uprising in Asturias in a few months, and carry it off perfectly, mercilessly, as things should be done . . . And within two or three years he'll become the strongest man in the country . . . I can tell you what I'd do to his pig of a father . . . Court martial, jail, the firing squad . . . zas, zas, zas, and zas! And I'm no fascist.

NICOLAS-SON: Whenever you're ready, Notary.

(*The Notary begins to read.*)

NICOLAS-FATHER: Agustina. Agustina!

AGUSTINA: (*Entering.*) Can't you leave me alone a minute? What do you want now? I don't turn up in this scene.

NICOLAS-FATHER: Do you know what they're up to? What they're thinking while they listen to the reading of the will! A legal way to take from me what is mine!

AGUSTINA: You jump to conclusions, Nicolás. Surely you're mistaken.

(*Now the children have approached the table to sign and are surrounding the Notary.*)

NICOLAS-FATHER: But don't you see them? Huddled together like judges. Even Ramón! They and I. The law and those of us who're outside the law. We're the criminals, they're passing judgment on us.

AGUSTINA: Why? What harm did we ever do to anyone?

NICOLAS-FATHER: But they're going to hear from me, you bet they will!

AGUSTINA: Careful, Nicolás.

NICOLAS-FATHER: One moment! I want things to be clear. I have 40,000 pesetas, 40,000 miserable pesetas that are all I've managed to save in a lifetime. And they'll never go to you, but to the person who helped me save them one by one . . .

AGUSTINA: But what's the use of all this now?

NOTARY: No one's trying to take anything away from you.

PILAR-DAUGHTER: Though if you want my opinion, Papa, it doesn't seem nice for you to have that much stashed away while your wife and children were in need in El Ferrol.

NICOLAS-FATHER: Thirty years of work and doing without! Or do you think we didn't suffer hardships to send you your allowance every month?

PILAR-DAUGHTER: It was a situation that you chose of your own free will . . .

NICOLAS-FATHER: And has it never occurred to you that I must have had some very good reasons if I chose it and never regretted it?

NICOLAS-SON: You can't complain. Mama never even denied you the right to see your children.

NICOLAS-FATHER: Because for that a lawsuit would have been required, and a lot of dirty linen would have been aired.

RAMON: Please, Papa, that's enough.

NICOLAS-FATHER: No, it's not enough! Now let's talk about the house in El Ferrol. I don't intend to give it up now or ever. It belonged to my parents. It's mine . . . and therefore, Agustina's, for as long as she's at my side.

NICOLAS-SON: Do you intend to set up . . . that woman . . . there?

AGUSTINA: Why are you doing this, Nicolás, when we live so comfortably in our own little apartment?

NICOLAS-FATHER: Because I feel like it. Didn't Pilar occupy it as long as she lived?

PILAR-DAUGHTER: You're not going to start comparing her to Mama.

NICOLAS-FATHER: Of course not. I would be unfair to Agustina if I did. Because she's given me what I never got from the other one . . .

AGUSTINA: Nicolás, for God's sake, you're talking about their mother.

NICOLAS-FATHER: You've also given me a daughter, with as much right as they have to live in the house. Go on, tell them what you've had to put up with from me during these thirty years: coming home drunk after an all-night binge, shouting, fighting, I've even struck you, God forgive me. But you love me as I am with all my shortcomings, because you know very well that I love you too. That's the reason, and the only reason, that we go on sleeping in the same bed. Speak, tell them, for Christ's sake, tell them or you'll be sorry.

AGUSTINA: What do you want me to tell them?

NICOLAS-FATHER: Just that, what it takes to put up with my bad temper.

AGUSTINA: Don't exaggerate, I have a temper too. (*To the children.*) In El Ferrol, when I got to know your father, there were two classes of people . . . like everywhere, I guess . . . you, the gentlemen and ladies . . . and those of us who weren't. I still find it difficult not to address you servilely as my mother did her whole life . . . We were there to serve . . . and you, to show off your money and your pretty clothes. Do you know what made me fall in love with your father? It was because —as conceited as he always was—he was the only gentleman who didn't seem like one, or never tried to be one . . . and no one with him, no matter who, ever felt inferior.

NICOLAS-SON: And what does that have to do with anything?

AGUSTINA: A lot. Because all the other "gentlemen" were like purebred horses locked up in their narrow stables. (*To Nicolás-Father.*) But you couldn't be limited that way. You complained and kicked like a wild animal because you were too full of life to stay there. My accomplishment, and forgive my lack of modesty, was opening the doors for you.

PILAR-DAUGHTER: Papa, it's very late.

NICOLAS-SON: We've already taken too much of the Notary's time.

NICOLAS-FATHER: To hell with the Notary, the will, and time. Didn't you hear what she said? Are you all deaf?

RAMON: Papa, you've really said enough.

NICOLAS-FATHER: So, now you feel yourself one of them . . . Well, son, if you stand up for the people who elected you the way you do for your father, it's no wonder you're a failure in congress.

RAMON: Sometimes you're unbearable.

NICOLAS-SON: Silence! Francisco is going to speak to us.

NICOLAS-FATHER: Oh no! I refuse. I don't want to hear anything he has to

say. I'll cover my ears. Now I'm deaf. Deaf and blind. I don't want to
see any more of you. Out, all of you out. Everybody out! (*They exit.
Only Nicolás-Father and Agustina remain onstage.*) They're all alike, a
selfish, ambitious bunch . . .who're only out for themselves . . .
Power, money, popularity, and all the rest. I wish they'd all drop
dead! Forgive me, Agustina, but for the first time since I've lived with
you I'd like to die myself . . .

AGUSTINA: Well, it would be a shame, for we're having your favorite
tuna pie for dinner . . . and if that's not enough, I plan to wear my
new transparent nightgown, the one we bought at the flea-market. Just
wait till you see me! Besides, we still have the war to live through.

NICOLAS-FATHER: Another war?

AGUSTINA: I should say! This one is going to be the worst of all. Civil War.

NICOLAS-FATHER: No! I refuse.

AGUSTINA: Since when do storms frighten a sailor? Nicolás, will you let me
kiss you?

NICOLAS-FATHER: Have you ever needed my permission for anything? (*She
kisses him with great tenderness. During the kiss, a bugle is heard. A
Sergeant appears.*)

SERGEANT: Stop! What are you doing in a military zone?

NICOLAS-FATHER: We're here because we feel like being here.

SERGEANT: Your documents.

NICOLAS-FATHER: I'm not carrying any.

SERGEANT: Name?

NICOLAS-FATHER: What does it matter to you?

SERGEANT: Don't answer a sergeant of the Galician volunteers in that
manner! We're at war, a holy war to free our country from its enemies.

NICOLAS-FATHER: And we all know who they are.

SERGEANT: I don't like the way you're talking.

NICOLAS-FATHER: And I don't like the way you're talking, so we're equal.

SERGEANT: I'll take your declaration at headquarters. Let's go!

NICOLAS-FATHER: Agustina . . . the suitcase. (*Agustina picks up an old
satchel.*)

SERGEANT: What are you carrying there.

NICOLAS-FATHER: Don't answer him.

SERGEANT: It's got to be inspected. You, bring it here.

NICOLAS-FATHER: Keep calm.

AGUSTINA: Forgive me, but he frightens me more than your rifle. You
don't know how he can get over this confounded bag.

SERGEANT: Don't force me to fire.

AGUSTINA: I don't advise it. You'd find yourself in a real fix.

SERGEANT: I'm not afraid of anybody or anything!

AGUSTINA: Just remember what I said.

SERGEANT: All right. I'll trust you with the suitcase until we reach the guardhouse. Let's go.

SERGEANT: (*Writing his report.*) Two prisoners apprehended in suspicious behavior near the gun emplacements.

AGUSTINA: We were only kissing each other, sergeant.

SERGEANT: The new law forbids public indecency, and that includes kissing.

AGUSTINA: Christ!

SERGEANT: Where do you live?

NICOLAS-FATHER: In Madrid.

SERGEANT: An enemy zone.

NICOLAS-FATHER: We came to El Ferrol on a vacation before anybody was the enemy of anybody else . . . and the squabble caught us here.

SERGEANT: You're calling the most heroic action of all time a squabble! I could shoot you for that! The suitcase. (*Agustina looks at Nicolás-Father, and he motions to her to comply. the Sergeant opens it.*) Money. Where did you get this fortune?

NICOLAS-FATHER: From the bank.

AGUSTINA: You'd never imagine it, but we carry these 40,000 pesetas with us everywhere we go. A real trial! Watch out, Nicolás, I've said to him time and again, we're going to lose them, they'd be safer in a bank . . . but, yes indeed . . . He went and withdrew them.

SERGEANT: Why?

NICOLAS-FATHER: Because I don't trust them. Neither the bank or my sons.

SERGEANT: What do your sons do?

NICOLAS-FATHER: They all have different professions. But if I tell you, you won't believe me.

SERGEANT: Any more disrespect and I'll shoot you. You wouldn't have some kind of document to certify that this amount of money came from the bank, would you? Ah, you're in luck. Here's the receipt! It appears to be in order. Is this your name?

NICOLAS-FATHER: I suppose so.

SERGEANT: But, the way it is here? There's no mistake? (*Changing his attitude radically.*) At your orders. Won't you have a seat, please. Would you like something to drink? A cup of coffee, a glass of cognac?

AGUSTINA: Well . . .

NICOLAS-FATHER: No!

SERGEANT: A cigarette? A caramel for the lady? Here is your suitcase, sir. All closed up properly. With not a single bill missing, so that you can carry it back and forth, to your heart's content, wherever you wish . . . (*He hands it over to them.*) At your orders.

NICOLAS-FATHER: You take charge of it again, Agustina.

AGUSTINA: Not on your life. I'm not ready to get shot for that stupidity.

SERGEANT: Please, lady. What do you take us for?

AGUSTINA: You, of course, can pull your son out of your sleeve when the need arises.

NICOLAS-FATHER: You know very well that I am against everything he stands for, and I'll shout it to the world!

SERGEANT: Please, don't!

NICOLAS-FATHER: You don't know what's in store for you . . . You're not a very bright bunch, and he's going to walk off with all the power. God himself won't be able to take it away from him then.

SERGEANT: If you don't keep quiet, we'll have to detain you!

NICOLAS-FATHER: If you had any sense, you'd listen to what I'm saying. I've known him since he was born. Instead of making war, you'd stand up and demand peace and freedom. In fact, I'm prepared to contribute my 40,000 pesetas to such a noble cause.

SERGEANT: Are . . . you suggesting that I desert? Get out of here! Both of you! Kiss wherever you like and go where you please! But for God's sake just forget that you ever set foot in the headquarters of the Galician Volunteers.

*(The Sergeant exits. A bugle call.)*

NICOLAS-FATHER: You see, Agustina. There's no hope for this country.

*(The Servant Girl enters.)*

SERVANT: Sir, your son has arrived.

NICOLAS-FATHER: Ramón! Do you hear that? Ramón has finally come to see us.

RAMON: *(Appearing.)* Papa!

NICOLAS-FATHER: How wonderful to see you, son!

*(Ramón lifts him in the air as he embraces him. Then he will do the same with Agustina.)*

RAMON: Agustina, love of my life, I adore you. If you weren't my father's girl, I'd ask you to run off with me right now.

AGUSTINA: Ramón!

RAMON: How's your daughter? I've brought her candy and dresses and gifts from America. As soon as the war is over, we'll never be apart again. You are my real family!

NICOLAS-FATHER: But how have you come to fight against all that you believed in?

RAMON: It's only a strategem, Papa . . . to help our people from within. Like a time bomb . . . boom!

NICOLAS-FATHER: You're smart.

RAMON: It's all planned to the smallest detail. Only one thing is lacking. Money. 40,000 pesetas.

NICOLAS-FATHER: I have that much in this suitcase.

RAMON: I know. That's why I've come. Our cause needs your money.

NICOLAS-FATHER: It's yours.

RAMON: It's your life's savings!

NICOLAS-FATHER: Accept them.

RAMON: Your generosity is heroic, Papa. The revolution will be indebted to you for its triumph.

NICOLAS-FATHER: I'm only doing my duty.

RAMON: We'll name a street after you. And we'll decorate both of you. (*Miming the presentation.*) "For the world renown that you have achieved and your accomplishments, which history will remember." (*He embraces him with ceremony.*)

SERVANT: Sir, your son has arrived.

NICOLAS-SON: (*Appearing.*) I've come on an official mission.

NICOLAS-FATHER: (*To Ramon.*) Then you . . . you haven't really come to see me?

RAMON: I could never go to El Ferrol. You know that. It was impossible for me.

NICOLAS-FATHER: Then all this has been a dream?

RAMON: I was in charge of the air base in the Balearics, I couldn't leave the service. But I'll write you a long letter . . . one of these days. I promise!

NICOLAS-SON: I'm in a great hurry. I'm supposed to return to Burgos this evening.

RAMON: It was a pity. I would have liked to talk with you too . . . before dying.

NICOLAS-FATHER: I had so many things to ask you! What happened? Why did you let yourself get involved with them?

RAMON: Yes, Papa, we would have talked about a lot of things . . . I'm sorry.

(*Ramón exits. Nicolás-Father grabs his head with his hands.*)

AGUSTINA: Nicolás!

NICOLAS-SON: What's wrong, Papa?

(*Nicolás-Father lets his hands fall and he faces his son with great dignity.*)

NICOLAS-FATHER: He's come on a special mission, you heard him. Say what you have to say and go.

NICOLAS-SON: I'm very busy, Papa. I handle the affairs of the Secretary General.

NICOLAS-FATHER: Get to the point.

AGUSTINA: First I'll get you a glass of brandy.

NICOLAS-SON: Thank you, ma'am . . . I have here a long report of your activities of late. (*He takes some papers from a briefcase.*)

NICOLAS-FATHER: You mean you've been spying on me?

NICOLAS-SON: In August of '36, you induced a sergeant of the Galician Volunteers to desert after you had attracted attention by entering a military zone.

NICOLAS-FATHER: That squealer!

NICOLAS-SON: In April, when leaving a bullfight, you expounded your outlandish political theories by shouting.

NICOLAS-FATHER: Not liking dictatorships is hardly outlandish.

NICOLAS-SON: In February, in a local bank, you incited people to withdraw their accounts while standing on a counter from which you had to be forceably taken down by the Civil Guard.

NICOLAS-FATHER: Don't continue . . . I know what I'm doing.

NICOLAS-SON: I doubt it. In El Ferrol no one wants to come close to you for fear of being accused of sharing your opinions. I don't know whether you realize it but anyone else except you would have been brought up before the high court.

NICOLAS-FATHER: I'm ready to appear before your judges.

NICOLAS-SON: You know very well that's not possible. You are the father of the Supreme Head of State. It would create a scandal.

NICOLAS-FATHER: So what do you want of me? That I become a turncoat and lick your asses like the others.

NICOLAS-SON: Simply that you keep your mouth shut.

NICOLAS-FATHER: For that you'd have to cut out my tongue. The official interview is over. Goodbye.

NICOLAS-SON: Papa, be sensible.

NICOLAS-FATHER: The only sensible thing would be to punish you by making you stay under the sofa, the way I did when you were a boy.

AGUSTINA: I'm going to punish you myself, like a naughty child, if you don't watch out. You spend your life longing to see your children . . . and you treat him this way when he comes to see you.

NICOLAS-FATHER: With a file of accusations in his hand.

AGUSTINA: (*Referring to the brandy.*) You probably don't drink this anymore in Galicia.

NICOLAS-SON: Papa, let's put aside the official papers and talk frankly. Get used to the idea that Francisco is the leader of this country and will continue to be for many years.

NICOLAS-FATHER: You're to blame for that.

NICOLAS-SON: I've helped him all I could, I don't deny it.

NICOLAS-FATHER: Why?

NICOLAS-SON: Because he's my brother.

NICOLAS-FATHER: Some excuse.

NICOLAS-SON: And because Germany has demanded it as a condition for giving us their support.

NICOLAS-FATHER: Germany will end up starting another world war and will come out of it the loser.

NICOLAS-SON: I don't think so. But that's not the question. Right now their aid is indispensable for us. It's very late. I have to go.

AGUSTINA: Take the bottle with you. That way you'll remember your homeland and your father.

NICOLAS-SON: I'll come back very soon and we'll drink it up together.

NICOLAS-FATHER: When I write to Ramón, I'll tell him to come too to drink with us. He's capable of flying halfway across Spain for a drink. We'll have a great time.

NICOLAS-SON: Count on me. Goodbye, señora.

AGUSTINA: You've made your father happy with your visit . . . In spite of what he says, he loves you all deeply. Even the other one.

NICOLAS-FATHER: That's a lie. I hate him.

AGUSTINA: Don't believe him. It's the strict, hypocritical Spain, that has made him the way he is, that your father hates. Not him.

NICOLAS-FATHER: Take good care of yourself, son . . . And tell Ramón to be very careful. Not only in the air but on the ground. Especially on the ground. It won't be easy for them to forget his political past.

NICOLAS-SON: Everything is forgiven by higher order. Don't worry.

NICOLAS-FATHER: That one has all sorts of ways to neutralize annoyances . . . like Ramón and me.

NICOLAS-SON: Please, we've agreed that you'll keep your opinions to yourself.

NICOLAS-FATHER: I haven't agreed to anything.

NICOLAS-SON: It seems certain that they're going to send me to the embassy in Lisbon . . . You'll get news of me from there, and I'll send you a little amount each month.

NICOLAS-FATHER: You can forget about that. I don't need help from anyone.

NICOLAS-SON: You know that I'm not very good at writing letters . . .

NICOLAS-FATHER: I'll never accept anything from any of you.

NICOLAS-SON: All right, if you say so . . . Señora . . . I'll see you soon, Papa.

NICOLAS-FATHER: And don't forget. We have a bottle to finish off.

(*Nicolás-Son withdraws.*)

AGUSTINA: That was the last time he saw Nicolás. He would never see Ramón again or any of his children. (*To Nicolás-Father.*) Don't drink any more. Do you think I don't know?

NICOLAS-FATHER: Spy!

AGUSTINA: This happened in April or May, I don't remember too well . . . The year the war ended and we returned to Madrid. Of course, the old rascal kept on speaking his mind to his son and to the morning star, until he died in 1942. For all the good it did!

(*Nicolás-Father is stretched out motionless in the armchair.*)

PILAR-MOTHER: (*Appearing.*) Agustina, you have nothing else to do with this place. Take your nightdress, your perfumes and all your things and leave. My children and I will have the house on Maria Street scrubbed from top to bottom until it's what it used to be . . . before you came. Quickly!

AGUSTINA: You can't throw me out . . . the house is mine.

PILAR-MOTHER: Not any longer. The farce has ended at last.

AGUSTINA: What?

PILAR-MOTHER: Don't you understand? He used you and your daughter to insult the good people of El Ferrol whom he hated.

AGUSTINA: Nicolás, tell her it's not true.

PILAR-MOTHER: So you wanted to be my equal! To sit in my chair, to be respected, to act as if you were the mistress of the house . . . I realized that when you came as a girl to look for your mother, the seamstress. But at last everything is mine again!

AGUSTINA: You died many years ago.

PILAR-MOTHER: Marriage and family go beyond life and death. Divine Providence always ends up separating the wheat from the weeds . . . wives from servant girls.

AGUSTINA: I am not his servant.

PILAR-MOTHER: You are a nobody who exploits her body without shame.

AGUSTINA: My body is old now . . . and he is over eighty. And what have I gotten from all this, will you tell me? What the wife didn't want . . . what she cast aside like a worn out piece of clothing.

PILAR-MOTHER: Please, for heaven's sake!

AGUSTINA: I was naked the first time I gave myself to him, and I've gone on being naked and trusting in his arms.

PILAR-MOTHER: Hold your tongue.

AGUSTINA: I have not had brilliant sons, like you, and I haven't been an honorable woman . . . which in all modesty I could have been. And no law, divine or human, has been on my side.

PILAR-MOTHER: What about me? What was left for me, tell me that? What did you leave me? My loneliness, a bed that was too big for one person, and a few letters from my sons, always far away.

AGUSTINA: Then why did you let him leave? Did you love him?

PILAR-MOTHER: He was my husband . . .

AGUSTINA: You see? There's the difference. You loved him because you were supposed to love him. In my case . . . it was just the opposite.

PILAR-MOTHER: There are things more important than love.

AGUSTINA: I doubt it.

PILAR-MOTHER: Religion, family, convictions . . .

AGUSTINA: And you, señora . . . Didn't you ever think that you might be sacrificing your own life . . . that you were the victim of your own beliefs? Or of your own selfishness?

PILAR-MOTHER: God has given me the consolation of an untroubled conscience.

AGUSTINA: Why weren't you more generous to him? Haven't you ever regretted it?

PILAR-MOTHER: Never. Almost never . . . But soon they'll be burying his body beside mine and everything will finally be in place again.

AGUSTINA: They won't be able to separate us.

PILAR-MOTHER: You're mistaken. My son's laws have brought back decency and dignity to this country . . . Nothing is yours, it never has been. Now get out!

AGUSTINA: Nicolás, don't keep silent, answer her.

PILAR-MOTHER: He can't. Don't you see him? Now you're the one who is alone.

AGUSTINA: You won't be capable of treating me so shabbily.

PILAR-MOTHER: Don't go on this way. He's already one of ours.

AGUSTINA: He'll never be like you! You were born dead and you've gone around in mourning all your life! Do you hear her, Nicolás? Doesn't it make you want to laugh?

PILAR-MOTHER: Please . . .

AGUSTINA: Laugh hard as you've always laughed at everything. Do it for me.

PILAR-MOTHER: It's ridiculous.

AGUSTINA: Say something to me, for God's sake, wake up, speak, shout.

PILAR-MOTHER: You're wasting your breath. But do show a little more composure, if you can. (*She exits.*)

AGUSTINA: Nicolás . . . Nicolás! Please! I'm going to call the doctor.

NICOLAS-FATHER: No, don't do that, traitor! You know very well that I can't stand priests and doctors.

AGUSTINA: You're a shameless clown.

NICOLAS-FATHER: If you'd let me sleep in peace!

AGUSTINA: Oh, so you were sleeping, you rascal! Look, if you do that to me again, I'm leaving you for good.

NICOLAS-FATHER: Do you know how many of my old friends from El Ferrol are still around? Not a one. Only me. I feel like following them to the gathering place on the other side.

AGUSTINA: Don't you think we've had enough of your melodrama? (*Changing her tone and manner.*) This time it wasn't a joke, was it?

Stupid of me not to realize it! You used to make a joke of things so that I wouldn't see that you were afraid. Forgive me.

NICOLAS-FATHER: But it happened quickly. It was like fainting. For some time now everything has been mixed up here inside . . . Hand me the bottle. Wine curses everything. I'm going to lie down for a while.

AGUSTINA: Rest will do you good.

NICOLAS-FATHER: Be sure, when you lay me out, to put my dress uniform on me, with the silk sash and white gloves. Like the night at the dance pavilion. Do you remember the dance?

AGUSTINA: How could I forget? I was mad about you. Like all the girls in El Ferrol.

NICOLAS-FATHER: I'll have to settle for less this time. But above all, don't let anyone find out. Lock the door. Don't tell any of my children, and especially you know who. It would be grotesque if he set up a carnival with me as the attraction.

AGUSTINA: All right, but . . .

NICOLAS-FATHER: Ah, and one final thing . . . Let it be understood that when I die it's going to be by my choice. You can count on that!

AGUSTINA: Enough of that subject, for heaven's sake.

NICOLAS-FATHER: Hasn't your daughter returned yet?

AGUSTINA: It's early. Do you want me to call her?

NICOLAS-FATHER: I'll see her when she comes . . . A great girl your Pacita . . .

AGUSTINA: Her name's not Pacita.

NICOLAS-FATHER: Well, what difference does it make?

AGUSTINA: Nicolás . . . (*She goes over and kisses him several times.*)

NICOLAS-FATHER: (*Wiping his face.*) Uuf! You've always been a sloppy kisser. Yes, indeed! . . . Don't forget the wine. (*He exits.*)

AGUSTINA: (*Telephoning.*) Is that the shop? This is Agustina . . . Would you call my daughter to the phone? Child, your father . . . I think he's very sick. Come home quickly, and bring a doctor with you. And let the priest know too, just in case . . . I think he's slipping away from us!

(*Blackout. A doorbell keeps ringing. When the lights come up again, Agustina's Daughter appears. She is the same actress who plays the part of Pilar-Daughter. The Messenger also appears. Agustina remains onstage.*)

MESSENGER: I have another letter for you from Lisbon.

DAUGHTER: All right.

MESSENGER: Somebody has to sign the receipt, like every month.

DAUGHTER: Where?

MESSENGER: If you want, I'll do it for you. So it won't upset your father.

DAUGHTER: (*After signing.*) Is that all?

MESSENGER: That's all, I guess. Can you think of anything else?

DAUGHTER: Goodbye.

MESSENGER: Well then . . . I'll see you next month. Goodbye. (*He exits. The Daughter goes over to her mother.*)

DAUGHTER: The envelope . . .

AGUSTINA: This time we'll have to tear it up ourselves. (*She takes out the thousand pesetas and tears them into pieces.*) Throw the pieces in the toilet. And, as your father would say, pull the chain so that they'll go straight to the sewer. (*The Daughter exits. We hear the sound of the toilet being flushed. The Servant appears.*)

SERVANT: Señora, the neighbors are at the door. They've heard about the passing of Don Nicolás, and they want to pay their last respects.

AGUSTINA: Didn't I tell you that no one, not even God, is to come in? Is that clear?

SERVANT: I told them. And I double-locked the door, but they're still out there.

AGUSTINA: What do they want? Everybody in Madrid will know! Don't they understand that if people find out we're going to have serious problems? Make them go away! And leave us alone!

(*The Servant exits and returns almost immediately.*)

SERVANT: Señora . . . there's an official here with these papers for you.

AGUSTINA: I don't want to see him.

SERVANT: What do I do with these?

AGUSTINA: Give them back to him. I don't want to even touch them.

OFFICIAL: (*Entering.*) I'm sorry, señora. It's by higher order.

AGUSTINA: But why did you let him in, you fool?

SERVANT: He threatened me with a pistol.

OFFICIAL: I ask your pardon. But we can't disobey orders. Neither of us. I advise you to read them.

AGUSTINA: No.

OFFICIAL: I've been charged with the mission of removing the body of the Commandant to the Palace, to render him the honors due him by his rank and station. This is the document that authorizes the transferral.

AGUSTINA: Nobody is going to take him. Do you hear me? Do you all hear me? He's mine. For better or worse, alive or dead. And not you or a whole army can take him away from me.

OFFICIAL: I respect your feelings, señora . . . very understandable in these sad circumstances.

AGUSTINA: What do those papers say about my daughter and me?

OFFICIAL: Nothing. You're not even mentioned.

AGUSTINA: As if we didn't exist! As if we could be erased from his life just by signing a piece of paper.

OFFICIAL: Señora . . .

AGUSTINA: He can lock us both up, or kill us . . . but he'll never change the fact that we lived.

OFFICIAL: I urge you very sincerely not to leave this house under any pretext until after the funeral. I'll leave a guard at the door to protect you.

AGUSTINA: What does he have to protect us from?

OFFICIAL: It wouldn't be advisable, at this delicate moment, for you to do something rash that my superior doesn't wish and which I, personally, would deplore because of the grave consequences it could bring upon you.

AGUSTINA: Are you threatening us?

OFFICIAL: I'm only warning you for your own good.

AGUSTINA: And just what is our own good? Separating us from him and keeping us prisoners?

OFFICIAL: Only in seclusion for a few hours and treated with the courtesy that you deserve.

AGUSTINA: If he were alive, you wouldn't have dared . . . cowards!

DAUGHTER: I'll go to the Palace. They can't refuse to receive me.

OFFICIAL: That is impossible.

SERVANT: The street is full of police.

OFFICIAL: Don't be alarmed. It's a company of naval cadets, as is appropriate for the rank of the deceased.

AGUSTINA: Go get the bottle of wine, daughter . . . And you, lift up your skirt and show him the bloomers he used to like so much. Surely as soon as we tell him about the doctor and the priest he's going to wake up, protesting.

OFFICIAL: I'm sorry, señora. It's time.

AGUSTINA: You're not entering that room. You'll have to take me too and bury us together.

OFFICIAL: Señora, I beg you.

AGUSTINA: (*To the Servant.*) Open the door and let the neighbors in, the people in the street, the vendors . . . Let all his friends come in, the thousands of friends he made during his life . . . they will defend me.

(*Blackout. A spot comes up on Pilar-Daughter who has entered.*)

PILAR-DAUGHTER: My brother called me and he said to me: "Pilar, it looks like Papa may be dying. Are you going to look in on him?" I told him yes, that it was my duty. The moment I got there I told the girl: See that Agustina doesn't put in an appearance again because a priest is on the way, and I don't want him to see that . . . well, it's a simple matter of repentance . . . Tell her to go off somewhere and read . . . Steal the body? That's a lie the historians dreamed up. As if one goes around stealing bodies! We wrapped him in a blanket, put him in an ambulance . . . and drove off straight to the Palace! No, we never had any dealings with her. Not one of my brothers or I ever did anything about the financial situation they were in. The girl wasn't my father's child. Indeed! Another lie. She was Agustina's niece. And it's not true that she looked like me when I was her age. We were an ordinary middle-class family, no different from a lot of others. Normal you might say, except that certain circumstances of life made us a part of History. Nothing more.

(*Blackout. When the lights come up again, Nicolás-Father is seen seated centerstage, with his back to the audience. Immediately, Agustina and the Daughter appear.*)

NICOLAS-FATHER: What a dirty trick. The notice of my death on the fourth page so that no one will see it. The censors must have had something to do with that!

AGUSTINA: I don't say he didn't have his faults . . . what person doesn't? But living beside him was a celebration that never ended. Because he loved life, he adored life . . . and freedom above all else.

NICOLAS-FATHER: The body lay all night in the very room of the Palace where Alfonso XII died and which his widow, Queen Maria Christina, then turned into a chapel. What do you think of that? After treating me like dirt while I was alive, they put me in there as a joke. As if they didn't know that I was always a republican!

AGUSTINA: Drink . . . he liked to drink, there's no denying that. And women . . . But he was always loving to me.

NICOLAS-FATHER: Do you know who sent his condolences? Hitler! Doesn't that grab you where it hurts? (*Throwing down the newspaper.*) What a masquerade!

AGUSTINA: History, which won't spare the pages on his family, will hardly mention him . . . But with all his peculiarities, he was the best of them, I can tell you that.

(*Ambrosio, Nicolás-Son, Ramón, and Pilar-Mother begin to appear.*)

AMBROSIO: An eccentric!

NICOLAS-SON: Anyone else would have been tried for treason.

PILAR-MOTHER: A fake!

RAMON: A spunky little cock . . . though he couldn't fly.

DAUGHTER: I feel so proud of him! (*To Agustina.*) How did you meet him?

AGUSTINA: At a dance. Where else but at a dance would I meet a man like your father?

SERVANT: (*Entering and sitting near them.*) Go on, tell us.

AGUSTINA: In those days they used to play very gay music at the dances in El Ferrol . . . He would put on his dress uniform, with his sword, his silk sash, and his white gloves. He was very sure of himself, the most gallant and attractive man at the dance. Like a proud strutting cock.

SERVANT: Where is he?

DAUGHTER: Over there, in that box, don't look now.

AGUSTINA: With his glasses in his hand, he began to look in our direction, quite boldly, not caring what anyone might think.

DAUGHTER: He didn't take his eyes off us.

SERVANT: He's very good-looking.

AGUSTINA: Keep quiet. Don't get nervous. (*Nicolás-Father has stood up and is coming toward them. He is wearing a dress uniform, with a silk sash, and white gloves.*)

AGUSTINA: I wonder what he was thinking? That we'll fall into his arms like a bunch of ninnies the minute he comes over to us?

SERVANT: I will, of course.

DAUGHTER: So will I.

AGUSTINA: Well, keep him away from me.

NICOLAS-FATHER: (*Facing her.*) Señorita . . . may I have the honor of this waltz with you?

AGUSTINA: No . . . yes . . . I mean, of course you· may . . . (*Agustina stands up and almost collapses with emotion.*)

SERVANT: Be careful, your legs are shaking.

AGUSTINA: What do you expect? It is the brightest moment of my life!

(*They begin to dance.*)

NICOLAS-FATHER: You dance marvelously . . . Do you know what I'm wishing right now? That this waltz would last a lifetime . . .

AGUSTINA: And why not, Nicolás . . . Why not?

(*They dance blissfully. The lights slowly fade.*)

END

# Coronada and the Bull

## A Spanish Rhapsody

## Francisco Nieva

CORONADA AND THE BULL [Teatro María Guerrero, Madrid, 1982]
Directed by Francisco Nieva

CHARACTERS:
Coronada Luscious, oversized and unmarried
Zebedeo Luscious, her brother and the diabolical mayor
Mairena, a bitter gypsy
Father Cerezo, a compliant small-town parish priest
Melga and Dalga, spontaneous feminists
Marauña, a young man sentenced to be a bullfighter
The Town Voice, commentator and chorus
Blackbelly and Brutus, obedient officers of the law
The N.M., of the Mixed-Up Order
A photographer
The Thin Boy
The Fat Boy
The Pale Girl
The Foolish Girl
The Crippled Girl
Townspeople: indistinguishable, using interchangeable masks. Roles could be
    played by two women and three men. They act as the 200 inhabitants of the
    town.

The Place: *St. Blaise's Candlelight, a village high in the Bullchute mountains.*

The Time: *That of Spain in a preserve jar.*

# ACT ONE

*Mayor Zebedeo enters.*

ZEBEDEO: The time has come for the annual fiesta of St. Blaise's Candle-light, a vintage town with a long bloodline, of which I am mayor for life by my own popular demand. (*A hidden trumpet blast underscores this affirmation. The mayor kneels.*) Sir Governor of the province, with your cigar and shiny shoes; Most Reverend Bishop, draped with so many curtains; Honorable Captain of the leaden Civil Guard, I kneel before Your Divine Authorities, and with the ancient Chinese formality of the Spanish nobility I ask your permission to raise my voice in the required rejoicing. Let us begin the annual brouhaha in honor of St. Blaise, the saint of olive wood, the oldest and most holy in all the Bullchute mountains. (*He pulls Coronada out by one hand.*) This super-woman I've got with me is Coronada, my older sister, who's still not married—and not likely to be—because she's such a moose, and has the bad habit of being something of a domineering know-it-all. But I've got her well-trained and I'm teaching her how to be pleasant. Her dowry is three farmhouses and a chestnut grove. Curtsy, smart-ass, and cross yourself in front of these gentlemen. Don't give me anything to regret!

CORONADA: Zebedeo, you're embarrassing me. Forgive him, your lord-ships. He's got no education and he's very crude. You're wrong, dear brother, if you think you've got me well trained. I've been waiting for this moment with my heart and soul pounding madly, and now it's here. My time has finally come. Yes, I've come with you, but I've come to beg forgiveness for this candlelit town, and justice for all the outrages committed here . . .

ZEBEDEO: You traitor! You phony! You slippery-footed lizard! I'm not going to forgive you this time. Don't pay any attention to her, Your Universal Powers. I think she went crazy by not getting a man while she was ripe. She's overripe now. She's just a dizzy old maid.

CORONADA: (*Very hypocritically and with a show of modesty.*) No. What

I am is a woman with an aching heart, a heart that's been chilled by the sanctity of all the Theresas and Mary Margarets of our holy religion. Yes, gentlemen, I beg forgiveness—urgently—for all the beastly outrages committed in this town. Father Cerezo, our pastor, has been scared half to death so that he won't make any accusations from the pulpit, and they keep him content each year with three pouches of tobacco for St. Blaise, who doesn't even smoke. A bit of blackmail, as the novels say. And, on top of that, every bull that fights here carries many deaths upon its horns. We are condemned to be brave; here everyone fights the bulls. Little children fight the bulls from their grandmothers' arms, the musicians in the band fight the bulls because they love the beat of the big bass drum, widows fight the bulls to avenge their husbands. Our religion has become warped and there's no dignity left, no more human kindness. We're not Chinese any more! It's time to be finished with our traditional Spanish formalities, and to forget about the ancient customs we inherited from Hernán Cortez.

ZEBEDEO: Shut up, you old slob! I've got to stop this mad woman!

CORONADA: I'll say it again: there's no dignity here. Everything is ridicule and cruelty. We don't really celebrate during our fiesta, we just wallow in slime. Just to give you an idea of what goes on here, they put panties on the bulls so they'll die in ridicule and they braid their tails with burning pitch so that they'll light up the fiesta from behind.

ZEBEDEO: Officers, get over here! Blackbelly, Brutus, take her away, she's vilifying us and she'll be the death of us yet! What a stupid idea it was to bring you!

(*Enter Blackbelly and Brutus, two canine constables who throw themselves on Coronada and hold her back. But she manages to break loose by giving them a good shove.*)

CORONADA: Let me go! Don't touch me, you murderers! (*She steps further forward and proclaims.*) Oh, Most Highly Placed Gentlemen, august Caesars of the province, I raise the standard of my cause and in the name of the Three Dimensional Rights I beg you most urgently to intervene in this enormous and anti-human savagery. (*Her voice trembles passionately as she speaks.*) May the dove of light arrive to illuminate the world from under the petticoats of the Pope, and may Peace, who is so patient, finally exercise her authority and assign responsibilities! (*Progressively wilder.*) Glory to God in the Highest and may the enemies of the public good get lost!

ZEBEDEO: Where did you learn to give speeches and where are you hiding my manual? Beat it, you rotten rabble-rouser, those ideas could cost you your hide! Can't you see it? Look at the frown on the Chairman.

You want to destroy me but you're in for a let down. Look at the Supreme Mandators consulting among themselves, and scratching each other's head. Now I'm going to consult with the Governor. Most Honored Sir, what should I do with her? Can I cut off her head on the kitchen chopping block?

CORONADA: You'll never get permission for that from these most polite authorities. They are fathers of families, with their hearts in the right places, and they speak in a cultured manner; they are sons of their wives and they know all about Queen Isabella, and Carmen, and all the other famous Spanish women throughout history. I know how to behave, and how one addresses herself to the most highly placed so that they extend a gentlemanly hand.

ZEBEDEO: A hand with a big stick is what you deserve, and a swift condemnation to the shadows, like that bullfighter friend of yours.

CORONADA: Marauña? Why are you bringing him up? That's another story, Dear Sirs! Don't you know about Marauña? Well, he's a poor young man, the son of a dead widow who is kept perpetually imprisoned because he did something or other wrong—no one remembers what—and whom they free each year at this time because he once said that he'd rather be a bullfighter than a prisoner. And why do they give him this intermittent reprieve? Well, just so he'll mess up, and satisfy the spectators' desire to see disaster and bad luck. Poor boy! When the fiesta is over, he'll be returned to prison again, humiliated and aching all over. This is just one of many reasons why I'm begging you for justice. Remove my vicious brother from office. Why, just this winter alone he's killed two of my lovers and all their friends with his thundering shotgun. And then he complains that I'm not married!

ZEBEDEO: Traitor! You've just dug your own grave. If the Most Highly Placed Ones don't say anything, I'll condemn you myself. Hearing no objections, I'll proceed. (To the officers.) Lock that bitch up in the house I gave her as her dowry, with six balconies facing the street, all painted on, of course, so she'd never show her face again. I never want to see her again in my life! (Blackbelly and Brutus take her by force.)

CORONADA: (Struggling to get free.) You're flying in the face of all human and divine rights! I hope you don't think that I'm going to idle away the hours at home. I'll embroider all my complaints on a napkin that, whatever it takes, I'll make sure reaches the very table linen of St. Peter's in Rome. They appreciate Spanish women's handiwork there. You insensitive bastard! They're going to send me my own personal angel Gabriel, who's going to set you straight! (She is led away by the officers, at the same time that the bitter gypsy Mairena arrives.)

MAIRENA: Now you've gone and done it, Coronada!, you cold fish, you— you librarian! You won't be back to throw around your scorn and curses at this poor gypsy, who although she wanders around alone and free, is pure as the driven snow. Long live our shining mayor! Zebedeo, I'm very grateful to you for granting me sanctuary, and for your charity. You know that we gypsies kill the devils of the air and that we filter the atmosphere.

ZEBEDEO: This is Mairena, the gypsy who moved into our town so that she wouldn't keep wandering around like a soul in purgatory. I tolerate her because, even though she's mad, she's a patriot.

MAIRENA: And clean, which is saying a lot. Look at this white petticoat, without a single tear, and washed in jug water. Tell me if I'm not trustworthy. I'm what you might call a lovely weed. I'm a good-natured person that comes and goes forever dancing to the paso doble, and I give this dispirited town a cheerfulness that it never had until I wandered in, attracted by the fiesta of St. Blaise. And don't pay any attention to Coronada. This mayor is a loving father. He's honest . . . but boy it hasn't been easy . . . and so afraid of God that he won't even mention him. This sister of his, now there's a rotten apple for you.

*(Melga and Dalga, small-town feminists in their own way, enter unexpectedly. They wear veils and low-heeled shoes.)*

MELGA AND DALGA: We object, we object!

ZEBEDEO: Beat it, you ugly shrews! This must be the end of the world, the unleashing of an evil conspiracy!

MELGA: *(Introducing herself.)* I am Melga.

DALGA: I am Dalga.

MELGA AND DALGA: *(In unison.)* We are the ladies' committee, we are the comforters, the tender ones and the nuns of the house.

MELGA: We aren't the paso-doble type, like those that sow scandal throughout the world.

DALGA: And we're here to stand in for Coronada, our teacher, who will bare her very heart and soul to gain justice for all.

MAIRENA: How indecent. Mayor, you'd better make yourself tough, or your fiesta is finished.

ZEBEDEO: Tough? Tough isn't the word for what I'll be. What do you two want now?

MELGA: Hear what we've got to tell you. Or listen, if you think that's more democratical.

ZEBEDEO: Democ-ratical?? There'll be nothing radical here! Officers, get ready to skin these rabble-rousers alive if they don't get out of here immediately—and on the double! Hunting season for trouble-making women is now open! *(The officers enter.)* Ah, there you are! Well, Blackbelly, you get rid of Melga and you, Brutus, get rid of Dalga. Get them out of town and lose this pair of Thumbelinas in the woods.

MELGA: They're going to get rid of us?

DALGA: (*With salacious subtlety.*) They're going to lose us? They must be joking . . .

MELGA: It would be easier for them to put the walls of Jericho back together by snapping their fingers. What do they think they're going to do? They'll never penetrate the defenses of our chastity belts, our protectors against all evil. So, let them test their bravery and see just how much it's worth. The rock will split open, and we'll turn into pillars of salt, or maybe even more exemplary things . . .

DALGA: Then they'll be so sorry that they'll wish they hadn't.

ZEBEDEO: Why would they wish they hadn't if I don't order them to? I'm sick of all your revolutionary women's nonsense! Get them! Tear their honor into pieces!

MELGA: Scoundrel! Just let him try to set his dogs on Melga! (*She leaves without warning.*)

DALGA: Try setting your dogs on Dalga! (*She escapes, and the officers follow the two of them.*)

MAIRENA: Look at this! They're driving this man out of his mind. It's no wonder he acts a little like Herod now and then. Your Honorable Authorities should understand that. You don't have to be suspicious of him.

ZEBEDEO: (*Less resolutely.*) Shut up, Mairena, your tongue is a perpetual motion machine.

MAIRENA: But it's clean, just like the bottom of my skirt. Look at my tongue, gentlemen of the jury, and tell me if it isn't a little rose petal. (*She sticks it out.*)

ZEBEDEO: Great Balls of Fire! Shut up, or I'll lock you up too! If these Divine Authorities are in agreement, there's nothing left but to start the fiesta. Let's give the signal.

(*He fires a pistol taken from the folds of his sash. All the townspeople, squalid and sad, led by Father Cerezo, now appear. Whistles and bells, but feeble and faint. Zebedeo joins the group with a festive air suited to the occasion, but casts suspicious glances at his flock. An old-time photographer, with an unstable, junky, old-fashioned camera covered with black cloth, is trying to capture them on his photographic plate. The magnesium, however, is insufficient to the task and goes up in a puff of black smoke. The poor photographer, all blackened, and coughing, removes his head from under the cloth.*)

PHOTOGRAPHER: This is the third one that's gone out on us. Father Cerezo, since you haven't blessed the magnesium, the photographs won't come out for us this year. And the plates are costing our Supreme Municipality five pesetas apiece.

ZEBEDEO: Last year's will do perfectly well. We'll just have a less expensive tradition. Father Cerezo, take these three pouches of tobacco for St. Blaise, and burn them parsimoniously.

DON CEREZO: Thank you, my son. May God reward you in matches, and may he stock the hills this year, and may the mornings you greet with rifle shots be many. (*Confidentially.*) But don't go around liquidating all of Coronada's lovers, or that woman's fangs are going to tear you apart.

ZEBEDEO: What are you insinuating, Father Cerezo? Look, if I give the word, St. Blaise will smoke no more. (*He tries to snatch the donation away.*)

DON CEREZO: (*Pocketing it.*) My son, what a violent temper you have! Anyhow, you know that my advice only holds until you get the bishop to overrule me.

MAIRENA: (*To the photographer, wiggling her hips.*) Miguel, take a picture of me in motion, and make sure it captures my very soul. Let them hear me laughing at Coronada, without a man and still growing, the poor dear.

ZEBEDEO: Great Balls of Fire! Let's not lose any more time. Bring the bullchute for the gentlemen to see; it's time to put it to use again.

(*The boys, a little livelier, bring out the ingenious contraption called a bullchute. It is a tunnel of dirty canvas held up by hoops, through which the bulls of the meadow are served to the consumer.*)

TOWNSPEOPLE: Long live the bullchute! Viva!

TOWN VOICE: Long live the dark fiesta and the town of St. Blaise's Candlelight!

TOWNSPEOPLE: Viva! Long live our rich Zebedeo! Viva!

TOWN VOICE: Long live blood pudding and pickled bullshit!

TOWNSPEOPLE: Viva!

ZEBEDEO: (*Pointing to the bullchute.*) This is our most typical typicality that we've been waiting to show you. Of all our antiquities, this is our most modern, and it's the envy of all the surrounding villages. Through this long bullpen, all the way from their grazing land, come the bulls of death, unmolested, to the smell of tragedy. A reporter told us that it was the "cat's meow" of Spain, the pipeline of fear . . . Listen, and see if you don't hear footsteps that make your hair stand on end. And bring Marauña; I want to see him and give him a chance to cleanse his honor by putting on a good show for us! (*The officers, defeated and worn out, enter.*) Hey! You're back already? What did you do with those two runaways?

BLACKBELLY: Most Honored Mayor, despite your summary orders there's been a miracle.

ZEBEDEO: A miracle? A miracle against me! Explain yourself, Blackbelly, or I swear I'll tear off your badge.

BLACKBELLY: A miracle that scared us so much that it proved that even officers of the law can get goose-bumps.

ZEBEDEO: Everything's coming out backwards today. Someone's trying to play a nasty trick on us. Father Cerezo, you've got such an honest face, could it be you?

DON CEREZO: Me? God spare me! I have nothing to do with miracles. Miracles happen by themselves; they're scientific.

MAIRENA: It must be a trick of St. Blaise, to show himself off on his feast day. But why is he being so good to those two useless nobodies?

ZEBEDEO: What happened?

BLACKBELLY: Well, to sum it all up, and without beating around the bush, they got away from us by jumping a barrier more than seven feet high, as if they had been carried away in the air. What a leap!

BRUTUS: A miracle! And afterwards, they began to sing, with sweet, chirping voices:

Dear Saint Martha, sewing away,

Thank you for your help today.

And they accompanied the verse with the sound of two castanets that I'm sure they didn't have before.

ZEBEDEO: That's not a miracle or anything, and you two are a pair of dumb bunnies. They must have got the castanets from a tree. They grow the castanet tree just over the town line. Those are Coronada's lands.

MAIRENA: St. Martha? So it wasn't St. Blaise? They've jumped the fence of another parish, and they've brought off their miracle on foreign soil? Don't they have any shame?

DON CEREZO: All we can say is that this is an uncertain case. But it's been such a long time that we haven't had any miracles. . . ! All that talk in the pharmacy has been harmful to them.

ZEBEDEO: Come on, you good-for-nothing bastards, and bring the prisoner from his jail cell. By now he ought to be ready to meet his fate.

(*The townspeople perk up fatalistically, getting wind of the tragedy. The two officers go to get the prisoner. The Town Voice breaks into a mournful saeta merged into a cheerful jota.*)

TOWN VOICE:

To the bloody red spot

That won't blot.

To the sail black as night

Out of sight.

Past the World's end I'll head

With my crew, good as dead.

To eternal jail
Whether
Head or tail.
Jesus Lord
Please
Go our bail.
Long live the dead Christ and the rescued Marauña!
EVERYONE: Vivaaa!

*(They bring in Marauña, a wasted youth wearing a bullfighter's outfit that is a complete travesty. His hands are tied together with a short cord, and there is a noose around his neck, held by the officers. He comes to center stage, greets those present, and then, on his knees, lowers his head before the audience.)*

MAIRENA: Look at the tragedy of a young man in jail, with a chest that is nothing but a bag of bones. Tell us your troubles, Marauña, and start stirring compassion. We're very anxious to shed a tear.

MARAUNA: *(Casting his eyes upwards.)* I come to offer my very breath—labored as it is—to Your Authoritarian Highnesses. Here you see Marauña, dragged down by shame, to dedicate to you whatever beast it's my luck to draw, even if—as in past years—you've decided to make matters worse by cruelly attaching a barber's razor to both of his horns. And because of that, if I'm to die, I want the dedication I make today to be heard. Afterwards, may ashes rain upon Spain. I dedicate this effort to the tranquil sea, which my eyes have never seen; to the starry eyes of Mary Most Holy, to my trip to the heavens, and to the bubble bath that I'll finally give myself there. And, in the end, I'll die like a humble chicken shit, to please the crowd, and to cleanse myself for having been born gutless. If only I had wings!

MAIRENA: Yes, that's what bullfighters need the most. And that's all you would have needed, my boy, to emigrate to the Americas.

ZEBEDEO: Death to the pessimists! We got you out of prison for that toast of gloom and doom? Goddam it!

DON CEREZO: Calm down, Zebedeo, and be grateful to this abandoned child who has touched our hearts, and who has provided such instructive entertainment for the people.

MAIRENA: And how! My God, what heroism! Why don't we all agree to show him some compassion and shed a few tears over his fate. *(On the contrary, the townspeople laugh sarcastically.)*

TOWN VOICE: Let's see if you screw up again this time, Marauña. You know if you don't die you'll go right back to jail. Maybe you should take advantage of the opportunity.

MARAUNA: You're the one who should take advantage of it, shithead.

What a shame I don't know Latin, or I could get away with calling you a real son of a bitch.

ZEBEDEO: Shut up! Bring on the prisoner. You two, be careful that the rope doesn't come off. If it comes loose, he might forget his manners and run the hell out of here.

BLACKBELLY: (*With his ear to the end of the bullchute.*) Be careful, Your Honor! I think I hear hoofbeats. If we untie the knot, a wild and crazy beast will come running out of this chute.

ZEBEDEO: He's come right on time. Let him out, and we'll see the ugly face of the unexpected. Let the bullfight begin. You'll be his host, Marauña. And all the rest of you, if you can, climb up and sit high on the stairways to the sky. And another piece of advice, my children: if you run, you'd better not fall. (*The townspeople run and shout, and find places to hide behind, or climb to safe heights, leaving a small area for the bullfight.*)

TOWN VOICE:
Let the hollow bell toll
Damning every conformer
Dearest Death, she is cold
With my cape I will warm her.
Silence! and say: Amen.
And then
On her stretcher, supine
Nursed on soup mixed with wine,
After traveling through Spain
May she once again reign.
Don't let them kill our Death,
Neighbors.
Everyone hold your breath!

BRUTUS: Should I untie the knot?

ZEBEDEO: On with it, bring on the thunder! Father Cerezo, accompany me to the balcony.

DON CEREZO: I'm right behind you. There's nothing better about a bull-fight than to taste the pleasure of getting the hell out of the way.

MAIRENA: Marauña, remember your mother, who must be spinning wool with Saint Anne and can pray for you.

(*Brutus has untied the knot and hidden behind the chute. Some sort of form begins to take shape in the chute. A rumbling in the chute stops as quickly as it began.*)

BRUTUS: (*Again showing his pale white countenance.*) I think the big monster got lazy and won't come out. (*He gives the form a kick and, seeing that it doesn't budge, harasses it with the point of a knife.*) Hey, toro! Maybe this will cheer him up a little . . . He's coming! (*Very anxious anticipation. The N.M., dressed in black trailing robes, enters through the chute. An indescribable prophet whose gentle manners contrast with a long graying beard. Astonished, all the townspeople climb down from their hiding places. Like a gentle wave, they approach the N.M. with curiosity.*)

N.M.: Brothers and sisters, stop!

MARAUNA: It's got to be either my pardon or St. Blaise!

MAIRENA: Gypsy virgin! This man's got real presence! Demands respect.

ZEBEDEO: (*Coming closer.*) Hey! Who are you? And why did you take that passage? That's only for bulls, damn it!

DON CEREZO: (*Amazed and scratching his head.*) My Lord, what a sight! There's got to be a sacred mystery here. Although it looks like a poor imitation of St. Veronica, it could also be our own dear St. Blaise.

N.M.: (*With exemplary gentleness.*) Jabed like a bull? Is that how I'm received in this human wasteland? Is this the way to greet a pilgrim who has lost his way? Oh, St. Blaise's Candlelight, you darkened village high on this menacing cliffside . . . (*Greeting them.*) Most noble gentlemen of the rooftops, Honorable Mayor and Sir Pastor: I am, if you would like to know, the Nun Man, of the Mixed-Up Order, who, traveling all the paths around here, was fulfilling my mission and chasing a vixen that had taken my bread in her mouth.

MAIRENA: My God, a man nun chasing a vixen! It's a funny world.

ZEBEDEO: (*Peeved and frowning.*) There must be an emergency exit from that passageway, because we didn't see any vixens. Everything's going to come out backwards this year! And what about my bull?

DON CEREZO: Don't be impatient, Zebedeo, he may have come from the altars of heaven. At least he's not just any old body. Nobody we know would go for a walk in an outfit as sacred as that.

MARAUNA: (*Throwing himself at the feet of the N.M.*) Reverend Father and Mother, wasn't it my pardon that you were bringing?

N.M.: Your pardon? And who's going to pardon me? Oh, Jesus Mary! No, my son, the world is more than lost.

DON CEREZO: Will Your Reverence tell us what in the world this Mixed-Up Order is? I've never heard of it?

N.M.: Father Cerezo, sharpen your eyes, and look at me closely. Take your time. Don't you recognize me? I'm the son of Juanita the Face-Smasher and that smuggler that they used to call Slippery González. You used to take me on your knees and treat me very kindly. Of course that was long before I took the veil.

DON CEREZO: (*Scandalized.*) I've had a male nun on my lap? (*He observes the N.M. for a while.*) Son of a gun, I know who you are. Weren't you that little boy with lots of freckles like lentils all over his face, who knew how to hemstitch before he knew how to read, and who put gold paint on the hens? Well, I'll be darned! You turned out to be quite a whim of nature, and you were almost the death of your mother. It was very diplomatic of you to leave town.

N.M.: Yes, I am she. I grew up with so many headaches and so much heart-sickness and so eager to exceed the speed of time that I went to Rome to look for help. And I found it, Father Cerezo. Cardinal Malaspina himself, amethyst ring and all, led me to the Mixed-Up Order. And from there I emerged, as much a rustic Mario Magdalene as a wandering priestess, like those that in their madness, go around taming the world. Oh, Jesus Mary!

MAIRENA: (*Imbued with eschatological faith.*) Finally! A saint and a man who is a trustworthy Mother Superior has arrived! (*Kneeling before him.*) Save me from this life, Oh Bearded Mother, and tell me why I'm forced to live like a dog.

TOWN VOICE: (*Also filled with hope.*)
A pilgrim has joined us.
Though rare he appears,
He'll lessen our fears
And he knows where to point us.
Neighbors, lend him your ears!
Neighbors, pray he'll anoint us!

DON CEREZO: Quiet! Dearest Mother of the Desert, are you sure Your Reverence hasn't come to warn us about some displeasure that we've caused the Vatican, perhaps by not doing something we were supposed to?

ZEBEDEO: Come on! We haven't done anything wrong. I can see it now: Coronada, all this trouble has been caused by you and your Friends of St. Martha!

MARAUNA: Oh dearest mother-in-law! Don't you have any news about a mixed-up prison where I can get rid of this macho commitment to kill bulls with a noose around my neck?

ZEBEDEO: Marauña, if you lose your courage I'll have you hanged. This is revolution, the coming of the Antichrist! The sky is falling! Father Cerezo, don't try to tell me that God approves of these annoyances. I don't want any more new ideas in my town. Therefore, Mother and Esteemed Sir, you will return to your Mixed-Up Order through the same tube from whence you came, because we don't want any more nonsense around here.

N.M.: Jesus Mary! Are you going to steer me away from my sacred course? I'm bringing you an urgent message. Reconciliation above all.

ZEBEDEO: There's no need to reconcile anything here. Out—and make it snappy!

DON CEREZO: Zebedeo Luscious, control yourself, and don't overstep your authority.

ZEBEDEO: Don't worry. No matter how far I go I never overstep it! This is my town! Get out of here! Blackbelly, Brutus, I want you to show our prophet the way . . . out of here! Now!

MAIRENA: Oh, no! That's spitting right in Heaven's eye!

MARAUNA: Motherly father, don't leave us without taking us out of our misery!

TOWN VOICE:
They're casting out the Ill-Discerned
Forever, through our chute!
This town from now on will be spurned,
Our danger is acute!
Our punishment is richly earned!

DON CEREZO: Calm down, Zebedeo, and at least ask the Highly Placed Ones permission to throw him out. Be careful, if you overstep your authority as mayor, you may be forging your own downfall.

ZEBEDEO: (Making a visor of his hand in order to see more clearly.) Damn the dried up sea! Can't you see that they've gone? They've cleared out of here, feeling sorry for us, to travel the roads far from this bramble patch without a fiesta. What an impossible turn of events.

DON CEREZO: This day has turned out so badly, there's no need to prolong it. The day was bound to come when the perennial bull wouldn't show up.

ZEBEDEO: And that in its place an arrogant man nun would come to bother us? Well I won't stand for it!

DON CEREZO: Counterorders from heaven and a change of destiny. If you resist, you'll pay through the nose, that's for sure.

ZEBEDEO: Keep my nose—and your nose—out of this! I don't take counterorders from anyone! And nobody's going to embarrass me! The Nun Man is leaving this town or I'll kill him with my own hands. Worthless cops! And to think that I raised you like a mother without having to be a Mother Superior!

N.M.: There's no need to speak any more. No one is a prophet in his own country, brothers and sisters! The Mixed-Up Order has the admirable policy of resigning itself humbly in the face of adversity in this cruel world. Your disillusionment is yet to come. I'll bless this assembly, and I'll go, but I do announce, with my barometric finger, the arrival of bad times for this heartless town; and I'll go back to where I came from, repeating the sentence that the good thief directed to his dissolute companion: He who laughs last laughs best. (The N.M. retreats through the tube, full of dignity, and leaves the townspeople submerged in uncertain darkness. The darkness increases and the wind whistles occasionally.)

ZEBEDEO: How can you be so ungrateful! If you don't stop sulking I won't have any choice but to shoot myself! Did you hear me? (Their silence *answers him eloquently enough.*)

DON CEREZO: I need my scarf. (*He puts it on.*) It's windy. These high-land regions have cold hearts because of the lack of roads and poor communications.

ZEBEDEO: And with our current lack of merriment we're disgracing our-selves more and more.

MAIRENA: (*Who has been seated on the ground, looking into celestial infi-nity.*) When I was a young girl, I came here alone, running over the en-tire world chasing a black butterfly, and now I can't even find the road back to Granada. The tourists must have obliterated it. Nobody here understands our gypsy rhythms. They think they can cure everything with all their sissy tangos and fandangos.

ZEBEDEO: (*Pacing restlessly back and forth.*) Coronada is involved in all of this. She and her troop of harpies.

MARAUNA: (*Also sitting on the ground, looking more defeated than ever.*) Boys, loosen the noose a little, there'll be another chance. There'll always be time to die, goddam it! (*Two shadows from among the townspeople loosen the noose.*) What a clear sky, Dear Lord of the Martyrs!

DON CEREZO: Clear and tranquil. The evening star is up there winking at us. When I was a little boy we could hardly bear its brightness. What explosions on fiesta days! They could be heard from here, and look how far we are.

MAIRENA: This is the shivering hour. This is the time when the rosemary begins to nod its head, when the shadows begin to tickle it. God, how sad! I don't know what to think.

DON CEREZO: (*Yawns.*) Oh, Spain, how poorly you take care of your fiestas these days!

MAIRENA: You said it, Father Cerezo. We won't see anything come through that tube again. Not even a lousy Sunday family outing. Not even the sound of a whistle. What a silence!

TOWN VOICE: It's a silence of emigration. The Moors and the Christians have gone together to New York. And now, on top of all this, the Nun Man will wander alone among these barren plains, with neither bread nor assistance. Tonight he'll sup on a cup of river water.

DON CEREZO: That's life. And God, who giveth and taketh away, has even taken away the desire to play checkers.

MAIRENA: That game's gotten a little too simple for the anxieties of this modern world.

DON CEREZO: Well, if I thought St. Blaise wouldn't complain, I'd kill some time by smoking some of his tobacco.

(*The large shadow of the mayor stands out threateningly. He raises his pistol and fires into the air. The townspeople move around in unrecognizable clusters. From now on, everything occurs in an ambience of sinister fantasy.)*

ZEBEDEO: Great Balls of Fire! Isn't there anyone here with the guts to challenge this evil fate that's threatening us?

MAIRENA: Oh, my dark-eyed gypsy virgin, he's fired his pistol! Now there'll be trouble for sure!

MARAUNA: Well, even if the earth opens and swallows us, we won't lose a thing. And on top of that, I'll be out of prison. *(Another shot.)*

DON CEREZO: My God, Zebedeo! You're going to make the world stand still, and we'll all fall into one another from the jolt. *(A bell tolls.)* Listen! That bell is ringing by itself! Look—there's the bell ringer! It must be announcing a disaster. *(The two officers, united in an embrace, let out a blood-curdling howl.)* How far have we sunk, that officers howl. You're turning them into wolves with your bad example. Now what are we going to do to get out of this mess?

TOWN VOICE: Father, when everything is going wrong, when the crops are lost, and when the whole town is afraid, there's only one thing we can do . . .

DON CEREZO: What's that? Not that it's going to do us any good, but tell us anyway.

TOWN VOICE: Well, it's a remedy from ancient times, and it's so reliable, that sometimes it works and other times it doesn't.

DON CEREZO: Out with it, my son.

TOWN VOICE: Well . . . We perform the . . . Dance of Darkness.

DON CEREZO: May God have mercy on us! It's been a long time since anyone's performed that incredibly wicked dance. I'm getting the shivers already.

ZEBEDEO: Aha! I knew we wouldn't be lost! Dance! Dance, and don't stop! There's no greater defiance, no greater audacity in these mountains, than the infamous dance of darkness. Come on, neighbors! Go to it! Aha! I can hear guitar strumming already.

DON CEREZO: That dance was condemned for being too fanatic! Zebedeo, that dance is poisonous! If you agree to it, may God have mercy on your soul!

ZEBEDEO: Dance, damn it! Or I'll fire into the crowd of you! Get a move on!

*(The sound of a horn and the rhythm of the bass string of a guitar. Guitar strumming. Muffled stamping of feet. The dance of darkness, a menacing jota, begins. Everything is structured into a procession of shadows and inexplicable lightning flashes.)*

TOWN VOICE:
> Where have you taken my lungs and my liver
> That you stole from my grave by the deep black river?
> (*Pause and drumroll.*)
> I've eaten entire your lungs and your liver
> That I stole from your grave by the deep black river.
>
> My razor-edged and trusted knife
> Lost in your flesh, eternally.
> All wine now tastes like blood to me
> And heaven has lost its life.
>
> Where have you taken my lungs and my liver
> That you stole from my grave by the deep black river?
> (*Pause and drumroll.*)
> I sowed the land, with your lungs and your liver,
> Of the sad, dark mountains by the deep black river.

(*Total darkness. The bellowing of a bull is heard.*)

BRUTUS: The bull! Just in the nick of time!

DON CEREZO: The bull! There you have the tragedy, Zebedeo. In this darkness, the beast won't know which one of us is the bullfighter. That's how you've unleashed the punishment for our guilt. A late night bullfight that surprises us without even the stub of a candle at our disposal.

MAIRENA: The bull! Dearest St. Blaise, hold your candle high and see how pale we are!

TOWN VOICE: Did they say the bull? (*Kneeling in front of the group of the most cowardly.*)

> Oh land where death is near
> I want to see you here
> Neighbor,
> Return the thread
> Of life. Seal
> Your fate,
> No time to wait!
> Let's follow the worms.
> Oh, God!

BLACKBELLY: The bull! Tell him to stop, good mayor. That beast will trample us like we were nothing! (*A gunshot in the shadows.*)

ZEBEDEO: What the hell. . . ? Who pulled the trigger on me? You've brought on your own ruination. I'm out of ammunition. We're going to fall all over each other and end up in hell. Take out your knives! Start walking, and keep stabbing into the night until you get home!

*(The clusters of townspeople, bubbling with excitement, penetrate more and more into the darkness. Now we can see the N.M. with Melga and Dalga, who have taken shelter under his robe, crouching very cautiously.)*

N.M.: Shh! Shh! With the blackness of my robe, and the help of the night, those uncivilized beasts will never find us. They must have mistaken us for the bull. Shh! Shh!

MELGA: Oh, Holy Bearded Mother, what will we do if they recognize us? My heart's pounding.

DALGA: Quiet, sister, and watch your step, because you're bringing up the rear. Take it easy, and keep the faith; this virginal cloak will get us across the frontier of danger.

N.M.: And all the prophecies will be fulfilled against this evil rabble, my beloved daughters.

DALGA: To help us, God has destroyed their rotten rowdy celebration and brought night upon this pancake we call Castile.

N.M.: We are the final bull. After the revelation and the purging of consciences, there will be new, and more suitable, fiestas.

DALGA: And more refined. Perhaps the return of the rigadoon and the minuet.

MELGA: *(Stumbling over a form in the darkness.)* Oh my God! It's alive! We're lost! *(Marauna, on the ground, can now be seen.)*

MARAUNA: Don't shout. It's Marauña, Most Ladylike Father. Help me, give me shelter, too. Help me escape from prison and bullfighting. I ask you in the name of Saint Veronica and her purple cape.

N.M.: My son, you here?

MARAUNA: I'm not sure if I ran away or if they abandoned me in the confusion. But there is a real bull; I've seen him, and he's right around here somewhere! If we don't get the hell out of here, he's likely to attack us from out of nowhere. Hurry! I know a hole in the mountainside that'll take us all the way to China.

N.M.: We don't have to go that far. Those are old wives' tales. Join us and we'll go to Coronada's house. Don't be afraid. Our path will be carpeted with all the palms of heaven. *(He straightens up suddenly and points to the black heavens.)* Spain belongs to me! God and I make thirteen!

*(Blackout and a whirlwind of sound. The light comes up on Coronada's bedroom. Grim, like the only officiant at a secret ritual, the poor giantess without a man commits all of her flesh and, trembling with fury and sensuality, raises her arms to invoke the darkest powers.)*

CORONADA: Ignorant Zebedeo, on our parents' grave I swear, and by the goat's milk that we both shared from the same hairy breast, that I will avenge myself someday. You don't know the half of what your sister Coronada is in the privacy of her bedroom. I was born both Spanish, and a witch, so I wouldn't be left out of the ranks of the great celebration that takes place every night, without your knowing it, in the realm of my fantasy. Do you really believe that I'm a fool? As a little girl, when I sucked my thumb, I was already sucking the evil, bubbling bad blood that rose from my feet, and putting on an innocent face. Hardly have I closed the door, and I am someone that scares even herself, and there are words that come out of me like naked acrobats cursing on their trapeze. (*Defiant and Bacchic.*) Eye that looks from above, eye that looks from below, look at me now and see just what Coronada is capable of when she begins her nightly, endless ritual.

(*She begins to disrobe. She strips off her negligee, and is seen to be wearing stockings with a garter belt and a pair of sleazily wicked lace panties; a bra and a slip of dismal, silvery satin. She walks to an old gramophone from which she takes a record that she raises with a ritual air. Bewitched by her imprisoned instincts, she turns the record into a Eucharistic object of a black mass.*)

Black wafer that reflects, pancake that shouts, I consecrate you to the itching and the scratching and the hustle and bustle in my belly. Give me all of your fire and inflame this frenzied dream that possesses me. (*She places the record on the turntable and turns on the record player.*)

> Though Heaven may hold you,
> Carlos Gardel
> I'll dance your tangos
> To satisfy Hell!

(*The sound of the vinegary accordion music seems very rarified. Gardel suffers from the other world, while Coronada presents herself shamelessly to an imaginary audience.*)

This is where I'd like you to be, Most Illustrious Highly-Placed Ones, gazing on the true woman, who swings her hips and crushes all modesty when she walks. Look at this circus of flesh where the woman's lion eats the trapeze artist alive. Watch me dance the tango, chewing on the devil's tail while he couples with me within . . . (*She opens a window and looks out, receiving the light of the moon.*)

> Beautiful moon
> That shines on my breast
> Turn me into
> Another Mae West!

(*She sighs under the pale shower of moonlight. Another inspiration overtakes her and she goes to her dressing table.*) Now to get in my drawers. (*She paints herself outrageously.*) Oh, how my hands are trembling! How good this make-up feels! Yes, yes, Coronada, hold your lips up to shame and cover yourself with beauty marks that will gnaw away at you throughout the night. How stunning and sexy you are! (*She takes down a large Spanish shawl and she puts it on like a picture on a theatre poster.*) And now on to the solemn ritual and to the adoration of the Most Holy Razzamatazz! (*She caresses herself sensuously from side to side and she lowers herself to the floor in the back and forth movements of the possessed.*) So indecently wrapped in this shawl, I give myself to this delicious frenzy with the speed of the great European express trains. Oh God, I'm hot . . . I'm so hot . . . I'm turning into a tunnel of fire and I'm racing all through my body without a stop until I collapse into the mirror. (*She holds a hand mirror in which she begins to examine herself for very choice details.*) Mirror with the world behind you, speak to me and I'll answer you. Why are you silent? (*Pause.*) Well, if you don't want to say anything, stick your blade on my tongue, and make it drip into an unending kiss. Kiss me, my lawless king, my shameless thing.

(*The music on the gramophone stops.*)

What awful silence! Break this silence, you wicked mirror, or I'll shatter you! (*From the silence a loud thump, then hinges squeaking. Indecisive hoofbeats are heard.*) Huh! Who is it? Oh, my God, listen to those monstrous footsteps! Did I forget to lock the door? I'm lost, if they find me here dressed like a silly whore, and they decide to hold me up to public ridicule. I'd sooner commit suicide . . . (*She listens. The steps stop, then begin again. Each time they are closer.*) Dear God, what heavy footsteps! What are you waiting for, executioner? Come in now, if you want to see how I hang myself by my own hair before you set a hand on me.

(*In the doorway appears the large head of a black bull, with a terror-producing, inexpressive, Asiatic eye.*)

My God, they've sent me a bull. . . ! A bull in my own house! This is the end of Coronada. This is my death and my dishonor. Couldn't it have been a man, even if he were more of an animal? Well, if that's the way it is, don't wait any longer. I'm yours, you cruel black beast! I'll close my eyes and give myself to you. May the light of the world go out forever for me . . . (*She surrenders herself, covering her eyes. Momentary blackout, with the sound of loud hoofbeats. The light returns, and at an opposite doorway, the hind quarters and the tail of the bull are*

*now seen, as if it had crossed from one end of the room to the other.*)
Where are you going, you wicked beast? Weren't you looking for me?
You mean you don't want to take me. . . ? (*She clutches his dangling
tail.*) Are you turning me down? Is it possible that a bull would refuse
to gore a sexpot like me? Or didn't he recognize me? I'm wicked, wicked . . . and I'm yours, you despicable creature! (*The bull breaks loose
from Coronada's grasp and exits.*) This is a mystery that doesn't have a
solution. Why would a bull stay out this late at night and then just
wander into my house as if he owned it? What is that animal looking
for in that dark and disoriented room? He must be sleepwalking.
Tough! You'll stay there till you rot, meathead! (*She locks the door
with a key that she keeps between her breasts.*) And I'm glad! Now luck
is on my side, and you're going to stay in there until you die. Did you
come here just on a passing fancy? Well, I'm going to keep you there,
and Zebedeo will learn how a woman can fight bulls too. Even
barefoot and pregnant! (*She puts her ear to the door.*) Huff and puff all
you want, you fat slob, you big load of meat. No one's going to know
your whereabouts. St. Blaise, you heartless town, this is how I'm going
to keep your fiesta and revenge myself on your mayor. Now it's my
turn! All I've got to do is lock the other door and enjoy this secret at my
leisure. (*She locks herself in and picks up a chair, which she places
against the door through which the bull disappeared.*) I'm going to
sleep by your side, you black villain. I'm going to enjoy dreaming
about you, and all your thousands of steps in this room will be a
delight. Ay, Marauña, you smudged little simpleton, bullfighting con-
vict, your good auntie Coronada has kept them from playing a dirty
trick on you tonight. Death to all the fiestas of fear, and the pains of
imprisonment, and let there be a new way of life in Spain, and no more
brothers obsessed with their honor, and where the law prohibits these
wicked carbon-black beasts with bodies like big fat jugs, and specifies
only nice white bulls that will eat from the bullfighters' hands. I'm so
excited!

(*Her neck droops and her hands fall lifelessly at her side in a swoon. In the
distance, guitar strumming. The room becomes magically clouded over in
Coronada's dream. Strange sounds and jingling of chimes. Softly, the
bullpen door opens, and, in a luminous haze, a procession arrives. It is the
N.M., on a rolling platform, pushed by Melga and Dalga. Marauña is at
the front, carrying a lighted torch. Their eyes are miraculously brilliant.*)

N.M.: Beloved daughter Coronada, there is no better nor more thoughtful way to listen to a good sermon than sleeping like a log. You're
dreaming, that's for sure. And you've got that kidnapped bull submerged in a fatal slumber. Take me for whatever you want, and realize that

I can just as easily be St. John of the Haystack as St. Mary of Mittens. I am the unexplainable. I have returned to Spain, my country, as a beatific blushing violet, but very few can even imagine what I am and what I know. (*He lifts up his robe and shows a foot wearing a brilliant satin high-heeled shoe.*) As you can see, I have a foot that steps very daintily. (*He shows the other foot, goat-like and hairy.*) And another that sinks into the earth like a cloven hoof. I've said it over and over again "If you understand me, I'm yours."

MELGA, DALGA, MARAUNA: (*In an almost mumbled prayer.*)
Most Holy Woman
Most Holy Man
Bring us from heaven
Whatever you can.

N.M.: But I've come here, Coronada, to tell you that you must suffer martyrdom for opposing your outrageous brother. By his authority we will be imprisoned as defendants, accused of the most serious of crimes, according to his judgment, and through him we will know the agonizing pains of death that will be an example for ages to come. Therefore prepare yourself and make an act of contrition. My daughter Coronada, you must be good, you must renounce the tango, and not give yourself any more to the frenzy of the Great European Express trains, because that is no more than frivolous. Put an end to this nonsense and rise above yourself through sacrifice. The four of us are here to celebrate with you a get-together for most holy after-dinner conversation, in which we will celebrate the peace of the world and the confusion of the wicked. (*He blesses her.*) Ego te absolvo, Coronada, because you are a poor wretch and have grown more than your share. Mayor Zebedeo killed your three lovers because he needed to prove that he was more of a man than anyone. His punishment will come. May this cruel world pay for its guilt as weighed on the scales of heaven and may its judgment be set to the music of the spheres . . .

(*The light increases irresistibly over the apparition and then goes out suddenly in an infinity of guitars.*)

# ACT TWO

*The cemetery walls. The Town Voice enters with a horn that he plays facing the public. He announces:*

TOWN VOICE: A proclamation from Mayor Zebedeo to the four winds and their children the whirlwinds! "Fourteen days have now passed since the fiesta of St. Blaise, and we still haven't found the lost bull. The letter of the law imposes a very severe sentence on whoever dares to commit an outrage against our ceremonious and traditional fiesta. All the townspeople are hereby summoned to report every suspicious action so that we may wash away this dishonor from the town. And it's not open season on a certain father-mother, a wandering slanderer, as well as on the bullfighter Marauña, who escaped from prison with the unhealthy intention of making a fool of his jailers. Whoever leads us to them and discloses the bull's whereabouts will be more than adequately rewarded." This is the end of the proclamation, and I'm going to leave so I won't be late . . . (*He leaves, then returns.*) To those of you watching from the shade, I announce the arrival of five children coming from school, to relieve their bellies at the cemetery walls. Whoever doesn't want to see this uncouth spectacle better leave for a while, and if you want, come back after these proceedings, which are as natural as they are filthy. (*He leaves by the opposite exit.*)

THIN BOY: After school, tired of counting our fingers, there's no better entertainment than to delay our arrival home by peacefully making doo doo in the field. That way we can forget how black the blackboard is and how lousy the chalk tastes. Down with shorts and panties!

FAT BOY: The best way to notice the way in which the clouds eat one another up is while performing this enjoyable chore.

PALE GIRL: I'd like to hemstitch while I do it, but then I wouldn't have any hands free and I'd fall. And that's not decent.

THIN BOY: But you can smoke. And I'm smoking a cigarette that I rolled myself; it's made of scouring powder and dry grass. It's so good. . . ! (*He lights up and chews on the cigarette.*)

FAT BOY: Smoking while you shit makes you more of a man. It's a shame that us kids don't start out grown up.

FOOLISH GIRL: And us daughters by being mothers.

THIN BOY: Yuck. I'm really ruining an anthill.

CRIPPLED GIRL: Really? And what are the ants doing? Can you hear them complaining?

THIN BOY: They don't know what to do. They're forming a committee to see if they can figure it out.

FAT BOY: But they won't. They'll say that what's falling on them is just bad luck and they'll leave.

THIN BOY: But they're not going. They look really interested.

FOOLISH GIRL: Maybe they'll take advantage of it. They're so industrious!

PALE GIRL: They're probably so bored at going to and from their house carrying junk, that they'll find in their mourning a reason to work a little less.

CRIPPLED GIRL: Just like us. At first, when the bull escaped, we spent all our time hiding and didn't go to school. I wonder where that vicious beast is now?

FAT BOY: He must be over the horizon. Everything you can't see is over the horizon. Geography's been that way ever since Columbus.

PALE GIRL: Can the bull see us from there? If he showed up now, he could give us a goring that would send all five of us to the other side, where death is waiting.

FOOLISH GIRL: Don't start with your scary proverbs.

THIN BOY: I'm not afraid. Even though they say that the hour of the setting sun is when the dead come out with a bell of smoke and a candle made out of rancid lard.

FOOLISH GIRL: Ooh, that's so scary it made my pee-pee stop. I'm going to sing you a riddle:

> It helps you to go
> But never to stay,
> In the month of October
> It's 'round twice a day.
> It's found in the country
> And also the town
> But not in the city
> Unless it's renown.
> But it's sad to remember
> Wherever you go
> If you're hoping for yes
> It can only be no.

FAT BOY: What the hell are you talking about?

FOOLISH GIRL: The letter O, silly!

THIN BOY: What a load of crap! That's just the kind of nonsense women say while they're embroidering. The men who piss and shit in the woods always sing a fandanguillo.

FAT BOY: I've got a dirty song for all the sissy girls.

Little sissy la-las
You're just like your aunts
You're all such scaredy cats
You pee in your pants

CRIPPLED GIRL: Well, I'm scared . . . Don't you hear it? I can hear long footsteps. (*The sound of footsteps through a hidden underbrush.*)

THIN BOY: If they find all of us sinning together, they'll tell our teacher. This is what Father Cerezo says is playing with fire.

FAT BOY: Well, we've played with fire, and now we're going to get burned!

ALL: (*They get up and curl themselves up into a ball against the wall.*)
We'll all stick together
None of us will tell.
If nobody catches us
We won't go to hell.

(*Mayor Zebedeo emerges from behind the wall. He is an imposing figure, covering up the rays of the setting sun with his cape.*)

ZEBEDEO: Here, among the dead men and women of my family, I swear that I will revenge myself on whoever swindled me out of a bull for which I paid exactly a thousand in hard cash. Corpses that rot, and souls that beg, listen to me, all of you. If I don't get the satisfaction of punishing the guilty party, may they take me to the hospital after I've been given a generous dose of microbes of tuberculosis and tetanus. Since I'm walking so bravely over your putrefaction, afflict me with apoplexy, scrofulous poison, anemial diptheria, and measles with diabetes. May I die of unnatural moribundity, and may the pain not leave until they read me the Bible; until they psalm me, liturgiate me, orthodox me, and de profundis and kirieleison me. And if after this oath I still don't get to punish the guilty party, I'll swear the same oath with three etceteras more, which I'll start thinking about tonight in order to calm myself down a little. Goodbye dead ones, goodbye, sun . . . (*The large puppet submerges himself once again among his witnesses.*)

PALE GIRL: It was the mayor, who came here to amuse himself because he's furious.

CRIPPLED GIRL: Did you hear how he talked? He sounded like an Egyptian king.

THIN BOY: He's mad because of the bull that got lost and because of the fiesta we never had. That's why he didn't see us, because he's blind, and wants to eat up the world.

FAT BOY: We were lucky to get out of that! OK, you guys, let's cover up all this crap and get home . . .

FOOLISH GIRL: I feel like crying.

CRIPPLED GIRL: Why?

FOOLISH GIRL: Because I've lost my pee-pee and I feel all alone.

PALE GIRL: I'm getting scared too. It's gotten so late, that I'm different from what I was this morning. What if I get home and they don't recognize me?

*(Captured in the twilight breeze, a long agonizing bellow is soon heard.)*

THIN BOY: Did you hear that? Cross my heart and hope to die if it's not a dead body breaking its heart because it's trying to rise from the dead but can't. (*Again they squeeze together.*)

FOOLISH GIRL: And . . . what if it's the bull? (*Another frightening bellow. The five little sparrows go off in all directions.*)

ALL: The bull! The bull's coming!

*(Deep night. The walls of the cemetery are parted and we can see a shallow landscape of roofs with a scattering of chimneys. Mairena is spying through the top of one of them. The two constables, who are following her, are moving about and crouching behind others.)*

MAIRENA: Come on out, you scuts! Don't think that I don't know that you're following me. Come on out of your hiding place, and grab me by the wrist to take me to jail, if that's what you want.

BLACKBELLY: And who told you you could wander around the roofs of town in the dead of night, you wingless horsefly.

MAIRENA: Because this is forbidden ground and I'm a gypsy anarchist without a passport. What did you think?

BRUTUS: I don't believe that. I think that you've got other ideas under that head of hair, Mairena. I know that as sure as my name's Brutus. We've seen you stick your little nose into each one of these chimneys. Do you keep yourself alive just by smelling the smoke of the food that's frying?

MAIRENA: I keep myself alive with the suspicion that somewhere in my prowlings I'm going to find a bull that bellows every night remembering the milk he sucked as a baby and the grass that made him wild. And I'm getting nearer to the person that has him hidden among her walls to ridicule my soul brother the mayor.

BLACKBELLY: You're too full of the mayor. Well, don't depend on it . . . You don't know how cruel Zebedeo is. He'll never marry anybody.

MAIRENA: Like the gypsy that I am, I'm split into pieces, and I'm torn between bitter affection, black sadness, and evil justice. Without that pleasure, I'm nobody.

BLACKBELLY: Then you can take us as your lovers, Mairena. We're going to hunt you down and make a martyr out of you.

BRUTUS: After her!

MAIRENA: Just wait a second and put your ear to this smokeless chimney. This is where the moaning of the beast and the preaching of that Mother Monk are coming from. And besides that, I can hear a gramophone talking through its nose and a lot of giggling and silly talk. That's got to be Melga and Dalga. You don't believe me? Well, I swear it to you by those stars scattered all over the sky with so much good taste and so little explanation.

BLACKBELLY: You're a liar! We've got orders from the mayor to take you to jail, as a suspect.

MAIRENA: Is that how Zebedeo is going to reward me? Oh, what injustice and what a blot on the law!

BRUTUS: Well, now you've got a reason for singing those mournful gypsy songs, and food for your yearning for torment.

MAIRENA: But, don't you believe me? This spot on which I'm standing is directly above Coronada's house, and that giant woman has been playing a rotten trick on her brother.

BRUTUS: The truth, in fact, is that your screeching hate for luscious Coronada, and towards all women that have a spare pair of panties and good manners, is killing you.

MAIRENA: Are you really going to arrest me? Can't I convince you? Dear God, how poorly you treat your dark-skinned gypsies! (*Furious, she raises her arms and invokes the heavens.*)

Dear Heaven on high
If you won't listen
To me when I cry,
I'll go straight to hell
Where my darkness will glisten
And your God I'll repel.
The Devil's each wish
Will be my command.
I'm leaving your winter
For summer's bright sand,
And for all of your blessings
I don't give a damn!

(*She bends her elbow into the international symbol of contempt. Just then the bellowing of the bull can be clearly heard. Mairena sighs, satisfied with the result of her challenge.*)

There you have him, oh men of little faith!

BLACKBELLY: So, it was true! Mairena, that denunciation is going to get you the best little gypsy cave around, with no rotten smells, and as many jasmines in flowerpots as you want. Let's go to Zebedeo with the alarm. There'll be no pardon for those bastards that ruined our fiesta.

MAIRENA: There better not be! All hell is about to break loose! I'm going to watch that judgment sitting in my rocking chair.

BRUTUS: It will be the restoration of Spain. Public humiliation and capital punishment, at least, for the Nun Man, for mistress Coronada, and for Marauña, the orphan bullfighter.

MAIRENA: And don't forget Melga and Dalga, as accomplices. They're all rebels!

BRUTUS: I'm going to get the mourning creeps and have the town square swept clean right now. There won't be any pardon! (*The scenery begins to change.*)

MAIRENA: What a night! And just when it seemed that there wouldn't be any more celebrations . . . I hope that from now on there'll be a holiday to celebrate during the week. I'm fed up with Sundays!

BRUTUS: Hey you, don't go too far; Sundays are all patriotic! What you're suggesting is just too much . . . There won't be any pardon!

MAIRENA: There better not be! Let them all fall into the trap, and long live Judas cursing rope!

(*They exit. Coronada's room can now be seen. The three women and the N.M. are seated on a large sofa, enjoying a pleasant gathering, while Marauña is demonstrating some indoor bullfighting passes to amuse them.*)

MARAUNA: In a bullfight, the first thing you've got to do is examine the bull carefully, to know how much steam he has and how much horsepower is stamping within his body. (*Practicing.*) This pass is called "Harmony," and it's been around for more than three centuries, since the time when all the bulls were dedicated to a famous duke of old. There is also the "Half-harmony," which can be lessened to a quarter, or reduced to a mere intention. (*He continues acting friskily and acquiring greater confidence.*) Then come the "Suspicions," the "Cornerings," the "Pass of Ingratitude," and the "Up Yours." And if the bull comes out sweetly, they tickle the "Arpeggios," like this . . .

CORONADA: Son, I don't understand a thing, but how well you express yourself!

N.M.: It's quite an art. Reproachable, but a fine art nevertheless.

CORONADA: And how does this complicated undertaking end up?

MARAUNA: At the end, assuming there's no catastrophe, you let your cape fall and drink from a jug, without looking back or letting your legs buckle.

MELGA: Oh, what a wicked world! We're seeing just how much better a living room bullfight would be in the public square, with a timid crowd engaged in needlework.

CORONADA: The risk in a bullfight is so great, that I don't know why, in the killing part, it's not done with a mop soaked in instant poison attached to the end of the sword.

DALGA: That's it. Without violence. So that the beast could taste it, if he wanted to.

MARAUNA: On the contrary, we kill in many different ways, dear Coronada, but the best is hitting the mark, and there's the difficulty. (*He gets a sword and a cape.*) You move the cape around with "happiness," because the brute is so brutish, that he's grateful that he's made happy before he dies. Then you "rub" him, and "jostle" him, and "spin" him around; you entrust yourself to your favorite saint and, in my opinion, the best way to finish him off is like this, with the "Assassin." (*He thrusts the sword through a crack in the door behind which the bull is suffering, and we can hear a gentle bellowing.*)

DALGA: My God, I think you got him where he lives! You're beginning to get lucky, Marauña.

CORONADA: His bellowing is getting weaker and weaker and, it seems to me, more and more resigned. He's been locked up for two weeks now with nothing to eat, except maybe for the straw covering from a chair or two. Marauña, come to the shelter of the brazier, and finish your hot chocolate.

N.M.: Yes, my children, there's nothing like gentleness, peacefulness, the "I won't budge an inch" with your eyes blank, and awaiting unjustified punishment in order to give a good example to the world.

DALGA: How exciting! If they had told me that, instead of getting married, I was going to be crucified, I would never have believed them.

MELGA: Me neither! And believe me, maternal father, I'm not afraid of the martyrdom that faces me either.

CORONADA: And what about me? I blush so happily when I think that I'll be able to enter into the distinguished academy of martyrs through this exemplary sacrifice.

DALGA: (*In ecstasy.*) You said it, mistress. Our death will be celebrated as a national holiday.

MELGA: And even an excellent vindication for the patron saint of Pamplona. How can he help but be grateful that a bullfighter has finally turned out to be gentle, and that they send him, with his hands tied together, to the land of glory where the saint awaits him. What do you say to that, Marauña?

MARAUNA: Well, I say that I'm going to dedicate this effort to my mother. And also to those bullfighters that struggled for Glory, although they didn't achieve it by following the "Lives of the Saints." They were good guys, but they were wrong. Today they would be St. Joselito, St.

Machaquito, Sts. Manolete and Belmonte . . .

CORONADA: Your brave comments will edify all of them, Marauña.

MARAUNA: Well, one does what one can, mistress Coronada.

CORONADA: How wonderful! I can see you now on a pedestal with your bullfighter's cap and a palm.

MELGA: Maybe you'll have as many embroidered slippers in the wardrobe of a sacristy as there are days in a year, give or take a day for leap year.

DALGA: Let's not think now about rewards, but about solidifying our resignation, and courage to suffer Zebedeo's insults and his rotten treatment of us.

N.M.: (Sipping.) This hot chocolate is very good, dear daughter Coronada. It seems incredible that something so dark could illuminate the soul with such warming rays. But that's the way of Divine Providence.

CORONADA: Drink, Maternal Father, and make up for so much humiliation in the wilderness of Adversity and Broken Glass.

MELGA: That really is wilderness, with so many broken soda bottles and old shoes without their mates . . . What awful hardships!

DALGA: And that onslaught of clouds and winds, that is nothing but living by fits and starts. Who can stand it?

CORONADA: And buzzing mosquitoes flying in hordes, and slimy, snotty scorpions that fall on you like spit.

N.M.: Spain is different in everything, and that's the will of God.

(*The bull pounds on the door and bellows gloomily and insistently.*)

MELGA: Ooh, how scary! It doesn't seem as though the wild beast is dying of consumption. It's enough to make your hair stand on end. (*They all get up with a start and form a group next to the door.*)

DALGA: There's a mystery here. Why was he quiet for so long, and now all of a sudden he's starting to let off steam?

N.M.: He must be passing on to the better life, and having a tough time of it.

CORONADA: Oh, sweet hairy-chested mother! I'm so nervous, and so full of doubts. After all these days, I'm beginning to feel as though it's my husband that's dying, and without me at his side because he's been so restless and bad.

N.M.: Who knows? Everything is possible in the poly-faceted mirror of divine affairs, where everything is good, and there are neither political prejudices nor any scruples. What's more: in the name of the mixed-up saint, I can marry the two of you "in articulo mortis."

DALGA: Heavens, that mirror of yours certainly allows tremendous liberties! And, to think they wouldn't even let that bull's herder court me, because of prejudice. How have we survived in such backwardness?

CORONADA: It's the ignorance in which woman wanders. In other words, one doesn't marry the person she wants because she doesn't want to? I've always suspected that in the Redemption there would be things that would give pleasure to even the rocks. (*Loud banging on the other, distant door. Noises.*)

BLACKBELLY: Open up! It's the law! (*Everyone turns noticeably paler, except the N.M..*)

DALGA: Dear God! Here come the assassins to seal our fate!

N.M.: Yes, dear children, the time has come. (*Kneeling down.*) Let the solution arrive soon, that we may understand instantaneously the mysteries of the universe, and laugh at how simple they are. (*The banging continues.*)

MELGA: That's for sure, Motherly Father; it's the least we could ask for.

CORONADA: (*Drying a tear on the sleeve of her gown.*) Should I open the door to those beasts?

N.M.: Let them get angrier and angrier and make them tear it down. Kneel down, Coronada, and meditate. Now all we can do is accept the passing of time. (*The noise of smashing is heard, together with the clear sound of a crowd.*) Are you listening? They're here. (*They are all kneeling, with visionary resignation, and they breathe a deep sigh. Blackbelly enters, very restrained and with an expression suited to the occasion.*)

BLACKBELLY: A very good evening to this ladylike gathering.

CORONADA: The same to you, Blackbelly.

BLACKBELLY: With your permission, if I may . . . (*He leaves, and returns carrying a coffin, which he places in a corner. Behind Blackbelly comes Brutus carrying another, and each in his turn continues this chore until five coffins have been piled up. This work doesn't keep them from joining the conversation.*)

BRUTUS: Good evening.

OTHERS: Good evening.

(*Despite their preparedness for martyrdom, the poor defendants—with the exception of the N.M.—can't help but be impressed by the growing pile of coffins.*)

BRUTUS: But cold and harsh. The crescent moon is so crescent that it's not healthy. There's a lump growing on its cheek, and I'm afraid that it might freeze. Let's pray that it doesn't burst open and that a drop of moon doesn't fall here and destroy our harvest. It would be a very hard year.

BLACKBELLY: But maybe that drop of moon could make us a pond, just like happened almost ten years ago. Do you remember, mistress Coronada?

CORONADA: Yes, my son. And it was thanks to the moon that we have electric current. If not, who would remember these poor mountains?

BRUTUS: Well, well . . . And what are you all doing down on your knees?

DALGA: It's funny that you should ask. Can't you tell? We're here waiting to die, and to suffer whatever other penalties you might inflict upon us. What do you want?

BLACKBELLY: You seem very devout, Marauña, and very resigned to your arrest.

MARAUNA: It goes with having been born at the jailhouse doors, and having cut my first teeth inside. That's impossible to forget.

MELGA: If you think all that machinery of death is going to make our blood curdle in our veins, you're full of it. Which you are even if it were true.

BRUTUS: If it were true? Well, now the most serene Zebedeo is coming to express his condolences to all of you.

MELGA: Well, we're certainly thankful for his consideration.

CORONADA: Let him come. He'll be very graciously received. After all, he is my brother.

BRUTUS: He's on his way, strolling through town. The people are crowded together with a lot of respect, so much respect, in fact, that it's scaring the very authorities themselves. Look at the street! It's a very solemn night.

TOWN VOICE: (*From within, distant at first and later nearby, accompanied by disquieting sounds and the ringing of bells.*)
Glory to all the suffering souls
Treatment shoddy
To the tributary body.

BLACKBELLY AND BRUTUS: (*In unison and with solemn fervor.*)
Miserere nobis
velis nolis.

TOWN VOICE:
A star is just a rotten egg
That's surrounded
By a silence that's unbounded.

BLACKBELLY AND BRUTUS:
Miserere nobis
velis nolis.

TOWN VOICE:
I'll make the sign of the cross
With the stain
That surrounds all human pain.

BLACKBELLY AND BRUTUS:
Miserere nobis
velis nolis.

CORONADA: (*Aside to the N.M.*) Our mother, who art in heaven . . . This is death. This personal justice of my brother's is beyond all reason. What are they going to say in Madrid about this violent behavior?

N.M.: I already warned you about that, beloved daughter. It's an incredible piece of stupidity, but they'll be sure to cover it up and feign ignorance, just so that we can be admitted to the "Society of Decent Nations." (*Steps and sounds.*)

BRUTUS: (*Looks through the door and announces.*) Here is the Great Zebedeo. Everyone rise, for with death all punishment is ended. (*Zebedeo enters.*)

ZEBEDEO: God be with you, brothers and sisters, and let everything we do be in God's name.

MELGA: You've finally named Him. Well, if it's in God's name, and you say it, then there's no one who can help us.

ZEBEDEO: Coronada, on what a sad occasion we meet.

CORONADA: I guess that's what fate had in store for me. Don't worry, I won't cause any trouble. Come on brother, sit down.

ZEBEDEO: And to top things off, here we are with the mixed-up, beatific Nun Man in the middle of this conspiracy. Well, take heart, and brute strength, in your souls, so that you won't weaken when the going gets tough.

N.M.: We are most resigned, my son.

DALGA: Yes, Zebedeo. And you find us already confessed to this womanly saint for two weeks now, which seems appropriate to your sentence.

ZEBEDEO: I'm very pleased, Marauña, that you accept the noose around your neck with such resignation.

MARAUNA: I am here to serve you, and more a prisoner than ever.

CORONADA: Zebedeo, you've finished with all the requirements of your tyrannical rules of etiquette. Now sit down, sentence us, and be done with it! (*The two sit down very solemnly on the sofa.*) If you say that God made you mayor as a token of his esteem, I don't want to get in any arguments about the will of God. Look after yourself and do your duty until you've stuffed yourself.

ZEBEDEO: I don't ration out my obligations, as well you know. And today I think I will stuff myself with them. I had to make a deposition to myself, acquainting myself with this case and acknowledging that you were the guilty ones.

MELGA: You've saved us the work.

CORONADA: You've done very well, Zebedeo. You're the man, and you decide.

ZEBEDEO: And, by the way, because I still trust my good taste, I also ordered you a shroud, just in case you didn't have any suitable clothes for the occasion. Melga and Dalga will be buried as maids of honor. The clothes are being finished now by some professional seamstresses-in-mourning that have very willingly offered their services. Let's hope they get here in time.

CORONADA: What? Without taking our measurements? You should have realized, brother, that I'm not the kind of person that can be buried in ready-made clothes.

ZEBEDEO: You don't have to worry about that, they'll be big enough. You'll have the perfect dress in which to be buried alive.

CORONADA: Alive. . . ! (*The accused try to conceal their shock.*)

ZEBEDEO: I have the sentence scribbled on this little piece of paper, but I didn't have to chew off too much of the pencil to write it all. It says: Seeing that Coronada Luscious—Most Serene Princess—has defamed her honor and mine . . .

CORONADA: Why did you call me Most Serene Princess?

ZEBEDEO: To treat you with respect and so as not to lose my serenity. It continues: her honor and mine, lending her house and her ears to a Father Sister that is going around sowing confusion throughout the Christian world because he can't tell his left foot from her right; and seeing that, influenced by the aforementioned man and/or woman, she locked a bull in her house with the worst of intentions . . .

CORONADA: The worst? God almighty! If I could only explain to you about the poly-faceted mirror . . .

N.M.: Now isn't the time for those subtleties; you'll just make him angrier and he won't let us die in peace.

ZEBEDEO: . . . and seeing that the young ladies Dalga Melgares and Melga Dalgares—who are first cousins—have joined in this anti-Spanish and dissipated conspiracy, together with the bullfighter-convict, alias Marauña, and seeing that . . .

CORONADA: Seeing that! Seeing that! Why do you keep on repeating yourself. We can see what you've been seeing, but your vision must be blurred.

ZEBEDEO: Well, seeing that all of this goes against dignified behavior and brazenly crosses the line of conception . . .

CORONADA: What conception?

ZEBEDEO: My own. And seeing that which has been seen, those that have passed over the line, who are the aforementioned men and the aforementioned women, and their confused companion, they will be given a first-class funeral and will be executed in accordance with the bygone custom of being buried alive. (*He rises.*) This is happening to you, Coronada, for straying off the beaten path and wandering into Wonderland, which isn't even in this jurisdiction. Are you all satisfied? Well, now turn the bull loose, and we'll see if there's still some tragedy left in that body after all the evil treatment he's received. (*A great commotion ensues.*)

CORONADA: You want to turn him loose? You're not even going to let him be mine, just like all the others you denied me for no reason at all? Oh,

I'm going to die before I reach the tomb!

ZEBEDEO: Shut up, you bestial bitch! I want bulls and I'll have bulls, even at the wrong time and in the wrong place, yes, even in a closed room. Let everyone find their own hiding place, if they can.

MELGA: He's a fiend. To fight the husband of the divine poly-faceted mirror "in articulo mortis."

DALGA: Shut up, Melga. Don't mention the mixed-up one or the poly-facted mirror anymore, because as far as he's concerned, you'll always be stepping out of line.

ZEBEDEO: Open the door, officers! And you, Marauña, stand in front of it and do your duty, right to the very end. Nobody leave!

MELGA: What a spot we're in now! (*To the N.M.*) Feminine father, give us all your blessing, and may God grant us a merciful death.

N.M.: (*Blessing them.*) Whatever the divine plan may be, it has my official acceptance. That which cannot be avoided should not be avoided by any means, because then it becomes cheapened.

(*Blackbelly opens the door of the bullpen and hides behind it.*)

BLACKBELLY: Hey, toro. . . ! (*Silence, followed by a mild bellow.*)

BRUTUS: (*Taking a chance and sticking his head into the darkness.*) Hey, toro. . . ! That dilapidated creature isn't even stirring.

BLACKBELLY: (*Overcoming his misgivings.*) He's already a soul in purgatory. He's only bellowing out of habit; he's dead and done with.

ZEBEDEO: Great balls of fire! Then push him out! Go in there, Brutus, and give him a good shove.

BRUTUS: In I go! But he doesn't have a breath left in his body. He's nothing but a moth-eaten wreck. (*He goes into the bullpen.*)

ZEBEDEO: Great balls of fire! The bull is done for! Did you know that this anti-death conspiracy of yours was digging your own graves for you?

(*Blackbelly follows Brutus, but Brutus returns with a broken off horn in his hand.*)

BRUTUS: Here's the proof. His defenses fell off, just like acorns when it's time. (*He drops the horn and exits again.*)

ZEBEDEO: Great balls of fire! Even with nine lives you wouldn't be able to pay for this!

(*Blackbelly appears holding up a long, skinny tail.*)

BLACKBELLY: It just took one yank . . . and here you have his tragic tail. (*Brutus races in as if he were being chased by the bull. The women*

*shout and crowd together. Brutus turns and looks back. Castanet-like
sounds can be heard, and some dust comes through the door.*)
BRUTUS: He just fell apart! Just like that! He disintegrated!
ZEBEDEO: Cowards! (*Furiously, he takes the sad taurine appendage from
Blackbelly.*) Aaahhh! I can feel this tail in my hands as if it were mine,
torn off so roughly. Mine, and Spain's, and our national bullfighting
dignity. This dishonor must be cleansed! You are officially sentenced!
Death, death, and penance! Everyone out of their houses and to my
judgment! Let the sky fall down and let the mountains be torn asunder,
turning all the world into a vacant lot! I call everyone together for the
Final Judgment, because I am the final mayor and the Supreme Con-
demnator!

(*The scene is blended together into a confused and thundering nightmare,
in which the entire town appears, led by the Town Voice—dressed as a
Roman centurion—and Father Cerezo wearing a celebrant's frayed
chasuble. It is a gloomy, mournful, emphatic processional. In summary, a
pitiful small-town Apocalypse.*)

TOWN VOICE: (*Accompanied by some penitent women sighing to suit the
occasion, while they shake some cowbells.*)
　　Ding, dong, ding, dong!
　　The destruction of bliss
　　For our joyless throng.
　　Our brave we will miss
　　Now there's only the hiss
　　Of the hurricane's song.
TOWNSPEOPLE: (*Praying.*)
　　Miserere nobis
　　velis nolis!
TOWN VOICE:
　　Ding, dong, ding, dong!
　　The rumbles persist
　　All the day long.
　　The lovers who kissed
　　Before dawn in the mist
　　Have vanished and gone.
TOWNSPEOPLE: (*On their knees, intoxicated with resignation.*)
　　Miserere nobis,
　　velis nolis!

(*The defendants arrive, carrying their own caskets. Crying and lamenta-
tions as they go by. Like solicitous Cyrenians, Blackbelly and Brutus help
them along, and later help to put the coffins into the trapdoor that*

*represents the tomb. Zebedeo leads his sister to the edge.)*

ZEBEDEO: This is where the yawning mouth of your tomb has opened for you, and here will be our farewell, until we meet in the other life. You can't complain of bad company or lack of ceremony.

DON CEREZO: (*Crushed by the situation, in confidence.*) Zebedeo, I have my doubts as to whether what you're doing will really reclaim the honor of the town, and the nation that surrounds it.

ZEBEDEO: You can pay homage to the destiny of the world whenever you please, but mind your own business, or you might fall into the tomb too. (*Addressing Coronada again.*) Coronada, you're very pretty and you're really dressed fit to kill. Speak your final words, and say goodbye to your sufferings, because your time has come.

CORONADA: All right. Don't be concerned. (*Solemnly.*) Townspeople gathered here, brother mayor, Father Cerezo, pastor in the wasteland: I am Coronada, a heroine, who enters her grave on her own feet, after having grown in body and developed in bosom beyond the low level typical of this Godforsaken land. I am more woman than I am delinquent and, because of that, my heart is full of new ideas, even more than a big-city department store. I am Spanish and simple, but misunderstood, because of the force of habit, by a blindly faithful rabble. I was once much more of a lady, but I went too far and forgot the way things are. I'm not sorry. And because of that I'm going back to the earth to which all of us will return and find ourselves packed together in paradise. The worms are freer than we. And if one day, you can understand the way I do, you'll see that I'm not lost somewhere in outer space but on the open road to freedom—both mine and yours. Bless me now, Father Cerezo, and let me smell the stink of that tobacco of St. Blaise as a remembrance of what I breathed regularly as a girl. And I bid you farewell, you poor wretches. (*She lowers herself with dignity. The townspeople are sobbing loudly.*)

ZEBEDEO: She's got no shame and she's just using all her theatrical talents to make her farewell more dramatic. It's absolutely right and necessary that she die. Down with the rest of them! (*Amidst prayers and murmuring, all lower themselves into the tomb.*)

DALGA: Fellow townspeople, I am Dalga and, like my soul brother Don Quixote, I'm an hidalga. I'm going to the tomb where my ancestors are already growing, to give me a family beyond reproach. (*She goes down.*)

MELGA: Well, if she's an hidalga, I'm an himelga, which makes me a super-hidalga, and I'm glad that I'll never look you in the eye again, you peasants! (*She goes down too.*)

MARAUNA: I am grateful to the law for this honor to my family, because as a poor man from a humble home, I never would have seen such a well-lit funeral with so many luminaries . . . (*He disappears as well.*)

TOWN VOICE: (*Screaming himself hoarse, and with even louder bells ringing.*)

> Earth, earth, dust and soil . . .
> Those who rest and those who toil
> Into your depths accept and broil!

ZEBEDEO: And now for the Incomprehensible One. Let's see what silly remarks he's got for us now.

DON CEREZO: My mixed-up child, although I held you in my arms once, I never have understood that fuzzy gospel that you go around preaching; furthermore, if the authorities have condemned it, I have no other choice but to give my consent without another word.

N.M.: Now I see that there is no escape, and that you have brought me to the doors of death without anyone to help me in this human condemnation. Zebedeo, wicked mayor, Father Cerezo, poor do-nothing priest, and you, miserable townspeople of Candlelight, since you have been so pigheaded and cowardly, the highest heaven, freed from its moorings, will have to teach you a lesson. It destroys more than the lot of you, and creates more than itself. Let it be done then, and let's get going.

(*Suddenly, to the terrified amazement of all those present, he is holding a ball of fire in his hand. He throws it into the mouth of the tomb, and the growling of the earth, whose very entrails are trembling, can be heard. The sound increases, until it becomes deafening. A dazzling jet of fire issues from that womb. General excitement.*)

Very exalted and very enlightened powers have given me the authority to show you, through the unfortunate group of people that you have condemned to death, the only glory of the world, the still-unseen spectacle of the resurrection of the flesh. Raise your heads and look at me. I am the Unnamed, because I contain all names, and the eternal unknown. Moreover, I am the senseless and glorious redemption of life and death . . . (*He points to the tomb, from which the fiery jet has ceased to issue.*) Coronada, beautiful leviathan, come out of that blind hole and show everyone how you will be, forever, in the shower of infinite light that I have prepared for you.

(*And now the victorious company emerges, transfigured, with white wigs and vaudeville costumes, all very handsome and claiming their right to participate for an eternity in the Carnival of Rio.*)

CORONADA: Oh, what's happening to me? With every step I take, I shudder with pleasure, as if I'd had quite enough of lovers.

N.M.: May you die of joy, and never finish dying; now you are a flame that can laugh without finding a shadow in your path. Look at her carefully! And don't forget the two handsome wenches that are following her, Melga and Dalga. Nor the wretched Marauña, who is finally a bullfighter with wings, and appears before you so jaunty and so light and airy that he is simply mist and fragrance of bullfighters long since gone to their rewards.

(*A new trembling of the earth. A distant bellowing. Everyone is frightened.*)

That bellowing that you hear and that scared you half to death is . . . the Snow Bull, who has come down from the tops of the purest mountains on which nobody walks. He will show you the way. There he is! (*A winged white bull appears among the veils of gliding clouds.*) Go on, my group of adventurers, follow that powerful white bull. I will follow you; I will teach you; I, your maternal father that no one can name, who doesn't even know himself, being so large, and so small, and so smooth, and so hairy . . .

(*He turns towards the group which, radiant with joy, is beginning to move away. Taking one step, his robes drop to the ground. He now appears as a figure of the ultimate wonder.*)

There lie the relics of my unacceptable presence among you and of my divine ridicule. Don't follow them or I will strike you with lightning, inhabitants of Candlelight, fruit of melancholy, miserable breed. (*They move away, ethereal, shining brilliantly. As this is going on, Mairena enters, anxiously, and flogs the earth with the bull's tail, which has ended up in her hands.*)

MAIRENA: I, who am a gypsy, I knew it, and I know it, and I was eaten up by envy, and I've shouted it alone on the mountainsides, and I've vomited it on the meadows, and I've sung it softly through all the keyholes, but nobody heard me, and nobody hears me, complaining, complaining in all my gypsy rhythms: complaining in fandangos, in soleares, in tonadas, and in seguidillas. I have been cursed by fate, which always leaves me outside the gates of Heaven! They're going, they're going and they're leaving me behind! Wait for me, my fortunate white brothers and sisters, tear me away from this agony, from the fingers of these jailers. Zebedeo, officers, to you I dedicate this gypsy song, to see if I can finally soften your filthy hearts, to see if, surrendering my soul, I can let out with the scream that will earn me the resurrection of my flesh. (*She wraps the bull's tail around her neck and squeezes with suicidal energy, while she begins to scream in the flamenco style of death.*) Ay, ayyy. . . !

END

## ON THE EDITOR

Marion Peter Holt is on the faculties of the College of Staten Island and the Ph.D. Program in Theatre of the City University of New York. His publications include *The Contemporary Spanish Theatre: 1949-1972,* a book-length study of the theatre of Jose Lopez Rubio, and articles and reviews in *Modern Drama, Hispania, Performing Arts Journal, Theatre Journal,* and *Estreno.* In 1981 he was awarded a grant from the National Endowment for the Arts for a translation of Buero-Vallejo's *The Sleep of Reason,* which was produced by Baltimore's Center Stage in 1984. Other Holt translations have been staged or given staged readings by The Writers Theatre, The Flat Rock Playhouse, and the Intiman Theatre.